MY SYSTEM

21st Century Edition

ARON NIMZOWITSCH

Edited and converted to algebraic notation by Lou Hays

Hays Publishing   Park Hill, Oklahoma

Original English translation of My System by Philip Hereford

Editor: Lou Hays
Book design and typeset: Lou Hays
Cover Illustration: Carolyn Hoefelmeyer
Proofreaders: John Hall, David Sewell, Luis Salinas, Mike Richards, Joe Drake, Al Sprague

Illustrative game computer files built on "Zarkov 2.5" (developed by John Stanback and distributed by *Chess Laboratories*). Diagrams created on "Zarkov 2.5" and "Diagram 2.01" (developed by Steve Kelly). Many of the examples in parts one and two of the book (particularly those with "nested variations") were created and processed on "ChessBase 3.0" (distributed by *ChessBase U.S.A.*).

PRINTED IN THE UNITED STATES OF AMERICA

Hays Publishing
P.O. Box 777
Park Hill, Oklahoma 74451

ISBN 1-880673-85-1 Softcover

*This edition is dedicated
to my parents, Bill and Dorothy Hays,
who in 1958 dragged me to the
Muskogee, Oklahoma public library
for Saturday chess lessons,
and to Frank Rogers, who taught me to play.*

A WORD FROM THE PUBLISHER

My System, by Aron Nimzowitsch, first published in 1925, has its place among the two or three all-time most instructive books in the literature of chess. Indeed, it is difficult to find a strong chessplayer who has not studied this great classic.

The current edition, *My System - 21st Century Edition*, incorporates many positive changes. To accommodate the modern reader, the chess notation has been converted to the algebraic format and the text has been updated to contemporary language. In parts one and two, paragraphs are double spaced to provide for easier reading, while the illustrative games section is peppered with new diagrams and liberal spacing to facilitate the study of variations. Aron Nimzowitsch comments in the preface to his book *Chess Praxis* (published 1936), *"I would have liked to see each game provided with four or five diagrams to facilitate the study of the variations which often are particularly intricate, but obese volumes are not in favor nowadays (slimming is the watchword)."* In this vein I feel certain that he would be most pleased to know that *My System - 21st Century Edition* contains 419 diagrams! This is nearly double the number found in the original 1930 English language edition from which this book is derived. In short, everything possible has been done to make the use of this book convenient and easy for today's chessplayer.

I wish to thank the staff of the John G. White Collection of the Cleveland Public Library for the photograph from which the cover illustration was created.

The goal of making *My System* as accurate and easy as possible for the contemporary reader has been achieved. The master work of Aron Nimzowitsch, after nearly seventy years of challenging and teaching thousands of the world's best chess thinkers, is now in a position to continue its noble task throughout the next century.

Lou Hays
Dallas, Texas
December, 1991

TABLE OF CONTENTS

PART 1 - THE ELEMENTS

PAGE

PART 2 - POSITIONAL PLAY

PART 3 - ILLUSTRATIVE GAMES

ILLUSTRATIVE GAMES LIST

INTRODUCTION

by International Grandmaster Yasser Seirawan

It is with the greatest of pleasure that I write the introduction to this edition of Aron Nimzowitsch's classic, *My System*. The effect of Nimzowitsch's writings and play has had a profound impact on chessplayers since his chess career began in 1904.

In his heyday (the years 1925-1931) Nimzowitsch was considered to belong to the company of the world's strongest players. It is a pity that he never got his chance to battle in a World Championship match. Chess is poorer for it. Besides being a powerful player at the chessboard, Nimzowitsch became even more famous for his writings and his *style* of writing. He followed in the scientific tradition of the first World Champion, Wilhelm Steinitz. After several devastating losses, Nimzowitsch looked deeply into the causes of his defeats. Besides a single bad move that pitched a game, was there something else to be learned? Yes, the plan was wrong. What was the right plan? How could that plan be found? Why should it work in this circumstance and not another?

By taking a detached look at his weak play, Nimzowitsch devised a scientific approach to the analysis of a given position. These ideas were unfolded in *My System*. He introduced and expounded upon bizarre strategic ideas such as "overprotection" and "prophylaxis." He coined such classic phrases as *"the passed pawn is a criminal that should be kept under lock and key,"* and *"the threat is stronger than its execution."* By mixing scientific jargon, wit, and humor, Nimzowitsch was able to create a challenging work that has tested and treated chessplayers since 1925 and will continue to do so for many generations yet to come.

Nimzowitsch's works, *My System, Die Blockade*, and *Chess Praxis,* ushered in an era described by Nimzowitsch as the hypermodern period. Today's chess has thoroughly absorbed its effects. Nimzowitsch's "restraining" defense, the Nimzo-Indian, is still the most popular way of meeting 1.d4. Most openings today feature the Bishop's fianchetto, a radical development that was introduced by Nimzowitsch and his contemporaries. Various strategies, such as blockading Knights playing on different colored squares, and many others described in the book, have all become part of the arsenal of today's Grandmasters. Nimzowitsch's ideas have stood the test of time and have prospered.

My own experience with *My System* is not a unique one. I first read *My System* during my teenage years - the years of rebellion. Of course I took issue with just about everything he wrote. But in this I had been tricked. Nimzowitsch had induced me *to think about his ideas*. Right or wrong it didn't matter. The fact that I was either forced to prove or refute these ideas had me thinking in a manner that was unexpected. What was this business of, "restraint, blockade, destroy?" Why try to "undermine" a "base pawn?" Why not just play for mate, I thought? Yes, indeed in those days, chess was as easy as check, check, and mate. But, what to do when the opponent's King is safe?

The years take their toll. Annoyed with *My System*, both because I didn't understand it and didn't know how to refute it, I put the book down and didn't look at it again for several years. The next reread had me bemused. Of course prophylaxis makes sense. Wasn't everybody playing h2-h3, escaping back rank mates when they couldn't find anything better to do? Certainly the conquering of the absolute 7th rank is a marvelous investment of a pawn. Maybe he hadn't been so wrong after all. The digesting process was, however, still difficult.

Several defeats later brought me back for the third time, and another quick reread. More happy surprises. Nimzowitsch had understood the advantage of space and how to use this to switch to attacks on a flank. He also understood that although a player has few squares for his pieces, it is acceptable provided that each piece has a good square.

This then, is the strength of *My System*. It is a book that provokes you to think differently about chess. It challenges you to consider a different approach and urges you to prove or refute Nimzowitsch's ideas. It is also a book that you can read and reread, each time coming away with different lessons and insights, leading to a deeper understanding of the game.

The biggest problem with my original copy of *My System* was that it was written in descriptive notation at a time when algebraic was taking over as the world's chess language. It was also written in a manner and style that was decidedly too "European" and "Scientific" for my young mind.

The next generation of chessplayers may be spared my experience with the current volume, *My System - 21st Century Edition*. The entire layout is in algebraic notation, making it much easier to use. The book has gone through a tremendous amount of editing to create an easier read with more of an "American English" flavoring. I'm certain you'll savor this great classic every bit more.

Yasser Seirawan, International Grandmaster
Seattle, Washington
November, 1991

PART ONE

THE ELEMENTS

CHAPTER 1

ON THE CENTER AND DEVELOPMENT

Contains a short introduction and what the less advanced student must know about the center and development.

In my opinion the following are to be considered the elements of chess strategy:

(1) The center.
(2) Play in open files.
(3) Play in the 7th and 8th ranks.
(4) The passed pawn.
(5) The pin.
(6) Discovered check.
(7) Exchanging.
(8) The pawn chain.

Each one of these elements will be as thoroughly explained as possible in what follows. We begin with the center, which we propose to treat at first with the less experienced player in mind. In the second part of the book, which is devoted to positional play, we will attempt to investigate the center from the point of view of "higher learning." As you know, the center was precisely the point around which in the years 1911-13 what amounted to a revolution in chess took place. I mean that the articles which I wrote, *(Entspricht Dr. Tarrasch's "Modern Schachpartie" wirklich moderner Auffassung?)* ran directly counter to the traditional conception and sounded the call to a revolt which was in fact to give birth to the neo-romantic school. The two-fold treatment of the center, which we propose to undertake on instructional grounds, would therefore seem to be justified.

First a few definitions:

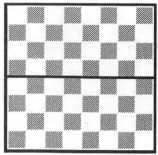
#1 The Frontier Line

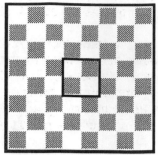
#2 The Midpoint / The small square
is the center

The line shown on Diagram 1 we call the frontier "line," and is of course to be taken in its mathematical, not in its chess sense. The square marked on Diagram 2 is the midpoint of the board, again naturally in its mathematical sense. The midpoint is easy to find, as it is the point of intersection of the long diagonals.

♦ *1. By development we mean the strategic advance of the troops to the frontier line.*

The process is similar to the advance on the outbreak of a war. Both armies seek to reach the frontier as quickly as possible in order to penetrate into enemy territory.

Development is a collective conception. To have developed one, two, or three pieces does not mean that we are developed. The situation demands that all pieces be developed. The period of development should be inspired by a democratic spirit. How undemocratic for instance, it would be to let one of your officers go for a long walking tour, while the others kicked their heels together at home and bored themselves horribly. No, let each officer make one move only, and . . . dig himself in.

♦ *2. A pawn move must not in itself be regarded as a developing move, but merely as an aid to development.*

An important rule for the beginner is the following: if it were possible to develop the pieces without the aid of pawn moves, the pawnless advance would be the correct one, for, as suggested, the pawn is not a fighting unit in the sense that his crossing of the frontier is to be feared by the enemy, since obviously the attacking force of the pawns is small compared with that of the pieces. The pawnless advance, however, is in reality impossible of execution, since the enemy pawn center, thanks to its inherent aggressiveness, would drive back the pieces we had developed. For this reason we should, in order to safeguard the development of our pieces, first build up a pawn center.   By center we mean the four squares which enclose the midpoint - the squares e4, e5, d4, d5 (Diagram 2).

The wrecking of a pawnless advance is illustrated by the following: **1.Nf3 Nc6 2.e3** (since the pawn has not been moved to the center, we may still regard the advance as pawnless in our sense). **2...e5 3.Nc3 Nf6 4.Bc4? d5.** Now the faultiness of White's development may be seen; the Black pawns have a demobilizing effect. **5.Bb3** (bad at the outset, a piece moved twice), **5...d4** and White is uncomfortably placed, at any rate from the point of view of the player with little fighting experience.

Another example is the following: White without QR, A. Nimzowitsch - Amateur (White's a-pawn is at a3). **1.e4 e5 2.Nf3 Nc6 3.Bc4 Bc5 4.c3 Nf6 5.d4 exd4 6.cxd4 Bb6.** Black has now lost the center, and in addition, by neglecting to play 4...d6, he allows White's center too much mobility. His development may therefore rightly be described as pawnless, or, more strictly, one which has become pawnless. **7.d5 Ne7 8.e5 Ne4 9.d6 cxd6 10.exd6 Nxf2 11.Qb3** and Black, who is completely wedged in by the pawn on d6 succumbs to the enemy assault in a few moves, in spite of the win of a Rook. **11...Nxh1 12.Bxf7+ Kf8 13.Bg5** and Black resigned.

It follows from the rule given (♦ 2, previous page), that pawn moves are only admissible in the development stage when they either help to occupy the center, or stand in logical connection with its occupation; a pawn move which protects its own or attacks the enemy's center, for example. In the open game after 1.e4 e5, either d3 or d4 - now or later - is always a correct move.

If then only the pawn moves designated above are allowable, it follows that moves of the flank pawns must be regarded as loss of time - with this qualification, that in close games the rule applies to only a limited extent, since contact with the enemy is not complete, and development proceeds at a slower tempo.

To sum up: In the open game speed of development is the very first law. Every piece must be developed in one move. Every pawn move is to be regarded as loss of time, unless it helps to build or support the center or attack the enemy's center. Therefore, as Lasker truly observed: In the opening one or two pawn moves, not more.

♦ *3. To be ahead in development is the ideal to be aimed at.*

If I were running a race with someone, it would be, to say the least, inopportune were I to throw away valuable time by say, rubbing dirt off of my nose, although I must not be considered as blaming that operation in itself. If, however, I can induce my opponent to waste time by a similar action, I would then get an advantage in development over him. The repeated moving back and forth of the same piece would be described as an action of this kind. Accordingly we force our opponent to lose time if we make a developing move which at the same time attacks a piece which he has already moved. This very typical situation arises after **1.e4 d5 2.exd5 Qxd5 3.Nc3** (Diagram 3).

#3 Typical win of a tempo

♦ *4. Exchange with resulting gain of tempo.*

The moves just given show in the most compact form a maneuver which we may call a compound one. For why (see Diagram 4) do we take the d-pawn? (2.exd5). The answer is to entice the piece which recaptures it on to a square exposed to attack. This was the first part of the maneuver. The second (3.Nc3) consisted in the utilization of the Queen's position which is in a certain sense compromised.

#4 2.exd5! forcing the Black Queen to recapture on d5.

The compound maneuver which we have just outlined is one of the greatest value to the student, and we proceed to give a few more examples. **1.d4 d5 2.c4 Nf6 3.cxd5!** and now two variations follow. If 3...Qxd5, then 4.Nc3, and if 3...Nxd5 4.e4, so that in either case White with his 4th move will have made a developing move of full value, which Black will be forced to answer by wandering about. But perhaps the beginner may say in his heart: Why should Black recapture? Many a skillful businessman displays in chess an altogether unnatural delicacy of feeling and does not recapture. But the master unfortunately knows that he is under compulsion, there's no remedy for it, he must recapture, otherwise the material balance in the center would be disturbed. It follows from the fact that this is compulsory that the capture retards, for the moment at any rate, the enemy's development, except in the case when the recapture can be made with what is at the same time a developing move.

A further example: **1.e4 e5 2.f4 Nf6 3.fxe5! Nxe4.** Forced, otherwise Black would be a pawn down with no equivalent for it. **4.Nf3** (to prevent ...Qh4), **4...Nc6 5.d3** (the logical complement of the exchange 3.fxe5), **5...Nc5 6.d4 Ne4 7.d5,** and after 7...Nb8 White will have the opportunity of gaining more tempi by 8.Bd3 or 8.Nbd2. The latter contingency must be carefully weighed. The exchange of the time devouring Ne4 for the new-born Nd2 means loss of tempo for Black, since with the disappearance of the Knight there will vanish also the tempi consumed by him - there will be nothing on the board to show for them. When a farmer loses a sucking pig through illness, he mourns not only the little pig, but also the good food he has gambled on it.

An intermezzo is possible in the maneuver: exchange with gain of tempo.

After **1.e4 e5 2.f4 d5 3.exd5 Qxd5 4.Nc3 Qe6**, the exchange maneuver 5.fxe5 Qxe5+ comes into consideration for White, since the square e5 must be looked on as an exposed place for the Black Queen. However after **5.fxe5** there follows **Qxe5** giving check, and White is apparently not able to make use of the position of the Black Queen.

In reality, however, the check can only be regarded as an intermezzo. White simply plays **6.Be2** (Qe2 is still stronger), and after all gains tempi at the cost of the Black Queen by Nf3 or d4. **6...Bg4 7.d4** (Not 7.Nf3 because of 7...Bxf3! and no tempo is lost, since the Queen need not move) **7...Bxe2 8.Ngxe2 Qe6 9.0-0** and White has 5 tempi to the good (both Knights and a Rook are developed, the pawn occupies the center, and the King is in safety), whereas Black can show but one visible tempo, namely the Queen on e6. Even this tempo, too, will later on be doubly or even trebly lost, since the Queen will have to shift her ground more than once (she will be chased away by Nf4 etc.), so that White's advantage is equivalent to at least five tempi. Exchange, intermezzo, gain of tempo: the exchange and the gain of a tempo are related, the intermezzo alters nothing.

◆ *5. Liquidation, with consequent development or disembarrassment.*

When a merchant sees that his business is not succeeding, he does well to liquidate it, so as to invest the proceeds in a more promising one. Translated into terms of chess, I mean by this that when one's development is threatened with being held up, one must adopt a radical cure, and on no account try to remedy matters by half-hearted measures. I will first illustrate this by an example. **1.e4 e5 2.Nf3 Nc6 3.d4 d5?** (Black's last move is questionable, for the second player should not at once copy such an enterprising move as 3.d4). **4.exd5 Qxd5 5.Nc3 Bb4.** For the moment Black has been able to hold his ground, the Queen has not had to move away, but after **6.Bd2,** Black would still appear to be in some embarrassment (Diagram 5), for the retreat of the Queen, who is now again threatened, would cost a tempo. The right course, therefore, is to exchange **6...Bxc3 7.Bxc3** (whole-hearted liquidation) and now with the same idea

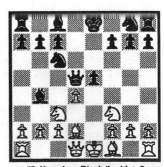

#5 How does Black liquidate?

7...exd4 (anything but a protecting move, such as ...Bg4, or a flight move, such as ...e4, for in the development stage there is no time for this) **8.Nxd4.** Black can now proceed with his development with **8...Nf6** and has relieved the tension in the center and is in no way behind in development. This relief of tension in the center, taken with the exchange, is a main characteristic of complete liquidation.

#6 Black's move. He must liquidate to relieve the tension.

After **1.e4 e5 2.Nf3 Nc6 3.d4 d5?** White can also embarrass his opponent by **4.Bb5!** (Diagram 6). Undeveloped as he is, Black sees that he is seriously threatened by 5.Nxe5. What is he to do? The protecting move 4...Bd7 is here as inadequate as 4...Bg4. Both of these moves have the common failing that they do nothing towards relieving the tension in the center. 4...Bd7 loses a valuable pawn after 5.exd5 Nxd4 6.Bxd7+ Qxd7 7.Nxd4 exd4 8.Qxd4, while 4...Bg4 could here be answered by 5.h3 (in this case a forcing move). **4...Bg4 5.h3!** Bxf3 (best to do it while he can! if 5...Bh5?, then 6.g4 followed by Nxe5) **6.Qxf3.** From here the Queen exercises a decisive influence on the center. **6...Nf6 7.exd5 e4** (or a pawn is lost) **8.Qe3! Qxd5 9.c4** with a decided advantage to White.

Relatively best for Black would have been (from Diagram 6) immediately **4...dxe4**, and he liquidates thus since his means do not allow him the luxury of maintaining a position of instability in the center. The continuation might be **5.Nxe5 Bd7** and Black threatens to win a piece by 6...Nxe5. **6.Bxc6 Bxc6 7.0-0 Bd6 8.Nxc6 bxc6 9.Nc3** f5 and Black has satisfactory development and does not stand badly. Or again, **6.Bxc6 Bxc6 7.Nc3 Bb4 8.0-0 Bxc3 9.bxc3** and now perhaps **9...Ne7.** After **10.Qg4 0-0 11.Nxc6 Nxc6 12.Qxe4**, White, it is true, has a pawn more, but Black seizes the e-file by **12...Re8** and now after **13.Qf3 Na5** (the process of development is over and maneuvering begins), followed later by ...c6 and the occupation of White's weak squares at c4 and d5 by ...Nc4, along with ...Qd5, Black stands better. Thus timely liquidation has brought the second player's questionable process of development back into the right track.

Another example is furnished by the well-known variation in the Giuoco piano. **1.e4 e5 2.Nf3 Nc6 3.Bc4 Bc5 4.c3 Nf6 5.d4 exd4** (forced surrender of the center), **6.cxd4 Bb4+ 7.Bd2** and now the Black Bishop is under the slight threat of 8.Bxf7+ followed by 9. Qb3+. On the other hand the White center pawns are very strong, and it is necessary to break them up. However if at once 7...d5 8.exd5 Nxd5 9.Bxb4 Ndxb4 10.Qb3 and White stands better. The correct play is therefore **7...Bxd2+** (getting rid of the threat to his Bishop) **8.Nbxd2** and now the freeing move **8...d5.** After **9.exd5 Nxd5 10.Qb3** Black equalizes with the strategic **10...Nce7.**

As we have seen, the exchange properly used furnishes an excellent weapon, and forms the basis of the typical maneuvers which we analyzed above: (1) exchange with consequent gain of a tempo, (2) liquidation followed by a developing or freeing move. We must, however, give a most emphatic warning against exchanging blindly and without motive, for to move a piece several times in order to exchange it for an enemy piece which has not moved, would be a thoroughly typical beginner's mistake. Therefore only exchange in the two cases outlined above.

An example of a wrong, unmotivated exchange: **1.e4 e5 2.d4 exd4 3.c3** (White offers a gambit), **3...Bc5?**. Curious that this move, which must devour a tempo, should be the beginner's first or second thought. He may consider 3...dxc3, but having perhaps heard somewhere that one should not go pawn hunting in the opening, and rejects it in favor of 3...Bc5. The continuation, a sad one for Black, will be **4.cxd4 Bb4+** (moving the Bishop again!), **5.Bd2 Bxd2+** (unfortunately forced) **6.Nxd2** with an advantage of three tempi. The mistake lay in 3...Bc5?, but (after 4.cxd4) 4...Bb6 would at any rate have been better than 4...Bb4+, which only led to a disadvantageous exchange.

♦ *6. The center and its demobilizing force. Some examples as to when and how the advance of the enemy center is to be met. On the maintenance and the surrender of the center.*

As we have already noticed, a free, mobile center is a deadly weapon of attack, since the advance of the center pawns threatens to drive back the enemy pieces. In every case the question is, whether the hunted Knight, losing all control over himself, will have to flit aimlessly from pillar to post, or whether he will succeed in saving himself or the tempi for which he is responsible. An example: **1.e4 e5 2.d4 exd4** (the White e-pawn is ready to march and is only waiting for an enemy Knight to show himself on f6 to put him speedily to flight), **3.c3 Nf6!**. Black lets what will happen, and this is what every beginner should do in order to gain

#7 Where does Black play the Knight to keep his tempi?

experience of the consequences of an advance in the center. **4.e5** (Diagram 7) **Ne4!** The Knight can maintain himself there, for 5.Bd3 will be answered by a developing move of full value, namely 5...d5. Not of course a further wandering by 5...Nc5?, for this move, after 6.cxd4 Nxd3 7.Qxd3 would yield an advantage of four tempi to White. On the other hand after **1.e4 e5 2.d4 exd4 3.c3 Nf6! 4.e5**, it would not be advantageous to move the Knight to d5, for the poor beast would not find any rest here. **4...Nd5? 5.Qxd4** (not 5.Bc4 because of 5...Nb6 and the Bishop in his turn will have to lose a tempo), **5...c6 6.Bc4 Nb6 7.Nf3**. White has here six tempi as against two or one and a half, for the Knight is not better placed at b6 than at f6, and the move ...c6 was really not a whole tempo, since no move of a central pawn is here in question.

#8 Where is the Black Knight to move?

Another example. **1.e4 e5 2.f4 exf4** (loss of time) **3.Nf3 Nf6! 4.e5** (Diagram 8) and now we have the same problem. 4...Ne4 would not here spell "maintenance," on the contrary there would follow at once 5.d3 Nc5? d4, etc. But here is an exceptional case when the square h5 is a satisfying one (as a rule, border squares are not favorable for Knights), **4...Nh5 5.d4 d5** (or 5...d6 to force the exchange of the White e-pawn for the d-pawn which has only moved once), and Black does not stand badly.

In general, the Knight seeks to establish himself in the center, as in our first example (Diagram 7), only rarely on the side. **1.e4 e5 2.Nf3 Nc6 3.Bc4 Bc5 4.c3** (a discomforting move which plans an assault on Black's center to disturb him in his mobilization), **4...Nf6 5.d4 exd4 6.e5 d5** (6...Ne4 would be a mistake because of 7.Bd5, but now the Knight can no longer maintain himself of his own strength so he calls in the aid of the d-pawn), thus: 6...d5 and if now 7.Bb3, then the Black Knight establishes itself on e4).

An example of how such establishment is maintained. In the position which we have already examined, after **1.e4 e5 2.d4 exd4 3.c3 Nf6 4.e5! Ne4! 5.Bd3 d5!** there follows **6.cxd4** and Black cannot hug himself with the thought that he is out of the woods, for a tempo gaining attack on the Knight is in the air (Nc3). Black, however develops and attacks at the same time, for instance by 6...Nc6 7.Nf3 Bg4 (threatening the d-pawn), or again by 6...c5, but not by the illogical 6...Bb4+?, as White answers 7.Bd2 and Black is forced into a tempo losing exchange.

It is nevertheless more prudent to hold the center intact. Even if we should succeed in breaking the shock of the advancing mass of pawns (by a proper withdrawal of the Knight as outlined above), the line of play is difficult, and what is more the "pawn-roller" need not advance at once, but may hold its advance as a continual threat over our heads. Therefore, if it can be done without counterbalancing threat over disadvantages, hold the center. (Diagram 9).

After **1.e4 e5 2.Nf3 Nc6 3.Bc4 Be7** (quite playable, though ...Bc5 is certainly more aggressive) **4.d4**, Black will do best to support his center by **4...d6** and thus hold

#9 Which is on principle the right move for Black, ...exd4 or ...d6? How is ...Bf6 met? Why is ...f6 bad?

it intact. After **5.dxe5 dxe5**, White's center is immobile. In order to maintain the center, support by a pawn is indicated (of course not by ...f6?, which would be a horrible mistake as the open diagonal a2-g8 would be decisive), since the pawn is a born defender. If a piece has to protect any attacked piece or pawn he feels himself under restraint whereas in similar circumstances a pawn would find himself perfectly at ease. In the case under consideration, protection by a piece, by ...Bf6?, would only support the e-pawn but not the center considered in the abstract. For instance, 4...Bf6? 5.dxe5 Nxe5 6.Nxe5 Bxe5 7.f4, and the exchange has occurred in accordance with our rule: Exchange followed by a gain of tempo (here by f4).

♦ *6a. Surrender of the Center.*

1.e4 e5 2.Nf3 Nc6 3.d4 exd4! (3...d6 would be uncomfortable for Black - 3...d6? 4.dxe5 dxe5 5.Qxd8+ Kxd8 (otherwise the e-pawn falls), and Black has lost the right of castling, and with it a convenient means of connecting his Rook). **4.Nxd4.** In the position now arrived at Black can, after mature consideration, play **4...Nf6**, since, after **5.Nxc6 bxc6,** possible attempts to demobilize the Knight by say **6.e5** can be parried by **6...Ne4** and if **7.Bd3 d5!** But with this Black will have solved only a part of his problem, namely the little problem of how to develop his King Knight, but not the larger problem of the center as such. To this end the following postulates are necessary. (1) If one has allowed the enemy to establish a free, mobile center pawn, the latter must be regarded as a dangerous criminal. Against him all our chess fury must be directed, so that the second rule follows at once: (2) Such a pawn must either be executed (d5, ...dxe4 must be prepared for), or be put under restraint. Accordingly we condemn the criminal either to death or to imprisonment for life. Or we can pleasantly combine the two by first condemning him to death, then commuting his sentence to life imprisonment; or, what is the more common case, we keep him under restraint until he is quite impotent, and then show our manly courage by executing the death sentence (arriving at d5 and ...dxe4). Restraint would be begun by 4...d6 and perfected by ...Nf6, ...Be7, ...0-0, ...Re8 and ...Bf8 by which procedure any violent advance is kept under close observation. White on his side will do all in his power to make the (criminal) e-pawn mobile, by, for example, f4, Re1, etc., as occasion offers. The game might run somewhat as follows: **1.e4 e5 2.Nf3 Nc6 3.d4 exd4 4.Nxd4 d6 5.Be2 Nf6 6.Nc3 Be7 7.0-0 0-0 8.f4! Re8!** (not 8...d5 because of 9.e5) **9.Be3 Bf8 10.Bf3 Bd7.**

#10 The fight in support of and against the pawn on e4

Each side has completed its mobilization. White will try to force e5, Black to prevent this advance. This situation (Diagram 10) gives rise to most interesting struggles, and we recommend that the student practice in games playing in turn for and against the center, as he will thus strengthen his positional insight.

#11 Lee-Nimzowitsch
Black to play and destroy
White's center

The restraining process is not easy, and to kill off the mobile center pawn seems simpler, though cases when this is feasible do not very often occur. A few examples follow. **1.e4 e5 2.Nf3 Nc6 3.d4 exd4 4.Nxd4 Nf6 5.Nc3 Bb4 6.Nxc6** (in order to be able to make the protecting move 7.Bd3) **6...bxc6! 7.Bd3** and now Black need no longer lay siege to the e-pawn by ...d6 ...0-0 and ...Re8, since he can at once resort to 7...d5, and after the further moves 8.exd5 cxd5 the disturber of his peace has disappeared. A like fate overtook the center pawn in the game Lee-Nimzowitsch, Ostend, 1907. **1.d4 Nf6 2.Nf3 d6 3.Nbd2 Nbd7 4.e4 e5 5.c3 Be7 6.Bc4 0-0 7.0-0** (Diagram 11) **7...exd4! 8.cxd4 d5!** and at a blow the proud e-pawn despite his freedom and mobility, vanishes, is pulverized! After **9.Bd3** (if 9.exd5 then 9...Nb6 followed by recapture on d5). **9...dxe4 10.Nxe4 Nxe4 11.Bxe4 Nf6** (here is our exchange with consequent gain of tempo) **12.Bd3 Nd5 13.a3 Bf6**, and now Black stands better because of White's weak d-pawn. For the continuation see illustrative game No.4.

As a third illustration take the opening moves of my game against Yates (White) at Baden-Baden. **1.e4 Nc6 2.Nf3 Nf6 3.Nc3** (or 3.e5 Nd5 4.c4 Nb6 5.d4 d6 and Black threatens to win back the 3 tempi he has sacrificed, though perhaps 6.e6 fxe6 might be played with attacking chances for White). **3...d5 4.exd5 Nxd5 5.d4** and White has established a free center pawn. There followed **5...Bf5 6.a3 g6** (the alternative was to restrain the d-pawn by e6, ultimately seizing the d-file and keeping the d-pawn under observation) **7.Bc4 Nb6 8.Ba2 Bg7 9.Be3 e5!** Black has thus not played to restrain the d-pawn, but to kill it. There followed **10.Qe2 0-0 11.dxe5 Bg4** and Black recovered the pawn with a freer game.

♦ *7. On pawn hunting in the opening. Usually a mistake. Exceptional case of center pawns.*

Since the mobilization of the forces is by far the most important operation in the opening stages, it strikes anyone who knows this as comic that the less experienced player should so eagerly plunge into an utterly unimportant sideline, by which I mean pawn hunting. This eagerness may be more readily explicable on psychological grounds, for the young player wants to give rein to the energy which smolders in him, which he can do by getting the scalps of perfectly harmless pawns, while the older player is - well, the older player is not loath to show how young he really is. In the end both come to grief. What, therefore, the inexperienced player, young or old, must take to heart is the commandment: *Never play to win a pawn while your development is yet unfinished!* To this there is but one exception, which we shall discuss later.

We begin by showing the best manner of declining a gambit, which we can do very shortly, since we have already considered some analogous cases. In the Center Gambit, after **1.e4 e5 2.d4 exd4! 3.c3** (Diagram 12). Black can play 3...Nf6, or any other developing move with the exception of course of 3...Bc5? For instance, 3...Nc6 4.cxd4 d5, or lastly even 3...c6 4.cxd4 d5. (It will now be noticed that the c-pawn stands in logical connection with the center). If 3...c6 4.Qxd4 Black still plays 4...d5 5.exd5 cxd5, to be followed by ...Nc6. Again, in the Evans Gambit **1.e4 e5 2.Nf3 Nc6**

#12 Black to move

3.Bc4 Bc5 4.b4 we decline the gambit with 4...Bb6 in order to avoid being driven around the board, which would happen if we played 4...Bxb4 5.c3. Black by playing 4...Bxb4 has by no means lost a tempo, since the move b4, which White was able to throw in *gratis* without Black being able in the meanwhile to develop a piece, was, in the sense of development, unproductive, unproductive as every pawn move must be in the nature of things, if it does not bear a logical connection with the center. For suppose after **4...Bb6 5.b5** (to make a virtue of necessity and attempt something of a demobilizing effect with our ill motived b-pawn move), **5...Nd4** and now if 6.Nxe5, then 6...Qg5 with a strong attack.

The beginner should decline the Kings's Gambit with 2...Bc5 (1.e4 e5 2.f4 Bc5) or by the simple 2...d6, a move which is better than its reputation. For instance: **1.e4 e5 2.f4 d6 3.Nf3 Nc6 4.Bc4 Be6!**. After **5.Bxe6 fxe6 6.fxe5 dxe5,** Black has good development and two open files for his Rooks (the d and f files), and in spite of his doubled pawns, stands better. If after 4...Be6 5.Bb5, then perhaps 5...Bd7, for since White has wandered about with his Bishop, Black may do likewise. The student should notice particularly that after **1.e4 e5 2.f4 d6 3.Nf3 Nc6 4.Nc3 Nf6 5.Be2,** the maneuver 5...exf4 is possible, and then if 6.d3 6...d5. This is timely surrender of the center and a speedy recapture of the same.

Acceptance of the gambit is allowable: **1.e4 e5 2.f4 exf4 3.Nf3 Nf6!**, not, however, with the idea of keeping the gambit pawn, but rather to subject the strength of White's center to a severe test (4.e5 Nh5), or to arrive at the counter thrust ...d5 (after 4.Nc3).

◆ *7a. A center pawn should always be taken if this can be done without too much danger.*

For example, **1.e4 e5 2.Nf3 Nc6 3.Bc4 Nf6 4.c3? Nxe4!**, for the ideal win (of a pawn), which the conquest of the center implies, is not high at the cost of a tempo. It is of less importance to keep the pawn. It is the ideal, not the material gain with which we are here concerned. Put otherwise: the win of a pawn anywhere on the side of the board brings no happiness in its train, but if you gain a pawn in the middle, then you really have something to brag about, for thus you will get the possibility of expansion at the very spot around which in the opening stages the fight usually sways, namely the center. (Diagram 13).

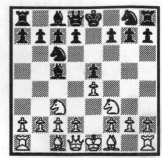

#13 Play continues 1.Nxe5 Nxe5 2.d4 in the spirit of gaining a center pawn

With this we close the first chapter, and refer the reader to illustrative games 1 and 2 at the end of the book.

CHAPTER 2

ON OPEN FILES

♦ *1. Introductory. General considerations and some definitions.*

The theory of open files, which was my discovery, must be regarded as one of the polishing stones of my system. I published the law of the establishment of outposts in open files about fourteen years ago in the *Wiener Schachzeitung,* but at that time I had not yet arrived at the perception that this maneuver must logically be subordinate to the main objective of any operation in a file, namely the eventual occupation of the 7th or 8th rank. In other words, in order to break down the enemy's resistance in it, but without for a moment relaxing our aim at the 7th rank, whose occupation must be regarded as the ideal to be arrived at in such an operation. The establishment of an outpost is therefore merely a subsidiary maneuver.

#14 The b, f, and h files are open for White's use, the latter from the point h3. The d-file is closed.

A file is said to be open for the Rook when no pawn of his is in it, or, if there is one, it is masked as, for example, it is in the h-file in Diagram 14. This definition implies that in deciding whether a file is "open" or "closed," we are not concerned with the question whether that file gives an avenue of attack on unoccupied, peaceful points, or on living enemy pieces (as a rule pawns). There is in fact no fundamental difference between play against a piece or against a point. Let us, for example, imagine a White Rook on h1, Black King on g8 and a Black pawn on h7. White is attacking the pawn on h7. Suppose that pawn were removed, White still attacks the point h7, which he wishes to conquer. In either case he will attempt, with the further material which he has at command (this was taken for granted: I give only the most important elements of the position), to establish a preponderance at h7, to bring up more pieces to the attack of this point than the defense can command. Having succeeded in doing this, he will ultimately play either Rh7 or Rxh7, as the case may be. That is to say our procedure is the same whether we are attacking the point h7 or a Black pawn at that point, for the measure of the mobility of the pawn will be reduced to nothing, since every object of attack must be made as nearly immobile as possible.

♦ *2. The genesis of open files: By peaceful means. By assault. The objective.*

From the definition of an open file, it follows that a file will be opened by the disappearance of one of our own pawns. This disappearance will be brought about peacefully if the enemy feels it incumbent on himself to exchange one of our well,

---

#15 Black playing ...Bxe3 opens the f-file for White

(because centrally) posted pieces, and the recapture is made by a pawn (Diagram 15). We must here stress the word "central," for it will be only seldom, and never in the opening, that you will be able to force your opponent to open a file by the exchange of a piece which you have posted on a flank. You will gain your object much more quickly if it is centrally posted, for pieces thus established in the middle of the board, and exercising their influence in all directions, are those which will be exchanged.

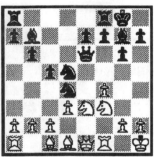

#15a Thomas - Alekhine , Baden Baden 1925. White moves

A position from the game Thomas-Alekhine, Baden-Baden 1925 (Diagram 15a). White to move. Black's Knights are centrally posted, and White finds himself forced to exchange them, so **1.Nxd4 cxd4** (opening of the c-file), and after the further moves **2.Nxd5 Qxd5 3.Bf3 Qd7 4.Bxb7 Qxb7** the significance of this file is considerable. There followed, **5.c4!** (On c2 the pawn would have been untenable), **5...dxc3 e.p.** with play in both the files. (see Game No. 11).

Therefore post your pieces centrally, as long as you can do so safely - without inviting the advance of the "pawn-roller." Thus will your opponent be provoked into an exchange which will give you an open file.

Let us in Diagram 15 imagine the continuation, **1...Bb6 2.Qd2 0-0 3.0-0-0 h6?** (see Diagram 16), we then get a typical example of an effective opening of a file. Thanks to Black's pawn on h6, White can now bring about the rapid disappearance of his g-pawn. 3...h6 was therefore bad, but hardly a waste of time, for Black had already completed his development, and after all there is a difference between going to sleep after or over our work! The mode of advance against h6 (the objective or object of attack) is h3, g4, g5. On hxg5 the pawn is then recaptured by a piece, whereupon Rg1 takes possession of the file which now is open. True, one of his own pieces is in the way, but this is of no consequence, for it is elastic. It is only a pawn which is obstinate, and we have our work cut out if we want to induce him to change his state.

As an example for practice, let us suppose that in the position shown on Diagram 16, the Bishops at e3 and b6 do not exist, and that Black's h-pawn is at h7, his

---

g-pawn at g6. The objective is now g6, and the h-file (always the one next to the objective) should be opened. The plan is h4, h5, and hxg6. But in this position after h4 we must, before going on, first give the Nf6 a dig in the ribs, since he is in the way, perhaps by 1.Nd5, and this done the pawn can advance to h5 in all comfort and without any sacrifice. As a last resort the attacked party may attempt to give the pawn the slip, that is on White's h5 to play ...g5, which, however, here would hardly answer since the square g5 is unprotected.

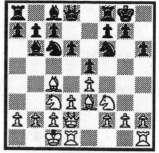

#16 The objective here is h6

♦ *3. The goal of every operation in a file. On some accompanying phenomena. Marauding raids. Enveloping operations.*

#17 Catastrophe on the h-file

The ideal which lies at the root of every operation in a file is the ultimate penetration by way of this file into the enemy's game, that is to say to our own 7th or 8th rank.

A very important rule is the following. Suppose that by operating in the d-file we reach the 7th rank by a roundabout way, by the maneuver Rd1-d4-a4-a7. This cannot be regarded as a *direct* exploitation of the d-file. A few elementary examples will now be given.

Line of operation the h-file. (Diagram 17) This will be seized by **1.Qh1+ Kg8**, and now according to rule either Qh7 or Qh8, the latter not being feasible, **2.Qh7+ Kf8 3.Qh8+** followed by a marauding expedition (for we thus designate every forking attack on two pieces), which is here not a chance raid, but rather a typical example of an entry by force at the 7th or 8th rank. If in Diagram 17 the Black Q were at d7 instead of b8, our method would be **1.Qh1+ Kg8 2.Qh7+ Kf8 3.Qh8+ Ke7 4.Qxg7+ Ke6 5.Qxd7+ Kxd7 6.g7**, and the result would be no less unpleasant. We may describe this triangular maneuver of the Q (h7, h8, g7) as an enveloping attack. Putting it briefly, we may say: Given deficient resistance the attacker, after safeguarding the lines of invasion, raids the 7th and 8th ranks, and, doing so, will not seldom be rewarded by the chance of a marauding expedition or an enveloping attack. So far the operation has been as readily intelligible as it is easily executed. Unfortunately in real life there are often great obstacles to overcome, as ♦4 will show.

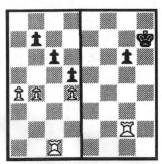

#18 On the left, Black's c-pawn guarded by his b-pawn is a protected obstacle. On the right, the g-pawn is an unprotected obstacle.

We have seen how great may be the significance of a forced entry into the 7th and 8th ranks. This being the case, it is natural to presume that nature herself may have done something for the protection of this sensitive area, just as good wise mother nature has given the human heart a place magnificently protected behind the ribs. The characteristic and natural defensive position is shown on Diagram 18 (right side). Here the pawn on g6 prevents White from invading the 7th rank. The road to the 7th or 8th rank leads only over my dead body, the valiant pawn seems to say.

If, however, this enemy g-pawn were protected by another pawn, it would be futile to run one's head up against such a block of granite by, shall we say, tripling our forces in the file. Rather would it not be the path of wisdom first to mine it by, for instance h4-h5, followed by hxg6, after which the granite block will have shriveled up to a defenseless pawnling? In Diagram 18 (left side), 1.b5 followed by bxc6 would have the effect of such a mining operation.

The pawn, as we have before insisted, is to be regarded as a sure defender. Protection by pieces may almost be called a confusion of terms. The pawn alone will stand on guard solidly, patiently, without a grumble. Therefore a "protected pawn" means a pawn protected by a fellow pawn. If our pawn has been enticed away from the confederation of pawns he will be subject to attack by many pieces.

The obvious idea is then to win the pawn by piling up our attacks on it, first for the sake of the gain in material, but secondly in order to break down the resistance in the file. This will be technically managed by first bringing up our pieces into attacking positions. A hot fight will then be waged around the pawn. As often as we attack, Black covers, so we now seek to obtain the upper hand by thinning the ranks of the defending forces, which can be done (a) by driving them away, (b) by exchange, (c) by shutting off one of the defending pieces. I mean that we transfer our attack from our opponent to his defenders, a perfectly normal proceeding, often practiced at school (in rough-and-tumble, I mean). The following endgame, (see Diagram 19) will illustrate the method, **1.Rh2 Kh7 2.Reh1.** White can pile up the attack since the obstructing pawn at h6 is without pawn protection, **2...Bf8 3.Nf5 Rb6.** Attack and

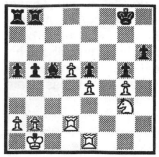

#19 Converging attacks on the Black h-pawn (evolutionary attack)

defense balance each other, but by White's next maneuver, 4.d6, the defending Black Rook on b6 will be shut out of the fight, and the h-pawn will fall, while simultaneously the entry into the 7th and eighth ranks via the h-file will be made possible. Had two Black Rooks stood on their 3rd rank,(a6, b6) the sacrifice of the exchange by ...Rxd6 would have been possible, but with the Rooks so placed, such a move as ...Bxd6 would have been very bad, after 4.d6 Bxd6 5.Rxh6+ Kg8 6.Rh8+ Kf7 7.R1h7+ Kf6, and now a waiting move, which after the preceding blows - one Rook now holding the 7th, the other 8th rank - is really intelligible, i.e., 8.Rg7! with mate to follow.

Or take the skeleton position: White Rooks f1, f2, Knight d4. Black pawn f6, Bishop d8, Rook c8, King f8. Play would go **1.Ne6+ King any 2.Nxd8 Rxd8 3.Rxf6.** The ranks of the defenders are thinned by exchange. The maneuver against the obstructing pawn so far considered is contained in the conception "evolutionary attack." The whole manner of concentration against one point, in order eventually to get superior forces to bear upon it, implies this. The goal, too, was symptomatic. It was, in fact, partly material gain (the win of a pawn was welcome) which tempted us, partly the ideal hovering before us of conquering the 7th rank. This mixture of motives was significant.

Quite another picture is revealed in the process employed in Diagram 20 (only the significant pieces are shown). Granted that play in the h-file by Rah1 would be idle because of ...Nf6 or h6 (with a granite block in the file). How may White otherwise make use of the h-file? The answer is that he gives up all idea of material profit, and instead does everything, stops at no sacrifice, in order to get the offending pawn out of the way. Therefore 1.**Rxh7** Kxh7 2.**Rh1** mate. Simple as this ending is, it seems to me to be of the greatest importance, as it brings clearly before us the difference between the "evolutionary" and "revolutionary" forms of attack.

#20 Breakthrough at h7 - example of the Revolutionary attack

We will therefore give yet another example (see Diagram 21). An evolutionary attack would, after **1.Rah1 2.Nf8 Be7** (thinning defender's ranks by exchange), lead to the winning of the objective. The revolutionary attack on the other hand would dispense with the winning of the Black h-pawn as follows: **1.Rxh7 Kxh7** (there can be no talk of having won the pawn here for White has given up a Rook for it)

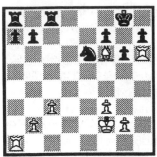

#21 How would the "evolutionary" and the "revolutionary" attacks proceed in this example?

2.Rh1+ Kg8 3.Rh8 mate. The idea of the revolutionary attack lies, as is here clearly shown, in opening by sheer force an entry to the 7th or 8th rank which had been barred to us. One Rook sacrifices himself for his colleague, in order that the latter may reach the objective, the 8th rank. Yes, even on a chess board there is such a thing as true comradeship!

In what chronological order are these two methods of attack to be employed? The answer to this is: First try the converging attack. Attack the obstructing pawn with several pieces. By so doing opportunity may be found to force the defending pieces into uncomfortable positions where they will get into each other's way, for the defense will often be cramped for space. Afterwards see whether among other things there is a possibility of a breakthrough by force, in other words of a revolutionary attack.

♦ *5. The restricted advance in one file with the idea of giving up that file for another one. The indirect exploitation of a file. The file as a jumping-off place.*

In the position in Diagram 22 the direct exploitation of the f-file, with eventual Rxf7 (after first driving off the protecting Rook), would be impossible with the scanty material available. The simple **1.Rf5**, however, clearly wins a pawn, and later Rb7 may follow. It is important that we examine this maneuver to see its logical meaning. Since 1.Rf7 was impractical, there could be no question of a direct exploitation of

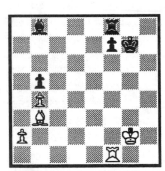

#22 The simplest example of the restricted advance in a file followed by the maneuvering of the Rook to another file 1.Rf5, 2.Rxb5, 3.Rb7

#23 The file as a "jumping off" place: a positional example. White can play Rc5-a5, menacing the Black a-pawn

the f-file in our sense. On the other hand it would be pushing ingratitude to an extreme length if we went on to assert that the f-file had no bearing whatever on the b-pawn. Where then does the truth lie? The answer is: The file was here used not directly, nor to its fullest extent, but indirectly, as a kind of jumping-off place. See Diagram 23, where another instance of the use of a file in this manner is given.

As a further example consider the skeleton position: White: Rook g1, Bishop e3, pawn h2. Black King h7, pawn h6. The maneuver 1.Bd4, 2.Rg7+ would be a direct, and 1.Rg3, 2.Rh3, 3.Rxh6 would be an indirect exploitation of the g-file.

♦ *6. The outpost. The radius of attack. With what piece should one occupy an advanced position on a center file, and on a flank? Change of roles and what this proves.*

Let us glance at Diagram 24. White has the center and the d-file. In other respects the positions are equal. White with the move will now attempt some operation on the d-file. This presents some difficulties since the protected Black pawn at d6 represents a "granite block." If White, in spite of the rules laid down in No. 4, proceeded to assault Black's d-pawn by Rd2, and Red1, not only the esteemed reader but the Black d-pawn himself would deride him, so we had better keep to the rules, and perhaps try to undermine the position by e5. But this too proves to be impossible, for the enemy's possession of the e-file is a quite sufficient

#24 White establishes an outpost on the d-file

bar to any projected pawn move to e5. Accordingly let us give up the d-file as such, and content ourselves with an indirect exploitation of it by the restricted advance Rd4, to be followed later by Ra4. But this maneuver, too, is here somewhat weak, for Black's Queenside is too compact. Note that if Black's a-pawn were isolated it would be totally in place to bring up by a similar process the King Rook to the a-file via the d-file. Since all attempts have so far broken down we begin to look for some other base of operations, and we would be wrong in so doing, for the d-file can be exploited in this position. The key move is 1.Nd5 and the Knight placed here we call the outpost. By this we mean a piece, usually a Knight, established on an open file in enemy territory, and protected (of course by a pawn). This Knight, protected and supported as he is, will, in consequence of his radius of attack, exercise a disturbing influence, and will, therefore, cause the opponent to weaken his position in the d-file, in order to drive him away, by ...c6. And therefore we may say -

    (a) An advanced post forms a base for new attacks.
    (b) An outpost provokes a weakening of the enemy's
        position in the file in question.

After **1.Nd5 c6** (1...Rc8 would also be good, and in fact in the position given would be the defense adopted by a strong player, but it takes iron nerves to let a Knight so threateningly posted remain in his place hour after hour! Moreover, there may come a time when Black will be forced to make the weakening move ...c6) there follows: **2.Nc3**, and now the Black d-pawn, after White's Rd2 followed by Red1 will certainly not laugh any longer.

It is important for the student to know that the strength of an outpost lies in its strategic connection with its own hinterland. The outpost does not derive its strength from itself, but rather from this hinterland, namely from the open file and the protecting pawn, and if suddenly one or other of these points of contact failed, it would almost entirely lose its prestige and significance. For instance, in Diagram 24 let us place a White pawn at d3, the d-file would in this case be closed, and then if **1...c6 2.Nc3**, the Black d-pawn would not be weak, (for how should a body be weak if it is not exposed to attack?). Or again (from Diagram 24) suppose the White pawn were at e3 instead of e4. Contact with the pawn now fails, as is painfully evident after the moves **1...c6 2.Nc3 d5!**, and White has achieved nothing, whereas with the White pawn at e4 the Black d-pawn would remain paralyzed (backward), at any rate for a considerable time. Therefore the file to its rear and the protecting pawn are essential accompaniments to an advanced outpost.

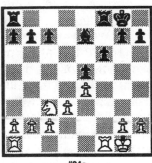

#24a

In a skeleton position arising out of the Giuoco Piano (Diagram 24a. We can imagine *x* other pieces on each side), White has the f-file with an advanced post at f5, Black the d-file with an outpost on d4. Both files at the moment "bite on granite" (on protected pawns). To sap this strength White will direct his Knight via e2 and g3 to f5. The obvious course for Black is to drive the Knight away by g6, but by inducing this the strategic mission of White's outpost will have been accomplished, for Black's f-pawn becomes a weakness. It is important to notice that moving the Knight to f5 was the starting point of a new attack, namely on g7.

Very often the outpost will be exchanged at his station. If the attacking player has played correctly, the retaking piece or pawn will yield full compensation for the piece which has been taken. Here a conversion of advantages is the order of the day. For instance, if after Nf5 a piece takes the Knight, this will be recaptured by the e-pawn, and White now gets the point e4 for a Rook or his other Knight, and in addition some possibility (after g4-g5) of opening the g-file. Further the pawn now at f5 will effectively render immobile the Black pawn at f6, which is the object of attack. (see Diagram 25, also Game number 5, Haken-Giese).

In a flank file the advanced post should be occupied by a piece of heavy metal. Flank files are the a, b, g, and h files. Center files are the c, d, e, and f files.

In Diagram 25 a flank file is in question, and the occupation of an advanced post in it by a Knight would have little effect, for the attacking range of a Knight at g6 would be small, (still smaller of course on a Rook file). 1.Rg6 is in fact indicated since thus we go some way towards gaining control of the g-file, which so far has been in dispute, or towards getting some other advantage. It should be noted that the file was disputed since neither side could move up or down it unchallenged. Freedom to do this is the only sure sign that a file is controlled. It therefore remains for White to find a suitable point on which to double his Rooks.

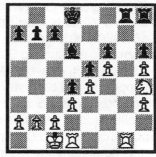

It can be found if we seek it. 1.Rg2? Rxg2 2.Nxg2 Rg8 and Black holds the file. Or, 1.Rg4? Rxg4 2.hxg4 Rg8 3.Ng6 and White will hardly be able to make anything of his backward extra pawn. But **1.Rg6!** (outpost), **Rxg6** (otherwise 2.Rdg1 doubling the Rooks) **2.hxg6** with a giant of a passed pawn and the possibility (after the Knight moves to f3) of the maneuver Rg1-g4-h4. So though because of 2.hxg6 White's open file is dead, there has arisen from its ashes a passed pawn, along with possibilities of attack in the h-file. This is a good example of the conversion of advantages referred to above in the case of the exchange of an outpost.

Let us stop for a moment longer at Diagram 25, and we shall come after **1.Rg6! Rxg6 2.hxg6 Rg8 3.Rg1**, on the track of a characteristic exchange of roles. Before 1...Rxg6 the White h-pawn protected the Rg6. This action, in which gratitude and kindly feeling are beautifully displayed, shows, too, that there is a real strategic connection between the g-file as such and the pawn (here the h-pawn) which protects the advanced post in it.

We close this chapter with an example, chosen not for entertainment but for instruction, taken from a game Nimzowitsch-Amateur (Diagram 26). **1.Nf4.** Development is a principle well worthy of attention right into the endgame. It is one, however, which is neglected by less experienced players, even in the opening. **1...Rag8 2.Rh7!** For present purposes we would ask the reader to regard this move simply as the occupation of a advanced post, for of course it could also be regarded as an invasion of the 7th rank. **2...Be8 3.Rdh1 Rxh7 4.gxh7** (conversion of the "file" into a

"passed pawn," 4.Rxh7 Kf8 5.Nh5 with, at an opportune moment, sacrifice of the Knight at f6, would also have been good), **4...Rh8 5.Ng6+ Bxg6 6.fxg6** and the passed pawn has become a protected passed pawn. **6...Ke6 7.Rh5!** This "restricted" advance stops any attempt of Black to free himself by perhaps ...Ke5 or

---

...f5, giving access to White's g-pawn. **7...b6 8.c4** (still more paralyzing would be 8.b4, but White follows other plans), **8...c5 9.a4 a5 10.b3 c6 11.Kd2 Kd6 12.Ke3 Ke6 13.Kf4 Kd6 14.Kf5!** Now White's plan for breaking through is revealed. By *Zugzwang*, exhausting Black's available moves, so that finally his King is forced to break contact with e5, White is able to play e5, whereupon the Black f-pawn disappears, and the entry of the White Rook at f7 will become possible. **14...Ke7 15.e5 fxe5 16.Kxe5 Kd7 17.Rf5.** Now it will be clear that the move 7.Rh5! had all the elements of the maneuver which we have called a restricted advance in a file, since Rh5-f5-f7 must, despite the time intervening, be regarded as the maneuvering of the Rook from one file to a new one. Black resigned, since Rf7 followed by Rxg7 would have yielded two connected passed pawns.

CHAPTER 3

THE SEVENTH AND EIGHTH RANKS

♦ *1. Introductory and general. Endgame or Middlegame. The choice of an objective. "Thou shalt not shilly shally!"*

As we have seen in the second chapter the entry into enemy territory, in other words into the 7th and 8th ranks, forms the logical consequence of play in a file. I have sought to illustrate this entry by some particularly marked, because catastrophic, examples, but I must here, to offset this, emphasize the fact that, in the normal course of events, it will only be late, when we pass into the endgame stage, that the 7th rank will be seized, for catastrophes of whatever nature are, after all, only the result of serious mistakes of our opponent, and consequently cannot be regarded as the normal. We are therefore disposed to regard the 7th and 8th ranks as endgame advantages, and this despite the fact that numerous games are decided by operations in these ranks in the middle game. The student should, however, try to break into the enemy's base as early as possible, and if he at first finds that the invading Rook can accomplish nothing or is even lost, he must not be discouraged. It is part of our system to instruct the student at the earliest possible moment in the strategic elements of the endgame. Accordingly, after treating of the "7th and 8th ranks," "Passed pawns," and the technique of "Exchange," we will insert a chapter which, though properly coming under the heading "Positional play," must, for instructional purposes, find a place early. And after assimilating this, the 7th and 8th ranks will be to the student not merely a mating instrument, but much more, a keen-edged weapon for use in the endgame. As already remarked it is both, but its use as an endgame weapon predominates.

It is of the greatest importance to accustom ourselves to carry out operations in the 7th rank in such a manner that we have from the start some settled, definite objective. It is characteristic of the less practiced player that he chooses an opposite course, in fact he wanders about, looking first to the right, then to the left without any fixed plan. No, settle on your objective is the rule. Such an objective, as we have learned, may be a pawn or a point. Which one, it matters not. But aimlessly drifting from one to another, this will expose you to a strategical disgrace.

♦ *2. The convergent and the revolutionary attack in the 7th rank. The win of a point or pawn with acoustical echo (simultaneous check).*

In the position shown in Diagram 27 White chooses the c-pawn as his objective. After Black's ...Rc8, attack and defense balance one another, but by a procedure analogous to that used in a file, we now seek to disturb this equilibrium to our advantage. Accordingly let us suppose White to have a Bishop at e1 and Black a

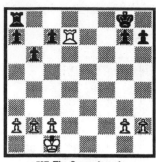

#27 The Seventh rank

Knight at g6, we would then attain our end by 1.Bg3, and if our Bishop had been at f1 (instead of e1), by 1.Ba6, driving away the defending Rook. Next let us suppose the forces on Diagram 27 increased by a White Rook at d1, and a Black Knight at g6, and that the White h-pawn is missing. The logical course would now be R1d4-c4, or perhaps 1.Rd8+ Rxd8 2.Rxd8+ Nf8 and White gets back to the 7th rank by 3.Rc8 c5 4.Rc7 etc. In Diagram 27 as it stands it should be noted the march of the White King to c6 would be the course to be aimed at, since the point c7 is our chosen objective.

The affair takes a similar course in the position on Diagram 28. White's objective is h7, since the win of this point would give the possibility of a deadly enveloping movement. **1...Rh6 2.Nf5 Rh5 3.g4 Rxh3+ 4.Kg2 Rxb3 5.Rh7+.** White has arrived on h7. The defender, the Black Rook had to flee. White wins the point h7 and gives mate. **5...Kg8 6.Rcg7+** followed by **7.Rh8** mate. The nature of a convergent attack on a chosen objective would seem to have been sufficiently illustrated by this example. Before, however passing to the "revolutionary" form of attack, we would underline as important the following rule: If the objective flees, the Rook must attack him from the rear. For example, a Rook on the 7th rank holds a Black pawn at b7

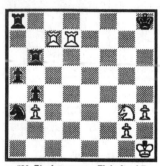

#28 Black to move. Fight for h7

under attack. If now 1...b5, then 2.Rb7, and not a flank attack on the 5th rank. This rule finds its explanation in the following considerations: (a) The 7th rank is to be held as long as possible, since it is here that the new objectives may present themselves. (b) The enveloping attack (and 2.Rb7 was such) is the strongest form of attack (ranged in ascending scale: i, frontal, ii, flank, iii, enveloping), which (c) often forces the enemy to undertake cramping defensive measures. It should be noticed that in the case considered above a flank attack on the b-pawn would be comfortably met by ...Rb8.

In Diagram 29 let us "choose" g7. The fact that this point is well protected does not frighten us. We concentrate our attack by means of 1.Ng3 a3 (the passed pawns are very threatening) 2.Nf5 a2 3.Qe5 (and now mate is threatened by 4.Rxg7+) 3...a1=Q+ and the g-pawn is now again protected and White loses, so our objective, g7, was a poor choice. The right choice is h7, and its conquest follows from a "revolutionary" attack. **1.Nf6+ gxf6 2.Qe6+ Kh8 3.Qd7.** Or **1.Nf6+ Kh8** (Black is stubborn) **2.Qxh6** (White is still more so!) **gxh6 3.Rh7** mate, and on the chosen spot! This example shows us the idea of a revolutionary attack applied to the 7th rank. One pawn is forcibly gotten out of the way in order that action on the seventh rank may be extended to that neighboring point which we had thought of as our objective.

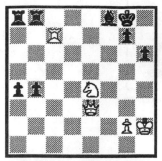

#29 Win of the the objective, h7

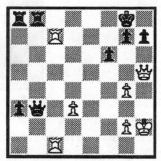

#30 Win of the objective, h7

Another example is shown in Diagram 30. Here the point g7 would be hard to attack successfully, though if the pawn on g4 were absent this would be easier: for instance by 1.Qg4 g6 2.Qh4 h5 3.Qxf6 etc. With the pawn there, however, matters are not so easy, for if 1.Rd7 (threatening 2.R1c7) 1...Rc8. Or if 1.R1c4 with the threat of 2.Qf7+) 1...Rf8. The right play is **1.Rxg7+** (h7 is our objective) **1...Kxg7 2.Rc7+ Kh8 3.Qxh7** mate. The capture on g7 extended the range of action in the seventh rank to h7. If 2...Kf8 3.Qxh7 would also have won, since the seventh rank could not be held by Black by any means. Still more precise, however, would be the employment of the Queen with gain of tempo, thus: (after 2...Kf8) 3.Qh6+ Ke8 4.Qe3+ Kf8 5.Qe7+ (enters the seventh with "acoustical echo"), 5...Kg8 6.Qg7 mate. This last maneuver deserves comment. It is typical, since by its means any approach of the enemy reserves can be prevented.

In Diagram 30a, White wishes to take the Knight with check. This he does by **1.Qg4+ Kh7 2.Qh3+ Kg7 3.Qg2+ Kh6** and now **4.Qxh1+.** We drive the King to the desired side of the board without losing contact with the piece or point we wish to win.

#30a The Knight is taken with check

In Diagram 31, the point to be won is e7. Either 1.Qh4 or 1.Qf2+ would fail miserably because of ...e3+ and Ra1 mate, e.g. 1.Qf2+ Ke8 2.Qxc5 e3+, etc. The right move here is **1.Qf1+ Ke8 2.Qb5+ Kf8 3.Qxc5+ Ke8 4.Qe7** mate. We could also state the problem as follows: White to take the point b5 with check. After 1.Qf1+, Ke8 2.Qb5+, White has contact with the point c5, and, at the same time, does not lose his driving effect on the enemy King, who is tied to his own square.

#31 Win of e7. White mates in 4 moves

♦ *3. The five special cases in the 7th Rank.*

1. "7th rank absolute" with passed pawns.
2. Doubled Rooks give perpetual check.
3. The drawing apparatus Rook+Knight.
4. The marauding raid in the 7th rank.
5. Combined play in the 7th and 8th ranks (enveloping maneuver in the corner of the board).

By "7th rank absolute," we mean that our control is such that the enemy King is shut in behind it. For example White: Rook at a7. Black: King at f8, pawn at f6. On the other hand, if the pawn were at f7 control would not be absolute.

(1) The first special case. The 7th rank absolute with well advanced passed pawns wins almost always. An example: White Kh1, Re7, pawn at b6. Black Kh8, Rd8. White plays b7 after which Rc7 and Rc8+ cannot be prevented. If the Black King had been at g6 the game would have been drawn.

The following is decisive in Diagram 32. **1.Qxh3+ Rh6 2.Qxh6+ gxh6 3.b6**, since the 7th rank is now "absolute". If it were not, if the Black pawn still stood on its original square, the game would be drawn. In Diagram 32a, (Tarrasch-Lasker, Berlin, 1918), Lasker in a note points out a win by **1...Ra2+ 2.Kf1? a5 3.Rxg7 a4 4.Rg6 a3 5.Rxf6 Rb2**. If White's g-pawn had been on g2 in the diagramed position, the idea of Kg1-Kh2 might still have given a drawing chance. As it is, however, the rank is "absolute" and Black wins. Interesting on the other hand would have been, after **1...Ra2+**, the attempt to neutralize the "absolute" 7th rank by **2.Ke1!** Lasker gives the continuation **2...a5 3.Kd1 a4 4.Kc1 a3 5.Kb1** with a draw.

#32 Example of the first special case

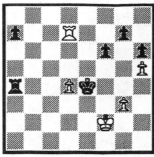

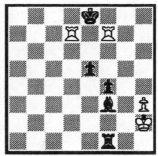

#32a Tarrasch-Lasker. Black moves

#32b Draw by perpetual check

(2) The second special case. Draw by perpetual check, which has an interest from a psychological error which is common. In Diagram 32b, White, a player of little experience, sees the desperate position of his King and plays for a draw by 1.Rfe7+, quite correctly recognizing the 1.Rde7+? would lead to the Black King's eventually reaching sanctuary. (1.Rde7+? Kd8 2.Rd7+ Kc8 3.Rc7+ Kb8 and White runs out of checks). After **1.Rfe7+ Kf8 2.Rf7+ Kg8 3.Rg7+ Kh8 4.Rh7+** (4.Rg1?? Rf2+!) **4...Kg8 5.Rhg7+! Kh8 6.Rh7+ Kg8**. Now he looks his opponent in the eye - does he really think he can escape? He repeats the checks as above a few times, and then just for variety's sake gives check with the other Rook, **7.Rdg7+??** after which his game is lost, since the King reaches sanctuary at b8. There follows a moral, that variety is not always profitable. The Rook at d7 was a sturdy sentinel, and as such should not have been needlessly disturbed.

(3) The third special case. The drawing apparatus (for perpetual check) Rook+Knight. White: Kh2, Rb7, Nf6. Black: Kf8, pawns c2, d2, e2. Black has three embryo Queens. White therefore seeks to draw by perpetual check. 1.Nh7+ Ke8 2.Nf6+ fails because of 2...Kd8. The solution is found in **1.Rd7**, since now after 1...e1=Q 2.Nh7+ and the drawing apparatus works to perfection. Observe that the key move, 1.Rd7 brings Rook and Knight into strategic contact.

Let us in the same position imagine a Black Rook at c8. In this case 1.Rd7 would not suffice, but would also be unnecessary, for the Rook on c8 stops the Black King's flight and makes a sentinel at d7 superfluous, so in this case **1.Nh7+ Ke8 2.Nf6+ Kd8?? 3.Rd7** mate. The Black King was a clever fellow. He committed suicide in the middle of the board, when a less talented sovereign would have been satisfied with the corner for this purpose.

(4) The fourth special case is quite simple, but is indispensable in view of the very complicated 5th case. It consists in a driving maneuver. The King will be forced out of his corner, and then a marauding raid will follow.

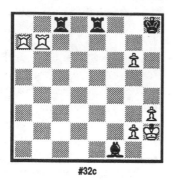

#32c

#33 The basis of the enveloping maneuver

Diagram 32c. **1.Rh7+ Kg8 2.Rag7+ Kf8 3.Rf7+** and wins the Bishop. A necessary condition for success was the protected position of the Rh7. Had it been otherwise 3...Kg8 would have prevented the capture of the Bishop. In this 4th case the capacity of the combined Rooks to drive the King from his corner (to c8 or f8) must be noted. This capacity provides the basis of the 5th case.

(5) The fifth special case. In the position, White: Rooks a7, d7. Black: Kh8, Qb8, White, who designs to seize the 8th rank, tries to do this by low cunning, since the direct road seems to be barred by the Black Queen. He seizes the corner, drives the enemy King out of it, and thus makes room for the enveloping attack of his Rook. **1.Rh7+ Kg8 2.Rag7+ Kf8 3.Rh8+** winning the Queen. The position arrived at after the two checks at h7 and g7 is the typical starting point of all enveloping maneuvers in the 7th and 8th ranks.

(Diagram 33). The analysis of this position shows us two Rooks each ready for a turning movement, but also a resourceful King, whose contact with the Rook at g7 protects him from the worst (mate at h8). As long as this contact is maintained mate cannot be given. The King's case is somewhat like that of a pedestrian who is set upon by a mugger. The latter raises his weapon to strike, but the former seizes his arm and keeps fast hold of it, knowing that so long as contact is kept up the robber cannot use his arm for the decisive blow. And so the rule runs: the King who is threatened by an enveloping attack must maintain contact with the nearer Rook as long as possible. The Rooks on their side must attempt to shake loose from the contact. The second rule follows: the King who is threatened must struggle towards the corner, the Rooks must and will drive him from it.

Starting from the typical position White can try three maneuvers: (a) for immediate material gain. (b) for a mating combination by breaking off contact between King and Rook. (c) for a tempo-winning combination.

(a) This has already been considered. If an enemy Queen stands anywhere in her first rank there will result 1.Rh8+ winning the Queen for the Rook at g7.

(b) Contact can be broken either through the protection of the Rg7 or by driving away the King by a check from another quarter. For example, White: Rooks g7, h7, Be1. Black: Kf8, Qa8, Ra2. There follows **1.Bb4+ Ke8** and now the Rooks have a free hand to deal the death blow **2.Rh8** mate. Instead of a Bishop at e1 we may imagine a pawn at e6, and the continuation would be **1.e7+ Ke8 2.Rh8+** The enveloping operation has been made possible, but the Black King now has a flight square which before was closed to him. **2...Kd7,** but this plays no role, for the air we have allowed him was alas!..poisoned. **3.d8=Q** double check and mate is not far off.

Now turn to Diagram 34. First White gets the typical position as shown on Diagram 33. **1.Rg7+ Kf8 2.Rh7** threatening mate, **2...Kg8**, the flight to the corner. **3.Rdg7+ Kf8** and now there follows **4.Ng5!** (less convincing would have been 4.Nf2) **4...fxg5 5.f6!** with mate to follow at h8. Or, **4.Ng5! d4! 5.Ne6+ Bxe6** (forced) **6.fxe6** followed by the driving of the King from f8 by e7+, and history repeats itself. This check at e7 which broke contact could only have been parried by ...Re8, leading to the loss of a Rook. **6...Re8 7.e7+ Rxe7 8.Rxe7** and White wins easily even if Black has

#34

one or two passed pawns to the good, for there would have been brought into play that capacity which Rooks possess, to which we have called special attention, that of attacking fleeing pawns from the rear in the 7th rank.

(c) Diagram 35. With **1.Rh7+ Kg8 2.Rfg7+ Kf8**, the typical position is reached, but how are we to proceed? Neither 3.Rh8 mate, nor a way of forcing a break in the contact, seems feasible. Of course if the White King were already at g5, then Kh6 would follow, but as matters stand it would seem as if White must content himself with perpetual check. However appearances are deceitful. There follows **3.Rxd7** threatening mate at h8, so **3...Kg8**. Now White repeats the little maneuver, **4.Rdg7+ Kf8 5.Rxc7** and again Black is forced to play to play **5...Kg8**. He has no time for the move a1=Q. (If our opponent has no time for something which otherwise would be most advantageous to him because he is forced to make some positional move irrelevant to his purpose, while we advance our project, then we have gained a tempo). White now plays **6.Rcg7+** and the ending runs: **6...Kf8 7.Rxb7 Kg8 8.Rbg7+** (8.Rxa7?? would be a gross

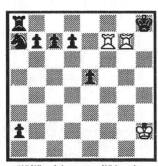

#35 Win of the tempo. White wins.

mistake because of 8...a1=Q), **8...Kf8 9.Rxa7 Rxa7 10.Rxa7** winning the Black a-pawn and the game. We may sum this up thus, that in (c) we have the case that White gathers new strength by touching the typical starting position, or more simply, by bringing about this position he creates a new mating threat and so a free tempo for gathering loot. We have now sufficiently illustrated the five special cases, and have made it clear that the first thing to do is to bring about the "starting point position". We will close with two more endgames.

Diagram 36 shows the position which White had obtained after 50 moves in the game Nimzowitsch-Bernstein, Wilna, 1912. My opponent here played **50...Rf8**, in order after 51...f6, to reduce the material on the board to such an extent that there would not be enough left to win with. I answered calmly **51.Rxb4 f6**, for now I manufacture out of its several components my 1st special case in the 7th rank (passed pawn and 7th row absolute), which was even at that date known to me. The continuation was **52.Bc5 Rc8** (forced, as 52...Rf7 fails after 53.Rb7 Rxb7

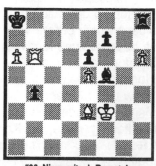

#36 Nimzowitsch-Bernstein

54.axb7+ Kxb7 55.exf6 and Black's Bishop has more work than he can do). **53.exf6 Rxc5 54.f7** (the passed pawn) **54...Rc8 55.Rb7** (the 7th rank absolute! The extra enemy piece is an illusion), **55...Bd3 56.Re7 Bb5 57.Kf4** (White avoided 57.Re8 Bxe8 58.f8=Q Bc6+ though he had treated himself to the pleasure of a new Queen, she would have vanished and with her also...all joy!) **57...Rh8 58.h7 Ba4 59.Ke5 Bb5 60.Kf6 e5 61.Kg7** and Black resigned.

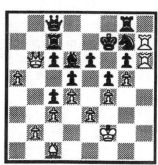

#37 Nimzowitsch-Eliasstamm
Riga 1910
White gave the odds of the QN

In the position in Diagram 37 there first occurred **1.a6 Qa8** (threatening ...Ra7 and ...Rxa6). In this difficult situation White saved himself by the following "subtle trap," as the *Dunazietung* called it, or by a combination based on a thorough knowledge of the terrain (7th rank!), as we would call it. **2.b3 Rb8** (better to be sure would have been 2...Ra7). Now followed the Queen sacrifice **3.Ba3!! Rxb6 4.Bxd6 Rc8 5.Rxg7+ Kxg7 6.Be5+ King any**, and the Rook gives perpetual check on h7 and h8. It is worth noting that after the Queen sacrifice, White has at least a draw in all variations. 4...Qxa6 (instead of 4...Rc8) 5.Be5 Ke8 6.Rh8+ Kd7 7.R6h7 Qa2+ (to leave the square a6 open) 8.Kg3 c5 9.Rxg7+ Kc6 10.Rxc7+ Kb5 11.Rxc5+ Ka6 12.Ra8+ winning the Queen. Or 4...Qg8 5.Bxc7 Rxa6 6.bxc4 followed by Be5. If 4...Qg8 5.Bxc7 cxb3 6.Bxb6 b2 7.Rxg7+! Q (or K)xg7 8.Rh1 and White has much the better prospects because of his strong a-pawn.

CHAPTER 4

THE PASSED PAWN

♦ *1. To get our bearings. The neighbor who is somewhat disturbing and the vis-a-vis who is totally unpleasant. The pawn majority. The "Candidate". The birth of a passed pawn. Rules for "Candidates".*

A pawn is passed if he has nothing to fear from an enemy pawn in front of him, i.e., in the same file, or from one on a neighboring file, and whose road to Queen is therefore open (see Diagram 38). If a pawn is only checked in his advance (blockaded) by enemy pieces, the fact does not prejudice our conception.

A special recognition is due to a pawn from the fact that enemy pieces must sacrifice a part of their effective strength in order to keep him under observation, and in fact under continual observation. If further, we bear in mind that the pawn enjoys another advantage over the pieces in that he is the born defender, we will slowly discover that even on the 64 squares the pawn, our foot soldier is worthy of all respect. Who checks an ambitious enemy pawn best? A pawn. Who protects one of his own pieces best? A pawn. And which of the chessmen works for least wages? Again, the pawn, for a steady job, such as protecting one of his own fellows or keeping in restraint one of the enemy's men, does not appeal to a piece at all, moreover, such occupation draws off troops from the active army. When a pawn is so employed this last applies in very much less measure.

In the position on Diagram 38 neither the b-pawn nor the g-pawn is free, yet the former seems to be less hampered than the latter, for the b-pawn has at any rate no direct antagonist. The *vis-a-vis* might be compared to an enemy, while the pawn in the next file reminds us rather of a kindly neighbor, who, as we know, can have his drawbacks. If, for instance, we are rushing downstairs to keep an important engagement, and a neighbor suddenly grabs us and involves us in a long talk, ranging from the weather and politics to the high cost of beer, he keeps us from our job, just as in Diagram 38 the Black c-pawn may be an annoyance to White's b-pawn. Nevertheless a somewhat gossipy chatterbox

#38 The White a-pawn and the Black d-pawn are passed. The White e-pawn is passed but blockaded

of a neighbor is far from being a bitter enemy, or to apply the analogy to our case, an annoying pawn on a neighboring file is far from being an antagonist. In our diagram, the White g-pawn's aspirations to greater things can never be satisfied, whereas the b-pawn can always dream of an advance.

Let us now turn to the passed pawn's family. In this connection we must first consider the question of the majority on one side or the other. At the beginning of the game after the first exchange of pawns in the center (After **1.e4 e5 2.d4 exd4 3.Qxd4**, pawn majorities loom up. White has now 4 to 3 on the Kingside, Black 4 to 3 on the Queenside). See Diagram 38a. In the course of the game if Black arrives at ...f5, thus killing White's free center pawn, the majority will be in yet clearer evidence, namely White's Pawns f2, g2, h2 against Black's pawns g7, h7.

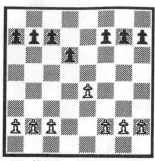

#38a Majorities on opposite wings

Rule: Every healthy, uncompromised pawn majority must be able to yield a passed pawn. Of the 3 pawns on the Kingside in Diagram 39, the f-pawn is the only one to have no opponent, he is therefore the least trammeled, and accordingly has the greatest claim to become "free" or passed. He is therefore the legitimate "candidate". Put more precisely, the rule takes the following shape. The spearhead of the advance is furnished by the candidate, the other pawns are only to be regarded as supports. So f4-f5, then g4-g5 and f6. If Black pawns are at g6 and h5, then

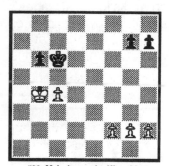

#39 Majority on the Kingside

White must play f4, g3, (not at once h3 because of h4 and White's majority is crippled), h3, g4, and f5. How simple! And yet how often we see weaker players in this position advancing first with the g-pawn, to which Black replies with g5, and White's majority is worthless. I have often racked my brain to discover why less experienced players begin with g4, yet the matter bears a simple explanation. The players in question are undecided whether to begin on the right (h4) or on the left (f4), and in their perplexity decide, after good respectable custom, to choose the golden mean.

♦ *2. The blockade of passed pawns. Proof of the obligation to blockade, and why the said proof must be of the greatest importance to the practical player as well as to the theoretician (chess philosopher). The exceedingly complicated, because ever varying, relations between the passed pawn and the blockader. On strong and weak, elastic and inelastic blockaders.*

In the position shown on Diagram 40, Black has a passed pawn, which can however be blocked by Nd4 or Bd4. By blockade we mean the mechanical stopping of an enemy pawn's advance by a piece, which is brought about by placing our piece directly in front of the pawn to be blockaded. Here and in all similar cases the question comes up: Does this blockade not connote an unnecessary expenditure of energy? Would it not suffice to keep the pawn fixed by the Knight or Bishop bearing upon d4? Is keeping up a blockade work worthy of an officer? Will not his nobility, so long as he takes his blockading problem seriously, be to a considerable extent diminished? Is he not thus degraded to the status of a stopped (immobile) pawn? In a nut-shell, is the blockade economical? I am glad to be able to offer you, I think, an exhaustive solution to this problem. The mediocre critic would settle the question by laying down quite briefly the general thesis that pawns must be stopped, but in my eyes this would be a proof of poverty of understanding. The why and the wherefore are of extraordinary importance.

#40 The problem of the blockade

There are three reasons which logically make the blockade imperative. In what follows, these will be analyzed under ♦2a, ♦2b, and ♦2c. Under ♦3 the effective strength of the blockader will be assessed in detail.

♦ *2a. First reason: The passed pawn is a criminal, who should be kept under lock and key. Mild measures, such as police surveillance, are not sufficient. The passed pawn's lust to expand. The awakening of the men in the rear.*

We return again to Diagram 40. The Black forces, Bishop, Rook and Knight, are as we should say, grouped around the passed pawn. They conform to a complex of which the d-pawn is the nucleus. Knight and Bishop guard the passed pawn. The Rook, however, supplies him with a certain impetus, gives him a supporting impulse in fact. So powerful is the pawn's desire to press on here, to expand (of which fact indeed visible recognition is given in the way the "officers," laying aside all pride of caste, picturesquely group themselves around this simple "foot soldier"), that our d-pawn often seems ready to advance on his own account, when to do so will cost him his life. So, for instance, **1...d4 2.N (or B) xd4**, and now all of a sudden the Black forces in the rear come to life. The Bishop from b7 commands a diagonal bearing on the enemy King, the Rook has a clear file, while the Knight has a new square for himself in the center. Such an advance at the cost of self sacrifice, for the purpose of opening a file, is, as a rule, only characteristic of a "pawn roller," a compact advancing mass of pawns in the center, and therefore furnishes a brilliant proof of the lust to expand inherent in a passed pawn, for the mobile center (the pawn roller) is endowed with an almost incredible energy. Again, the clearing of a square for one of his own Knights is a very special characteristic of an advance of this kind. Accordingly we say that the first consideration which logically compels the blockade, is that the free passed pawn is such a dangerous "criminal," that it is by no means sufficient to keep him under police supervision (by the Knight and Bishop in the diagram), the fellow must be put in prison, so we take away his freedom utterly by blockading him with the Knight at d4.

The example just considered, we mean the sacrifice of the pawn (for he is intended to die in the advance), is thoroughly typical, although it is not in the least necessary that a whole host of men to the rear should be freed by the operation. It is often just a single piece standing behind it that profits. In Diagram 41 Black, whose Queenside and center seem to be threatened, seeks to turn his "candidate" to account. Since the candidate is 90 per cent a passed pawn, the same rules apply for him as do for a passed pawn. Accordingly **19...f4! 20.gxf4 g4! 21.Bg2 Nhf5.** Sacrifice of a "candidate" with the result that the square f5 is cleared for the Knight on h6. The continuation was **22.Qb3 dxc4 23.Qxc4+ Kh8 24.Qc3 h5 25.Rad1 h4 26.Rd3**

#41 te Kolste-Nimzowitsch
Baden-Baden 1925
Black sacrifices a "candidate," and a
piece to the rear comes to life.
How is this accomplished?

Nd5 27.Qd2 Rg8. Black supports his pawn majority with vigor. **28.Bxd5 cxd5 29.Kh1 g3** and Black gets the attack.

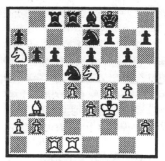

#42 Alekhine-Treybal
Baden-Baden 1925

In the game Alekhine-Treybal, Diagram 42, the following interesting maneuver occurred: **27.e4.** The mobile pawn center sets itself in motion. **27...f6 28.exd5 fxe5.** The passed pawn which has suddenly come into existence is clearly short-lived, the fruit of some sudden inspiration, and seemingly destined to as speedy a death, but appearances are deceptive, even this creature of a moment knows how to subject itself to the iron laws of chess, and so there followed **29.d6!!** The purpose of this pawn sacrifice was not to free the square from which it moved, and yet the advance completely fulfills the spirit, if not the letter, of our rules.

The pawn intends to lay down its life in advancing, and the main variation would be **29...e4+!** (so as to prevent fxe5 which could follow ...Rxd6) **30.Kxe4 Rxd6 31.Ke5!! Rcd8 32. Bxe6.** Note that the entry of the King into Black's game was made possible only by the pawn sacrifice.

For a complete game which shows in its full setting the very important operation which we have been discussing, see Leonhardt-Nimzowitsch, Game No. 12, which the reader is urged to study before proceeding further. We now pass on to an analysis of our second reason.

♦ *2b. The second reason. Optimism in chess, and the immunity of the blockading piece against frontal attacks. The enemy pawn as our bulwark. The deeper-lying mission of the blockading piece. The blockading point a weak enemy point.*

In my book on the "Blockade" I wrote on this point as follows: The second reason which we are now to analyze is of great importance from both the strategic and the instructional points of view. In chess in the last resort optimism is decisive. I mean by this that it is psychologically valuable to develop to the greatest length the faculty of being able to rejoice over small advantages. The beginner only "rejoices" when he can call checkmate to his opponent, or perhaps still more if he can win his Queen, (for in the eyes of the beginner this is [if possible] the greater triumph of the two!). The master on the other hand is quite pleased, in fact royally content, if he succeed in spying the shadow of an enemy pawn weakness, in some corner or other of the board. The optimism here characterized is the indispensable psychological basis of position play. It is this optimism, too, which gives us strength, in face of every evil, however great, to discover the faintest hint of a bright side of the picture. In the case under consideration we can lay it down as established that an enemy passed pawn represents an unquestionably serious evil for us, yet even this evil has its tiny gleam of brightness. The situation is this, that in blockading this pawn we can by good fortune safely post the blockading piece under the shelter of the enemy pawn itself, so that it is immune from any frontal attack. Consider a Black passed pawn at e4. A White blockader at e3 is not subject to an attack from an enemy Rook on the e-file (e8 to e3), and therefore stands there in a certain measure of security.

So far *Die Blockade*. And to these remarks there is perhaps only this to add, that the relative security outlined here - must in truth be symptomatic of that deeper mission which the blockader has to fulfill. If nature, yes, and even the enemy, too, are concerned about the safety of the blockader, he must have been set apart for great deeds. And in fact we are not incorrect in our reckoning, for the blockading point often becomes a "weak" enemy point.

I can imagine that the road to a real conception of "weak points" may have led across the blockading field. The enemy had a passed pawn. We stopped its progress, and now suddenly it appeared that the piece with which we effected this exerted a most unpleasant pressure, and the enemy pawn actually provided a natural defensive position which the blockader could use as an observation post. This conception once grasped was subsequently widened and dematerialized. Widened, because we now classify as weak every square in front of an enemy pawn, whether passed or not, if there were any possibility of our being able to establish ourselves on it *without risk of being driven away*. But the conception of a weak point was also dematerialized. When, for instance, Dr. Lasker talked of White's weak squares in the position on Diagram 43 (from the game Tartakower-Lasker,

Petrograd, 1909) the presence of an enemy pawn as a bulwark for the piece occupying a weak square was certainly not an essential condition.

♦ *2c. The third reason. The crippling induced by a blockade is by no means local in its nature. The transplanting of the crippling phenomena to the ground in the rear. On the dual nature of the pawn. On the pessimistic outlook, and how this can be transformed into the blackest melancholy.*

In game No. 12, Leonhardt-Nimzowitsch, the White Bishop on c5 blocked c6, one of the consequences being that Black's Bb7 was held a prisoner in his own camp. This state of affairs seems to be typical, only very often, a whole complex of enemy pieces is sympathetically affected. Large tracts of the board are made impracticable for any rapid maneuvering. At times, too, the whole enemy position takes on a strangely rigid character. In other words, the crippling effect has shifted from the

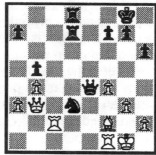

#43 Tartakower-Lasker
Petrograd, 1909
Weak White points

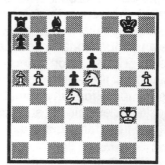

#44 Transplanting the effects
of the Blockade to the region
in the rear

blockaded pawn further back to its rear. In Diagram 44 the Black e-pawn and d-pawn are completely blockaded, and Black's entire position is numbed. Bishop and Rook are prisoners in their own camp, and White, in spite of his inferiority in material, actually has winning chances.

The state of affairs here sketched need not surprise us in the least. We have often pointed out that any pawn may be an obstacle in the way of his own pieces, and that to get rid of him may often be our dearest wish, as for instance, if we are planning to open a file or to free a square for a Knight. We see then that the blockade is not only embarrassing to the pawn itself, but much more so really to his comrades in arms, the Rooks and Bishops. In connection, by the way, with the pawn, it is important for the student to appreciate a certain dual nature which he possesses. On the one hand the pawn, as we have shown above, is quite willing to commit suicide, while on the other he clings tenaciously to life. For the presence of pawns, as he knows, is not only of great importance for the endgame, but still more helps prevent the establishment of enemy pieces within his own lines, which but for them might be possible. Put otherwise, they prevent the creation of weak points in their own territory. The mobility of a passed pawn, particularly of a center one, is often the very life-nerve of the whole position. Its crippling must therefore naturally find its echo throughout the whole of that position. We have seen, then, that weighty reasons support the establishment of a blockade at the earliest possible moment, whereas those which seem to tell against it, namely the apparently uneconomical use made of an officer, seemingly degraded to being a mere sentry (blockader), will be seen on closer examination to carry weight only in certain cases. To be able to recognize these we must now consider the blockader himself.

◆ *3. The blockader's primary and secondary functions. The conception of elasticity. Various forms of the same. The strong and the weak blockader. How the blockader meets the many demands made on him, partly on his own initiative, and why I see in this a proof of his vitality.*

The primary function of a blockader is obviously to blockade in a businesslike manner the pawn concerned. In exercising this he has himself a tendency towards immobility. And yet, admire his vitality! He very often displays pronounced activity: (1) by the threats which he can exercise from the place where he is posted (see Game 12, Leonhardt-Nimzowitsch, in which Black's Ne6 prepared the way for ...g5), (2) by a certain elasticity which finds expression in the fact that he does on occasion leave his post. He seems to be entitled to a furlough, (a) if the journey promises much in results, when the connections must all be made by express, so to speak; (b) if he can be sure of returning quickly enough to take up the blockade again on another square, should the pawn have advanced in the interval; (c) if he is in a position to leave a deputy in his place to look after the blockade. It is obvious that such a deputy must be chosen from those pieces which are protecting the blockader. This last consideration, for all its apparent insignificance, is of great importance, for it shows clearly the extent to which elasticity, at any rate in the form considered under (c), is directly dependent on the degree of weakness or strength of the blockade.

In connection with (a) see the endgame Nimzowitsch-Nilsson (Diagram 61).

In connection with (b) see Diagram 44a. In this simplest of positions the blockading Rook takes a little holiday trip **1.Rxb4**. It goes without saying that the passed pawn will seize the opportunity to advance. **1...h4 2.Rb2 h3 3.Rh2**. Master Rook appears in the office, bows to the boss, nods to his follow employees, and as if he were fresh as paint and thoroughly rested (though he had to do some bustling to get back in time), takes his seat at the blockading desk. He has, however, changed his seat, from h4 to h2. The maneuver here shown may be found repeated in many examples.

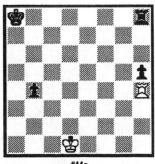

#44a
Change of blockading squares

In connection with (c), see the role played by the White Bishop at f4 in game Number 15, Nimzowitsch-von Freymann, White's 26th move.

From the above little discussion (under a, b, c), we see that elasticity is slight if the pawn to be blockaded is far advanced. The maximum elasticity is on the other hand developed when a half-passed pawn in the center of the board is the object of the blockader's attentions. In such a position as, for instance: White: Nd4, pawns e3, f2. Black: Bb7, pawn d5. The blockading Knight at d4 is here very elastic. He can take long journeys from his post and in all directions, and yet not neglect his primary duty which is to prevent the advance of Black's d-pawn. So much on the subject of elasticity. We will now analyze the actual effect of the blockade itself.

♦ *3a. Effect of the Blockade.*

The forces to maintain a blockade should be developed systematically and of set purpose, whereas elasticity often comes of itself without seeking. The blockading effect is intensified by bringing up supports, which in their turn must be safely stationed. Compare the two Diagrams, 45a and 45b.

#45a Black to move.
Is the Rc6 a strong blockader?

#45b Black to move
Can the blockader hold his own?

The Bishop in Diagram 45a will for motives of personal safety migrate to g6, though to be sure the blockading Rook will thus lose a powerful support. Nevertheless for the Bishop to play about on the long diagonal is a somewhat risky game, for the eye of the law (White's Queen) is upon him. After **1...Bg6** there follows, however **2.Kb5**, and now the attempt to restore the abandoned strategic connection by **2...Be8** fails badly after **3.Qe5+ Kd7 4.Qxe8+ Kxe8 5.Kxc6**. On the other hand in Diagram 45b, the Bishop can go to f3 where he stands safe and cannot be dislodged, and the Rook at c6 thus gains so much in importance that a draw seems inevitable. We have shown a similar state of affairs to exist in our study of outposts. In like manner here the blockader derives strength, not so much from himself as from his strategic connection with the country to his rear. A blockader who is insufficiently or imperfectly protected will not be able to hold his own against the enemy pieces which are hotly pressing him. He will be put to flight, and either taken or put out of action, whereupon the pawn whose road had before been blocked will resume his advance. In connection with the problem of the defense, the reader will find the rules (which will be treated in Part 2 of this book) on the overprotection of strategical points extraordinarily valuable. The blockading point is as a rule strategically important square, and therefore it is a part of wisdom to protect it even more than is absolutely necessary. So do not wait for attacks to pile up, but rather lay up a reserve of defensive force, just as before a dance one lays up a store of sleep.

And so a remarkable fact appears, that while the effect of the blockade can only be intensified or even maintained by laboriously bringing up supports, the other secondary virtues of the blockader, elasticity, and the threats he can exercise from his post, prove to be of hard growth. They come to fulfillment without any particular exertion on his part. This is explicable, (1) by the state of affairs in which a protecting piece takes the place of the blockader who has gone on his travels. (2) by the fact that, as explained under ♦2 the blockading square tends to become a weak point for the enemy. Keeping contact with a strategically important square must according to my system, work wonders. This will be considered in greater detail under positional play.

We can sum all this up in the following principle -

Though in the choice of a blockader elasticity and the threats he can exercise must be borne in mind, it is often sufficient merely to strengthen the blockade. Elasticity and the rest will then not seldom come of themselves.

It must now be clear that an officer in no sense compromises his dignity by answering the summons to act as a blockader, for the post proves itself to be a most honorable one, safe, yet allowing full initiative. The student should thoroughly test the truth of this observation from master games or games played by himself. He should compare the blockaders with one another, their respective merits, their ultimate fate, and how they came to fail or to succeed in their duty, and he will get more benefit out of a thorough knowledge of one "actor" than from a nodding acquaintance with the whole "troop". It is when working under limitations that the master reveals himself. *This true saying applies fully also to the aspirant to mastership, indeed to every student who is in earnest.*

♦ *4. The fight against the blockader. His uprooting. "Changez les blockeurs!" How to get a standoffish blockader replaced by one who is more affable.*

When we said that the blockader derived his effective strength from his connection with the country to his rear, this was an indisputable truth, yet he can, and should, contribute something of himself to the protection of the blockading rampart. This he does in that, thanks to his attacking radius, he wards off the approach of enemy troops from himself. It is also a merit if his origin be humble, the humbler the better. By this we mean that a blockader should have a thick hide. The rather exaggerated sensitiveness displayed by the King or the Queen would not fit with the role of blockader. A minor piece (Knight or Bishop) can stand up to an attack - in case of need he has only to call up aid, whereas the Queen reacts to the slightest attack to such an extent, that she at once, though with head proudly erect, leaves the field. In general the King would also be a poor blockader, but in the endgame his Royal attribute of being able to change his color is a big plus, so that if he is driven away from a dark blockading square, he can try at the next stopping place to establish a blockade on a light square. For instance: White Kg4, Bd1, pawn g5. Black: Kg6 Na7. The check **1.Bc2+** drives the Black King from g6, but now he takes up the blockade again at g7.

#46 From one of my games; the blockading Bishop at a8 will be replaced by the Rook

Since the blockaders as we have seen, may be of varying quality: strong or weak, elastic or inelastic, the obvious thing to do is to get one blockader replaced by another if this would suit us better. If I take a blockader, the recapturing piece takes over his role, and by so doing the command "changes les blockeurs" becomes a *fait accompli*. The following combination is typical: In Diagram 46 the opening moves would be **1.Rb8+ Rf8,** and now the attacking range of the Bishop renders the approach of the White King difficult, which would otherwise be decisive. There followed **2.Rxa8 Rxa8 3. Kb7.** This new blockader, the Rook on a8, now shows himself to be most accommodating, and nothing is further from his thoughts than to stay an attempt at approach, so **3...Rf8 4.a8=Q Rxa8 5.Kxa8** and the pawn ending is untenable for Black. **5...Kg7 6.Kb7 Kg6 7.Kc6 Kg5 8.Kd7! Kf5 9.Kd6** and wins. On the other hand (from Diagram 46), **1.Rb8+ Rf8 2.Kb6?** (instead of 2.Rxa8) **2...Bd5 3.Kc7 Kf7 4.Rxf8+ Kxf8 5.Kb8** would fail because of **5...Kf7 6.a8=Q Bxa8 7.Kxa8 Kg6** and this time it is Black who emerges victorious. In Diagram 47 Black would be perfectly safe if his King were not so far away. White makes the more accommodating Black Rook take the place of the embarrassing Bishop. **1.Rxf5 Rxf5 2.Kg4.** The White pawns become mobile and the Black King arrives too late. **2...Rf8 3.g6 Kb5 4.f5 Kc6 5.g7 Rg8 6.f6 Kd6 7.Kf5!** (stopping Ke6), and wins. The idea is this: The attacking party is prepared to come to an understanding with the blockading company but wishes first to see its apparently rather unsympathetic spokesman replaced by someone else. This done, negotiations may begin!

#47

The "negotiations," alias the uprooting.

How are the "negotiations" to be pursued? We concentrate as many attacks as possible on the blockader concerned. The latter will naturally call up reserves in his support. In the fight now raging around the blockader we seek, following the best practice, to bring to bear a superiority of forces by trying to kill off the defenders by exchanges, or to drive them away, or otherwise to divert them. Finally the blockader will have to retire and our pawn can move forward. In the endgame in the event of a blockade, we usually drive away the blockader's supports, in the middlegame on the other hand we seek to busy them. A very instructive example of all this is furnished by my game against von Gottschall, Breslau, 1925. See Game Number 13, which the student is advised to study at this point.

♦ *5. Frontal attack by the King against an isolated pawn as a Kingly ideal. The turning movement. The role of leader. The three-part maneuver, made up of frontal attack, the enemy's forced withdrawal and the final turning movement. The "reserve" blockading point. The superseded "opposition!"*

Many a stout fellow who has grown gray at chess will gasp at this: What? Is the "opposition" also to be abolished now? Yes, I am sorry, but this blow must fall. And first, to get our bearings, let us remark that to conceive the center arithmetically means counting the pawns standing there, and regarding a numerical majority as giving a guarantee of preponderance. This is a completely untenable conception. In reality it is only the greater or lesser degree of mobility which can be counted decisive in passing judgment upon the position in the center. Now if we look deep enough we find the opposition certainly has a relationship with the center "arithmetically" conceived, and the inner significance of both the one and the other is assessed on purely outward characteristics. In what follows I shall give my entirely new theory, which in eliminating the "opposition" analyzes the inner meaning of what is happening.

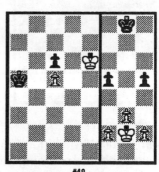

#48

Right: White wins an enemy pawn.
Left: White, himself threatened with an enveloping movement, turns the enemy position and wins his objective at c6. How does he do it?

In Diagram 48 (right side) the creation of a passed pawn by means of h3, f3, and g4 would not be sufficient to win, since the White King has lagged behind his

---

The passed pawn   41

passed pawn. The King must here play the role of leader, something like a pacemaker in a bicycle race, and not stay comfortable at home reading the news from the race track. The student, too must be fully aware of one point, that the King in the middlegame and the same King in the endgame are two totally different persons. In the middlegame the King is a timid soul, shuts himself up in his fortress (castled position), and only when he feels himself in contact with his Rook, with his own Knights and Bishops attentively grouped around him, does the old fellow feel himself doing well. In the endgame the King changes into a hero (not so difficult, as the board is swept almost clean of enemies!), and scarcely is it begun than he leaves his castled home and stalks slowly but imposingly to the center, clearly to be in the middle of things. More of this in Chapter 6. He shows, however, particular courage in a fight against an isolated pawn. Such a fight will be started with a frontal attack. For example, White: Kf5. Black: pawn f6. Such a frontal position is an ideal which the King aims at, and is one in fact well worth striving for, because given the necessary material, it can be attained, and thus the capture of the beleaguered pawn facilitated, or, in a purely pawn ending, it may lead to the eventual turning of the position.

And so, if fighting forces are still available, the Black pawn at f6 will be exposed to multiple attacks, which may lead to the protecting pieces having to take up less comfortable positions, while if it comes to a plain duel between the two Kings with no pieces left on the board, the weapon of exhaustion, *Zugzwang*, will be at the disposal of the attacker.

#48a

As an example suppose in Diagram 48a, after **1.Kf3 Kg7 2.Kf4** (the ideal position), there follows **2...Kf6 3.Bd3 Be6** and the difference in value between the active White Bishop at d3 and its passive Black counterpart on e6, who is chained to the pawn on f5, weighs by no means lightly on the scale. The purely pawn endgame on the other hand would run somewhat as follows. Diagram 48 (right side) **1.Kf3 Kg7 2.Kf4 Kf6 3.h4.** This is the first stage of the maneuver. Then comes **3...Kg6**, and this is the second stage, the enemy King must go to one side, a direct consequence of *Zugzwang.* And now follows the third and last stage, namely the White turning movement **4.Ke5** and wins. The frontal attack has developed into a turning movement, an advantage, for an enveloping movement is, as we know, the strongest form of attack (in ascending order: frontal, flank and enveloping).

That the enveloping attack is very strong in the endgame is impressed on us by the examples shown on Diagrams 48 (left side) and 49 (right side). In the latter there

---

follows **1.Kh6 Kf8 2.Kg6 Ke7 3.Kg7 Ke8 4.Kf6 Kd7 5.Kf7**. Notice the tortuous manner of approach of the White King, who works with *Zugzwang* as his weapon. In Diagram 48 (left side) the continuation is **1.Kd7! Kb5 2.Kd6** winning. But not 1.Kd6?, because of 1...Kb5 and White has no good move left, and is in fact himself in *Zugzwang*, in a strait jacket, shall we say? Or finally take the position White: Kh5, pawns a4, a5, f5. Black Kd4, pawns b7, f6. **1.Kg6 Ke5 2.a6! bxa6 3.a5.** Here White sacrificed a pawn in order to pass the unpleasant duty of moving on to his opponent.

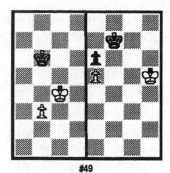

#49

Right: White turns the enemy position. Left: White wins the point b5 as a station for his King

Now that we have seen the significance of the enveloping movement, which, by the way, can only succeed against a stationary object (which in its turn limits the movements of its own King!), it will be intelligible to us why we should go to such trouble, in carrying out this three part maneuver, to bring off this type of attack.

We will now consider this maneuver in its three stages in a position where there are no enemy pawns. (See Diagram 49, left). The question at issue here is the win of the point b5 for the White King. Why precisely the point b5? Because the position of the King at b5 would insure the advance of the passed pawn as far as b6. If the King occupies this point, he has only to move to one side, say to c5, and the pawn whom we imagine as having already reached b4 will without question reach b6. In the same Diagram the square b6 is the first unguarded stage on the pawn's road to Queening. The points b4 and b5 are already secured by the King on c4. We therefore institute a frontal attack on the point b5. **1.Kb4** (first stage), **1...Ka6** (or Kc6) (the forced withdrawal of the King. This is the second stage). **2.Kc5** (or Ka5) (the third stage, the turning movement completed). Now as he wished to do, the White King reaches b5. For instance **2...Kb7 3.Kb5!**. In the position now reached, the White King's last move may itself be regarded as a frontal attack on the next halting place b6. The three-part maneuver directed against b6 will run an entirely analogous course, namely **3...Ka7 4.Kc6**, with Kb6 to follow.

The application of this method of thought to the defense is still simpler. In the position, White: Kc4, pawn b4. Black: Kc6. Black can draw because the White King has lagged behind. All that Black has to do is watch that the White King does not assume the role of leader, and next to keep well in mind that after the blockading point, the "reserve" blockading point is his safest position. (With a White pawn on b4, b5 is his blockading point, b6 his "reserve" blockading point). In the position under consideration Black's reply to **1.b5+** is **1...Kb6** (blockade). **2.Kb4 Kb7** (reserve blockade). **3.Kc5 Kc7** (but not 3...Kb8? or 3...Kc8? for that would allow the

White King to gain ground). **4.b6+ Kb7** (blockade) **5.Kb5 Kb8** (reserve blockade) **6.Kc6 Kc8 7.b7+ Kb8 8.Kb6** with stalemate.

To avoid any possibility of misunderstanding let us repeat that with a White pawn at b6, b8 is the reserve blockading point. If he is at b5 then b7 is the reserve point.

#49a

In Diagram 49a 1...Kb8?? would be a horrible move, for it would leave the whole field open to the White King and give him the chance of assuming the role of leader. **1...Kb8?? 2.Kb6** with a decisive frontal attack on the point b7.

The theory of the opposition is in its want of clarity only to be described as obscure, whereas the truth is so clear. The attacking King fights to get into the lead, his opponent strives to prevent this with the aid of the "reserve blockade point."

♦ *6. The privileged passed pawn: (a) two united, (b) the protected, (c) the outside. The King as a hole-stopper. On preparations for the King's journey.*

As in life, so on the chessboard, the goods of the world are not altogether equally divided, so that there are some passed pawns who have far greater influence than other, ordinary passed pawns. Such "privileged" passed pawns deserve to be highly regarded by the student, who should never miss an opportunity of creating one for himself. In what follows we shall attempt to explain the effect of the "privileged" pawns by a consideration of their characteristics, from which rules will be deduced for our direction, the pros and cons in the fight with or against the stout fellows we are going to consider.

#50
The c pawn is a protected passed pawn; the g and h pawns are united passed pawns in the ideal position

(a) The typical ideal position of two united passed pawns is shown on Diagram 50. The relationship between them is one of the truest comradeship, and therefore the position where the two pawns are on the same rank must be regarded as the most natural one.

The strength of passed pawns so placed lies in the impossibility of blockading them, for their positions (on g4 and h4) seem to rule out any blockade on the squares h5 or g5. However the march of events will cause the two passed pawns to give up their ideal position, for though they are, maybe, doing noble work at g4 and h4, the innate ambition towards higher things, common to all passed pawns, will drive them forward. And the moment one of them moves, possibilities of blockading them will arise. For instance after **1.h5** Black pieces could blockade them at h6 and g5. From this consideration, coupled with the fact that these united passed pawns can have no dearer wish than to advance together to g5 and h5, there follow these rules: the advance of a passed pawn from the ideal position must take place only at a moment when a strong blockade by enemy pieces is impossible of execution. Further: If the proper pawn has advanced at the right moment, any blockade which may be attempted will be weak and easily overcome, his companion must then advance as soon as possible, so as to recover the ideal position.

Accordingly (see Diagram 50) at the right moment, the proper pawn, perhaps the g-pawn, will advance to g5, a move which affords the enemy the chance of setting up a blockade at h5. The blockading piece, which by hypothesis was badly supported (for this reason, we use the term "weak blockade"), will be driven off, and the move h5 will bring about the ideal position again.

Very important service can here be rendered by the White King stepping into the breach which was caused by the advance of the first pawn. Thus, in Diagram 50, after **1.g5 Nh5**, the King, whom we imagine to be at hand, with **2.Kg4** will slip into the breach and close it. The maneuver here described we shall call hole stopping, and our King need never be afraid of being out of work, for at worst he can get a job as a traveling dentist and stop cavities!

Diagram 51 shows a position which occurred in a club match in Stockholm in 1921. White played 1.b6+? and thus allowed Black to establish an absolute blockade by 1...Kb7. Absolute, because from the nature of things the King can never be driven away. There followed 2.Kd6 and the White King wandered to g7 and refreshed himself with the h-pawn, but at that very moment Black played his Bishop to h5 and there was nothing more for the King to eat on the Kingside. Dolefully his Majesty then wandered back to the other wing, but here, too, there was nothing for him since Black's Bishop, now freed form guarding the pawn,

#51

made the board unhealthy. A fitting punishment overtook White for breaking the rules by his advance. Correct was **1.a6 Bd3 2.Bd4 Bf1 3.Kb4+!** (plans to stop the hole at a5), **Ka8 4.Ka5 Be2 5.b6**. Everything on schedule: the a-pawn advanced first, since the hindrance that can now be put in White's way (blockade is here almost too strong a term) can be easily brushed aside. The King stops the hole caused by the advance, the b-pawn moves on in his turn, and the two pals are again united.

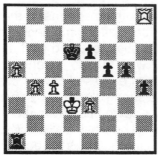

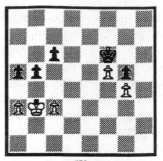

#52 Black to move. The g-pawn
shamefully leaves his friend the
h-pawn in the lurch. He got
high and mighty and forgot the
ties of friendship... so 1...g4!
2.Rxh4 g3 and wins

#53
White wins through the difference
in value between a protected and
an ordinary passed pawn

Thus like two trusty comrades on a battlefield, they will advance together, step by step, and it will be but seldom, and then only if far advanced, that it may happen that one of them will push on alone, ruthlessly leaving his friend to be slaughtered. Such an exceptional case is shown in Diagram 52.

(b) The difference in value between a protected passed pawn and an ordinary passed pawn is well shown in the following example (Diagram 53). White opens fire on the enemy's pawn majority. **1.a4 Ke5 2.axb5** (2.c4? would have been wrong because of 2...b4, with a protected passed pawn. The two Kings would then have had the scarcely pleasant job of walking up and down keeping an eye on the pawns, hardly an inspiring occupation for a King!). **2...cxb5 3.c4 bxc4+** (forced, 3...b4 would not help, for one of the White pawns would go on to promote), and now we have a position which is characteristic of the difference in value between the pawns, for, as is clear, the White King can munch the Black passed pawns one after another without any trouble, whereas the immunity of the protected f-pawn from any attack by the Black King is brilliantly in evidence. True, we have in our day seen players of little experience, ignoring this immunity. In the position White: Ka1, pawns f5, g4. Black: King e5, pawn g5, the second player, with a pleased grin on his face and flushed with the lust of battle, goes after the White g-pawn. After **1...Kf4 2.f6,** he sees his error and begins in all seriousness to chase the fleeing pawn. The last scene of the comedy runs thus: **2...Kf4 3.f6 Ke5!! 4.f7 Ke6!! 5.f8=Q** and Black Resigns. We may formulate the case thus: The strength of a protected passed pawn lies in its immunity from attack by the enemy King.

(c) In Diagram 54 the h-pawn is the "outside" passed pawn (that is, more remote from the midpoint of the board). After the indirect exchange of the two passed pawns, (after **1.h5+ Kh6 2.Kf5 Kxh5 3.Kxf6**) and the Black King is out of play, the White King is on the contrary, centrally developed. This is decisive. The more remote passed pawn is therefore a trump card with great power of causing a diversion, but like any other trump card must be hoarded, not played out too quickly, and this must be our rule. The exchange of pawns which drew off the enemy King was only the preliminary to the White King's journey which followed. This journey however, should be fully prepared for before the pawn advance takes place. Compare the position: White Ke4, pawns a4, c4, h2. Black: Kd6, pawns a5, e5, g7. White has the outside passer in the c-pawn. Its immediate advance would, however, be a mistake, for after 1.c5+ Kxc5 2.Kxe5, the King's journey to g7 would be a mere waste of time, for his traveling companion the h-pawn has been tardy. The right move is **1.h4.** The traveling companion reports himself! This induces **1...g6.** For this obliging advance we have to thank the *Zugzwang* weapon, of which we should make diligent use, particularly in the case of the more remote passed pawn. There now follows **2.c5+! Kxc5 3.Kxe5 Kb4** and Black arrives one move too late: **4.Kf6 Kxa4 5.Kxg6 Kb3 6.h5**, etc.

#54
The outside passed pawn, whose capture intices the enemy King away from the middle of the board.

Rules to be observed: Prepare for the King's journey before the sacrifice (or exchange) which is to divert the enemy King has been made. Make use of the *Zugzwang* weapon whenever possible. Let the traveling companion advance. The impediments to the journey (enemy pawns on the wings to which the King must travel) must be enticed forward. All this before the move is made which is to divert the enemy King out of action.

♦ *7. When a passed pawn should advance: (a) on his own account, (b) to win ground for his King who is following him (stopping the holes), (c) to offer himself as a sacrifice to divert the enemy. On the measure of the distance between the enemy King and the sacrifice which is to be offered him as bait.*

It is an old story that the less experienced amateur as a rule lets his passed pawn advance at the very moment least suitable to it. With two united passed pawns we saw him in Diagram 51 play 1.b6+? and thus allow an iron blockade to be set up. It may therefore be of practical use to note the cases in which an advance is indicated.

We have to ask ourselves: when is a passed pawn ready to march? We differentiate three cases.

(a) When the advance brings the passed pawn nearer to its goal (which will only be when there is a weak blockade), or when the advanced passed pawn gains in value in that he will then help to protect important points (see my game against v.Gottschall, Number 13, where 27.d6 helped to protect the point e7, with the threat

Ne7 or Re7). On the other hand it is wrong to push forward a pawn if he can be hopelessly blockaded, and in his new position will only be protecting unimportant points. It is easy to bring a passed pawn into the world. It is a much more difficult thing to provide for his future.

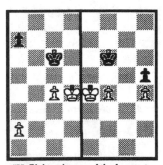

#55 Right: advance of the f-pawn to gain ground for the King to follow. Left: an affair of tempi

(b) When the advancing passed pawn leaves the ground clear for a following piece, and in particular gives his own King the chance of advancing against a new enemy pawn. See Diagram 55 (right side). The game proceeds: **1.f5 Kf7 2.Ke5 Ke7 3.f6+ Kf7 4.Kf5 Kf8!** The f-pawn has no future to look forward to. **5.Kg6** and wins the h-pawn. Here the advance was made simply and only to drive away the Black King, so that his own King might get near the h-pawn.

(c) When the advance takes place with the intention of sacrificing the pawn, so that the enemy King may be decisively drawn off from the field of battle. (See Diagram 54). Another example would be the following: White: Kg3, pawns a4, h2. Black: Kh5, pawn a5. Here the h-pawn is to be offered as a sacrifice, is to die for King and country. It only remains to decide how and, especially, where. Since the effect of the sacrifice as a diversion varies directly with the distance between the bait to be sacrificed and the enemy King, it would not be advantageous to let the h-pawn advance, for this distance would become smaller. The right course is to play the King at once over to the other wing. 1.Kf4 Kh4 2.Ke5 Kh3 3.Kd6, etc. Completely bad on the other hand would be 1.h4?? (Not content with sacrificing him, he actually serves him up on a platter! This I would call exaggerated politeness). After 1.h4?? there would follow 1...Kg6 2.Kf4 Kh5 3.Ke5 Kxh4 4.Kd5 Kg5 5.Kc4 Kf5 6.Kb5 Ke6 7.Kxa5 Kd7 8.Kb6 (threatening 9.Kb7) 8...Kc8 9.Ka7 Kc7 shutting in the White King and drawing. After **1.Kf4! Kh4 2.Ke5 Kh3** his Black Majesty may console himself with the fact that his walk from h4 to h2 has given him an appetite, so that the h-pawn becomes a pleasant meal after the fatigues of the tour, but this is all the consolation he will get. The student must take this to heart, that though the sacrifice to divert the enemy King is willingly made, it must occur under circumstances which will cause the maximum loss of time to the enemy.

It is not always so easy to recognize the motives of a pawn advance. See Diagram 55 (left side). Play proceeds: **1.c5 Kc7 2.Kd5 Kd7 3.c6+ Kc7 4.Kc5 Kc8** (reserve blockade) **5.Kd6 Kd8 6.c7+ Kc8 7.Kc6.** The pawn advance seems to be quite unmotivated, neither the cases a, b, or c, above, seems to apply, but there follows **7...a5**, for Black is now drawn into a *Zugzwang*. He must send forward his pawn, and with this the curtain rises on an exciting drama. The Black pawn goes a double stage, he storms ahead full of energy and youthful arrogance, but we choose instead the quiet **8.a3** for an answer, in order to prove to your youthful opponent that repose is a very valuable trait. After **8...a4 9.Kd6** (or 9.Kb6) the game is decided. Suppose that our young friend the Black a-pawn, recalled and soundly scolded for his impetuosity, now goes the modest route 7...a6. We then demonstrate to the luckless youth that energy is also a trump card, and we play 8.a4. Again after 8...a5 9.Kd6 Black is lost. The idea was the following: The stalemating of the Black King forces an advance of his a-pawn, and then White's a-pawn will time his advance to meet him so that after the a-pawns have run their course, White has the move. The latter then plays Kd6 or Kb6 and wins. This advance of the c-pawn may be classified under (a). He has advanced on his own account, for the affair of the tempi between the a-pawns makes of him a winning pawn, who otherwise, remembering the backward position of the White King, could only have been considered as a drawing pawn.

We close this chapter on the passed pawn with some endgame studies, reminding the reader that the chapter is to be regarded as an introduction to positional play.

♦ *8. Endgames illustrating the passed pawn.*

White (see Diagram 56a) had the move and sacrificed the exchange. The whole idea of the combination, throughout its weary length (there is no other phrase to use), lay in the one thought, the King must strive to attain the "ideal" position, namely

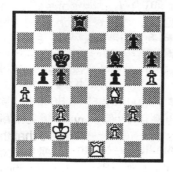 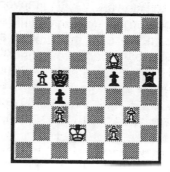

Diagrams 56a and 56b

Nimzowitsch-Rubinstein
Breslau 1925
The White King's struggle for a frontal
attack on an isolated pawn. Black
missed a win on his 7th move.

frontal attack on an isolated pawn (see ♦ 5). I succeeded in carrying out this hidden plan, although it could have been frustrated, because Rubinstein seemed to be handicapped by being not quite familiar with the postulates of my system, which were of course well known to me. I know of no other ending in which this struggle of

---

the King to reach the "ideal" position is more sharply brought out. The game proceeded: **1.Re6+ Kd5 2.Rxf6 gxf6 3.axb5 c4**, and now White took the h-pawn, although he had to give up his b-pawn and h-pawn for it. There followed **4.Bxh6 Rh8 5.Bg7 Rxh5 6.Bxf6 Kc5 7.Kd2!**, the point. All that has happened so far has been simply and solely to one end, to prepare the road for the King to go to f4. (Diagram 56b) **7...Kxb5?**, a mistake. Black could have here prevented the White King's contemplated journey by 7...Rh6 8.Bd4+ Kxb5 9.Ke3 Re6+ 10.Kf4? Re4+ followed by Rxd4 and wins. The student should observe that 10.Kf3 (instead of 10.Kf4) would not have saved the game for White either, since Black would then have played at his leisure ...Re4. The Black King would have then marched to e1 followed by the Rook's transfer to the seventh rank.

In the game the continuation was **8.Ke3 Kc5 9.Kf4!** Now all is right with the world again. **9...Kd5 10.f3**, with a draw in a few moves, since the Black King and Rook cannot both be freed at the same time. If this were possible, a double attack on the c-pawn with consequent sacrifice of the exchange would be feasible. An instructive endgame. If you ask why the White King struggled so obstinately for this frontal attack, the answer is that such a struggle responds to an instinct which is innate in him, moreover it must be remembered that in his action he was also obeying the blockade law.

#57 Hausen-Nimzowitsch
From a simultaneous exhibition in Randers, Denmark

Our second example shows a simple case of a turning movement. (Diagram 57). Black played **1...Kc7** (he must do something to meet the threat of c3, which would yield an outside passed pawn), and the endgame took the following very simple but effective course: **2.c3** (if 2.c4 Kb6 3.cxd5 cxd5 4.Kc2 Ka5! gaining a tempo), **2...Kb6 3.cxb4 Kb5 4.Kc3 Ka4** and the turning movement comes off to perfection despite the loss of a pawn, a result of the paralysis of White's forces.

The third example illustrates the diversion which can be effected by an outside passed pawn. (Diagram 58) The score of the game up to the exchange of Queens in the 36th move will be found in Game number 6. There followed **37.Kg1 Ke7 38.Kf2 d5 39.e5** (the simpler 39.exd5 Kd6 40.Ke2 Kxd5 41.a3 Kc5 42.f4 with eventually the diversion b4+ would also have won easily), **39...Ke6 40.Ke2** (40.f4 would have been weak because of 40...g5 41.g3 gxf4 42.gxf4 Kf5). **40...Kxe5 41.Kd3 h5 42.a3** (43.h4 first would have been preferable) **42...h4!** (creates a chance for himself later on) **43.b4 axb4 44.axb4 Kd6 45.Kxd4 Kc6 46.b5+** (White neglects the *Zugzwang* weapon which lies in his hand. 46.f4 would, after other Black moves were exhausted, have resulted in an obliging pawn move being made by Black, which would have furthered the subsequent excursion of the White King and the slaughter of the Black pawns). **46...Kxb5 47.Kxd5 Kb4!** Now this diversion has less significance than might have been the case, since after the win of the g-pawn and h-pawn Black will only need a few tempi for his h-pawn to get home. The ending is interesting because of the mistakes which were made. The position was in the end won by White after Black had overlooked a drawing chance.

#58 Tarrasch-Berger

The fourth example is significant as illustrating the method of advancing united passed pawns (see ◆6). The game proceeded (Diagram 59) **1.c6!** Here the choice of pawn to be first advanced rests not on the consideration of greater or lesser danger of a blockade, but on the reason that otherwise the c-pawn would be lost. **1...Qb6**

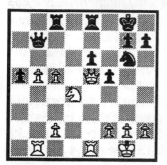

#59
Nimzowitsch-Alapin
Petrograd 1913

(if 1...Rxc6 2.bxc6 Qxb1 3.Rxb1 Nxe5, then 4.c7 with "passed pawn and 7th rank absolute." For instance, 4...Nd7 5.Nc6 and wins) **2.Qe3**, now the problem is to drive away the blockader from b6 so that the b-pawn who has lagged behind a little may catch up with his friend (see ◆6). **2...f4** (3.Nxf5 was threatened) **3.Qe4 Rcd8 4.Nf3 Rd6 5.h4!** holding the center strongly with the well-posted Queen, White intends now to prove that Black's defending pieces are somewhat in the air. **5...Qc5.** The idea has worked, the blockader is beginning to comply. **6.Ne5** (good results would also have come from 6.h5 Qxh5 7.b6 and the two comrades are happily united again) **6...Rd4** (the main variation would be 6...Rd2 7.Nd3 Qxc2 8.b6!, and despite the fall of the Knight, the pawns would have marched on to Queen) **7.Qe2 Nxh4 8.b6** (all according to book!) **8...Rb4 9.Rxb4 axb4 10.b7 Qc3 11.Qe4 Nf5 12.Nd7** Black Resigns.

The fifth example shows how impetuous a passed pawn can become. We do not as a rule regard him as being temperamental, yet knowing his ambitious nature this example will hardly surprise us. (see Diagram 60) There followed **1.g4 Bxg4 2.exf6+ Kf7.** The King is here a bad, because sensitive, blockader. The danger of mate makes his blockading effect illusory. **3.Bd5+!** (in order to give the Rook an effective range, without loss of time. The latter will now support the passed pawn with all his might). **3...cxd5 4.Qxe8+ Kxe8 5.f7+ Kf8.** The last attempt at a blockade. But now one of our supports, the Queen Bishop, comes to life. (5.f7+ has

#60 Nimzowitsch-Amateur
White played without the QN

The passed pawn   51

lengthened his diagonal) **6.Bg7+! Kxg7 7.f8=Q mate**. This endgame illustrates most pointedly the ambition of a passed pawn.

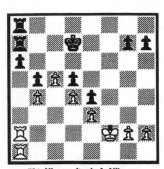

The sixth example (Diagram 61) is characteristic of an elastic blockade. This endgame was fully discussed in *Die Blockade*, so that we shall here only consider the more important points. White intends operations in the f-file, which he could start by 1.Kg3 and 2.Rf1. The breaking through point, f6, he will open by h4-h5-h6, and for this reason the White King's presence on the Kingside is required. In spite of the fact that the f-file controls the whole game, White had the courage to withstand the impulse to exploit it and calmly played **1.Ra5!!**, only taking up the fight in the f-file later. The blockade by the Ra5 is here possible because the blockader is elastic. He can at any moment be brought over to the Kingside.

The game proceeded as follows: **1...Kc6 2.Kg3 Kb7 3.Rf1 Kc6 4.Rf5 Re7 5.h4 Raa7 6.h5 Re6 7.Rf8**. The breakthrough, and still the Rook stands at a5 keeping guard, faithful, motionless. But the motionless watcher is prepared to intervene at any moment, whether by Ra2-f2 (proving his elasticity, or by Rxa6, if the Black Rook should move away. The possibility of Rxa6, it may be noted, should be classed under the threats exercisable from the blockading point. There followed **7...g6 8.h6 g5 9.Rb8 Kc7 10.Rbxb5 Rxh6 11.Ra4 Rf6 12.Rba5 Kc8 13.Kg4 h6 14.Ra2 Raf7 15.Rxa6** and White won after a further seven moves.

With this example we have suddenly found ourselves among the blockaders. The reader is asked to loiter for a while in this mixed company and to turn to Game numbers 14 and 15. We know that a blockader should: (a) blockade, (b) threaten, (c) be elastic, and we shall in number 14, be introduced to one who performs his manifold duties to perfection, while number 15 provides an interesting counterpart to this game.

CHAPTER 5

ON EXCHANGING

A short chapter whose purpose is to make clear the possible motives for exchanging

In order to show the student the danger lurking in indiscriminate bartering, we propose to enumerate the cases in which an exchange seems to be indicated. If an exchange does not come under one or another of these, it is bad. With the master the process of exchange is almost automatic. He holds files or safeguards his command of a strategically important point, and the opportunity of exchanging drops like ripe fruit into his lap. (See game No. 11, note to the 35th move).

In Chapter 1 we analyzed the "exchange with consequent gain of tempo." Again we often exchange in order not to be forced to retire, or to make time-losing defensive moves (liquidation with subsequent development). Both cases are in the last resort to be regarded as tempo combinations, though in fact the question of tempo plays an essential part in every exchange. A salient instance is the exchange of a newly developed piece for one which has wasted several tempi. In the middlegame the tempo motif finds expression when:

(1) We exchange in order to seize (or open) a file without loss of time. A very simple example. In Diagram 61a, White wants to seize (or open) a file in order to be able to give mate on the 8th rank. If to this end he plays 1.Bf3 or 1.Ra1, Black would have time to take steps against the mate with 1...Kf8 or 1...g6. The proper course is to exchange **1.Bxc6.** Black has no time to protect, for he must retake, and this "must" may also be taken in the psychological sense.

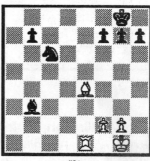

#61a

(2) We destroy a defender by exchanging. We destroy him, because we look on him as a defender. In the previous chapters we have made the acquaintance of defending pieces whose functions varied: pieces which protect a pawn obstructing the road in an open file, pieces which stand by to aid a blockader, and pawns which help to protect an outpost, etc. The destruction of any one of these is in every single case worth striving for. But by a "defender" we mean something much wider. A stretch of territory can also be defended, as for instance entry to the 7th rank, or a possible enemy approach can be warded off, as in game No. 14 where the Ne3 "protects" the points g4 and f5. Further it is well known that a Knight at f3 defends the whole castled wing (for example, preventing ...Qh4). So, too, in the case of a centrally posted blockading piece. In the position: White: Nd4, pawns e3, f3, g3, h3. Black: Be7, pawns d5, f7, g7, h7, the attacking radius of the Knight protects and safeguards for White a wide terrain, so that this Knight is also to be considered a "defender" in our sense. The rule therefore runs: Every defender in the narrower or wider sense of the word must be regarded as an object of our destructive wrath. In Diagram 62 where White wins by a series of exchanges, both kinds of motives are exemplified. A glance at the position reveals a Black Nh2 which has more or less gone astray, and his defender the Bb8. We play **1.exd5** (opening a file without loss of tempo), **1...cxd5 2.Re8+** (the Rook at c8 is a defender of the 8th rank and must therefore die), **2...Rxe8 3.Rxe8+ Kh7 4.Rxb8** (the arch defender now falls) **4...Rxb8 5.Kxh2** and wins.

#62 A series of exchanges
illustrating cases 1 and 2

(3) We exchange in order not to lose time by retreating. We are here as a rule concerned with a piece which is attacked. If we are faced with the choice whether to withdraw the piece with loss of tempo, or to exchange him for an enemy piece, we choose the latter alternative, especially if we can use to advantage the tempo we have saved ourselves by not withdrawing the piece. The question of tempo must therefore be actual in some form or another. The simplest example would be seen in Diagram 62a. **1.Ne4 a4 2.Rxb6** (to save a tempo) **2...axb6 3.Nxf6** and wins. If a major piece on each side is attacked, we have a special variety of this third case and we call it:

#62a

(3a) "Selling one's life as dearly as possible." In the position: White: Kh2, Qb2, pawns a2, e5, h3. Black: Kb8, Qd6, Nb7, pawn a4, the second player moves **1...a3.** White is prepared to exchange Queen for Queen, but if his Queen is really condemned to death, the wish to sell her life as dearly as possible is surely very intelligible. Like the soldier who is hemmed in on all sides, is ready to die, but carries on until his last cartridge is gone, wanting to account for as many enemies as possible, to sell his life as expensively as possible, so White plays **2. Qxb7+!**, in order to get at any rate something for the Queen. For some extraordinary reason such a commercial investment of the Queen is less intelligible to the beginner than a thorough-going heroic sacrifice. The latter is of common occurrence with him (though perhaps not the sacrifice of the Queen, since for her he has the most abject respect), whereas the former is quite foreign to him. Yet it is really no sacrifice, or at worst only a temporary one, and possibly it is in this amalgamation of sacrifice and sober conservation of material that lies the psychological difficulty under which the beginner succumbs.

#62b

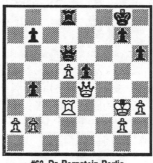

#63 Dr. Bernstein-Perlis
1909

(4) When and how exchanges usually take place. Lack of space forbids a detailed discussion of this question, and we will only quite shortly point out the following:

(a) Simplification is desirable if we have superiority in material. It follows naturally that exchanging can be used as a weapon to force the opponent from strong positions.

(b) When two parties desire the same thing a conflict arises. In chess this conflict takes the form of a battle of exchanges. For instance in Diagram 62b the key point is e4. White protects and overprotects the point with every means in his power. Black seeks to clear it, since a White piece on e4 is an annoyance to the second player because of its attacking radius. In the end it comes to a great slaughter on this point (e4).

(c) If we are strong on a file, a simple advance in that file is sufficient to bring about an exchange, for our opponent cannot suffer an invasion of his position, and at worst must seek to weaken it by exchanges.

(d) There is a tendency for weak points or weak pawns to be exchanged, one for the other (exchange of prisoners). The following endgame illustrates this. Diagram 63. The game proceeded **31...Ra8 32.Rb3 Rxa2 33.Rxb4**. (The weak pawns at a2 and b4 respectively have been reciprocally exchanged and have disappeared. The same happens to the pawns at d5 and b7). **33...Ra5 34.Rxb7 Rxd5 35.Rb8+!** (The simple exploitation of the b-file leads to the desired exchanges. **35...Qxb8 36.Qxd5+ Kh8**. As Dr. Lasker rightly pointed out, it would

---

have been better to maneuver the King to f6). **37.b3** and Bernstein won by means of his b-pawn in a brilliantly conducted endgame.

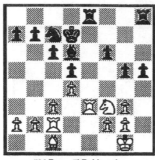

#64 Rosselli-Rubinstein
1925

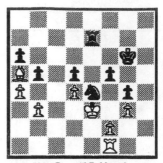

#64a Rosselli-Rubinstein,
1925 (at move 55)

We close this chapter with two endgames. Diagram 64 shows the position from the game Rosselli-Rubinstein after White's 21st move. There followed: **21...Rxe3** (or else White would double Rooks. Black, moreover had really no other sensible move). **22.Bxe3 Ne8 23.Re2 Ng7 24.Bd2 Nf5! 25.Re1 c5 26.dxc5 Bxc5**. (Now d4 has become the center of interest, and a battle will take place around it). **27.Kf1 h4 28.gxh4 g4 29.Nd4! Bxd4 30.cxd4** (see previous note) **30...Rxh4 31.Bc3 Rh1+ 32.Ke2 Rh2 33.Rg1 Nh4 34.g3 Nf5 35.b3 Ke6 36.Bb2 a6 37.Bc3 Nd6 38.Ke3 Ne4 39.Be1.** After some fruitless attempts by Rubinstein on the c-file, the position in Diagram 64a was reached after White's 55th move and the decisive breakthrough took place with **55...f4! 56.gxf4 Rh7 57.Bd2 Nxd2!** (kills the defender of f2 and f4) **58.Kxd2 Rh3 59.f3 gxf3 60.Rf2 Kf5 61.Ke3 Kg4 62.b4** (If 62.f5 Kxf5 63.Rxf3+ Rxf3+ 64.Kxf3 bxa4 65.bxa4 a5 and a successful turning movement against White's King will follow). **62...Rh1 63.f5 Re1+ 64.Kd3 Re4** and White resigned.

After this classic ending from a tournament game let us give one from a game at odds played in a coffeehouse, in which the exchange motif took an original shape.

#65 Nimzowitsch-Druwa
Riga 1919 (odds game)

Diagram 65. White, who had given the trivial odds of Queen for a Knight, "risked" the breakthrough **1.d5** and there followed **1...exd5** (safer was 1...Nxd5) **2.e6 fxe6** (he should have castled) **3.Ne5** (here we have the typical advance at the cost of self destruction. The Knight is the "awakened rear-rank man") **3...Nxc4 4.Bh5+ Ke7 5.Nxc6+!** (A surprise, for who would ever expect an exchange in the midst of a pursuit of the enemy King?!) **5...bxc6 6.Rf7+ Kd6 7.Nxc4+ dxc4 8.Rd1+.** Now the meaning is clear. The Bc6 was a defender, because of the possibility of Bd5 at this moment. **8...Ke5 9.Bf4+ Ke4 10.Bf3** mate!

CHAPTER 6

THE ELEMENTS OF ENDGAME STRATEGY

Some General Introductory Remarks

It is a well known phenomenon that the same amateur who can conduct the middlegame quite creditably, is usually completely helpless in the endgame. One of the principal requisites of good chess is the ability to treat both middlegame and endgame equally well. True, it lies in the nature of things that the student should gather his first experience in the opening and middlegame, but this evil, for such it is, must be rectified as early as possible. It should be pointed out to the beginner at the very start, that the endgame does not merely serve up untasty fragments left over from the rich feast of the middlegame. The endgame is on the contrary that part of the game in which the advantages created in the middlegame should be systematically realized. Now this realization of advantages, particularly those of an immaterial kind, is by no means a subordinate business. Very much the reverse, all the player's qualities as man and artist are demanded for it. In order to know, and to be able to appreciate what is happening in the endgame, one must be acquainted with the elements out of which it is compounded, for the endgame has its elements just as much as does the middlegame. One of these elements, the passed pawn, we have already analyzed thoroughly. There remain to be considered:

1. Centralization, with a subsection on the management of the King - the "shelter" and "bridgebuilding."
2. The aggressive Rook position and the active officer in general.
3. The rallying of all isolated detachments.
4. The combined advance.
5. The materialization of files. An element already touched on, to be understood in the sense that the file, which at first exercised an abstract influence, is narrowed down to a concrete point (protected by a pawn), or gains a concrete aspect.

The endgame would in fact, be in itself most interesting, even had Rinck and Troitzky never lived.

♦ *1. Centralization. (a) of the King, (b) of the minor pieces, (c) of the Queen. The journey to the King's castle.*

(a) The great mobility of the King forms one of the chief characteristics of all endgame strategy. In the middlegame the King is a mere "observer," in the endgame on the other hand - one of "the principals." We must therefore develop him, bring him nearer to the fighting line. This is often brought about by centralizing the King. Accordingly the rule runs: When the endgame is entered let the King set himself in

#65a

#66 Rubinstein-Nimzowitsch
Carlsbad 1907
The struggle of the Kings
for the center square

motion, and strive to reach the center of the board, for from this point he can, according to need, make for the right or left, in other words, attack the enemy King or Queen's wing.

First example: White: Kg1, Black: Re8 (only the most important actors are indicated). **1.Kf2**, pushing towards the center and at the same time protecting his base (the points e1 and e2) against the entry of the enemy Rook to these squares.

Second example: Diagram 65a. Here, too the first moves are Kf2-e2, and in this position White chooses the Queenside and plays Kd1-c2, thus protecting the b-pawn and releasing the Rook, which can now undertake something, perhaps by Rd7.

Third example: Diagram 66. White played **33.Nc3** since the immediate centralization of the King would have miscarried because of ...Bd5. For instance 33.Kf1 Bc4+ 34.Ke1 35.Bd5 and forces the exchange of pieces or the win of a pawn. After **33...Bc4 34.f4 Ke7 35.Kf2 Kd6 36.Ke3 Kc5**, the proper moment for White to get in touch with the point d4 had passed. If the Kings had been at d4 and d6 respectively, the win would have been much harder. The game, however, now plays itself. **37.g4 Kb4**. (This is the point. The central position c5 is to be regarded as a stepping stone to an attack on the wing, and therein lies the significance of centralization). **38.Kd4** - too late. **38...Bb3 39.g5 a4 40.Nb1 Be6 41.g3 Kb3 42.Nc3 a3 43.Kd3 g6 44.Kd4 Kc2!** and White resigned. In this example we have been able to look at this advance to the center from another side, and we have seen that it is meant not only to give our own King freedom to move about, but also to restrict the terrain accessible to the enemy King. For this reason the King will often fight for a point, as if a kingdom depended on it. The student should bear this carefully in mind, that he must leave no means untried to bring his King as near the center as possible, partly for his own King's sake, but partly also in order to limit the scope of the enemy King, who must not be allowed a place in the sun.

#66a

#66b

(b) Centralization must not be regarded as a purely Royal prerogative. The other pieces also develop a similar tendency. Take the position in Diagram 66a. Here White has two choices: King d2-c3-d4, or Nd4 followed by e3. As in the previous example, the centralization of the Knight has here a double effect. (1) He keeps, from d4, an eye on both wings. (2) He limits the liberty of the enemy King, bars, for instance, his journey via e6 to d5. If the enemy Rook is still on the board he will provide a rampart for his own King, who will take up a central position behind the Knight. Dr. Tartakower, the witty author of *Die hypermoderne Schachpartie* would have called this an island of pieces. A very simple example is one which would result from Diagram 66b. **1.Nd4**, followed by Kd3 with the central island of King, Knight and pawn.

#67 The centrally placed Queen allows the White King to journey into enemy land. His goal will be b6 or g6 with a frontal attack on an isolani.

(c) There is no more impressive proof of the importance of centralization than the fact that even the Queen, who in truth exerts sufficient influence even if posted on the edge of the board, herself seeks to attain a central position. The ideal one would be a centrally placed Queen defended by a pawn, and in her turn defending other pawns. Under such a protectorate her King can undertake long journeys into enemy country. So, for example the Kf3 in Diagram 67 will try to get to b6 or g6. After many

---

Elements of endgame strategy

and long wanderings he arrives at length on one of these squares, reaches safety, and wins.

♦ *1a. How his Majesty manages to protect himself against storms. The shelter. Bridge building.*

In order to have protection from the various dangers which may threaten, let the King provide himself in good time with a serviceable shelter. Such a refuge will protect him well should a storm come up. Consider the position of Diagram 68. Here 1.a7? would be an obvious mistake. After 1...Ra2 2. Kb6 (to free the Rook), the White King would have no protection against the storm, here the series of checks by the Rook, to which he is exposed. The right course would be to consider the point a7 as a shelter for the King, thus: **1.Kb6 Rb1+ 2.Ka7 Rb2 3.Rb8 Ra2 4.Rb6 Ra1 5.Kb7**. The sun is shining again now, so the old King can venture out. **5...Rh1 6.a7** and wins.

Events would take a similar course in the position in Diagram 68a. Here the point d6 would be the shelter, so this must not be made impracticable by 1.d6? The right move is **1.Ke6**, and if **1...Re2+**, then **2.Kd6** and Black has exhausted his checks, and is himself in danger since his King will be forced away from the queening square.

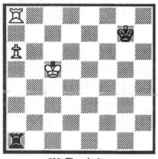

#68 The shelter

#68a

Endgame technique demands of us that we should be able ourselves to build our own shelter. In this, bridge building is useful. See Diagram 69. If White plays 1.Kf7, there will follow a series of checks, and in the end the White King will have to return to g8, his purpose unaccomplished. The key move is **1.Re4!**, one which at first sight is somewhat incomprehensible. There follows **1...Rg1** and now the King may venture forth into the light of day again. **2.Kf7 Rf1+ 3.Kg6 Rg1+ 4.Kf6! Rf1+ 5.Kg5! Rg1+ 6.Rg4!** The bridge has been built! The point g5 has become a perfect shelter. After 4.Kf6!, Black could also have marked time, thus: 4...Rg2 (instead of 3...Rf1+), and then there follows a delicious operation, which every bridge builder must envy. We transport in fact the whole bridge, with all that pertains to it, from one place to another with the move 5.Re5!!, and set up the bridge by means of Rg5 so that our shelter will now be at g6. This charming device belongs to the most common of every day maneuvers, a proof of the wonderful beauty of chess.

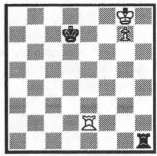

It will be interesting to see whether 1.Re5 at once might not serve. This as a matter of fact is the case. 1.Re5 also wins, though indeed less convincingly that the "author's" solution, 1.Re4. After **1.Re5** there would follow **1...Kd6 2.Kf7 Rf1+ 3.Ke8** (and not 3.Kg6 because of 3...Kxe5 4.g8=Q Rg1+), **3...Rg1 4.Re7 Ra1 5.Rd7+** and wins. Or 4...Rg2 5.Kf8 Rg1 6.Rf7 and

#69 Bridge building

wins. Bridge building for the provision of a shelter for the Royal traveler is a typical constituent in endgame strategy, and is very closely connected with the maneuver which will be treated in ♦3. For another example of bridge building see Game number 10, where 38.Nf5 creates a shelter for the White King at f3.

♦ *2. The aggressive Rook position as a characteristic advantage in the endgame. Examples and argument. The active officer in general. Dr. Tarrasch's formula.*

The advantage of an aggressive Rook position in the endgame is a most important one. See Diagram 70a (3 examples). On the far left, assuming that both players still have

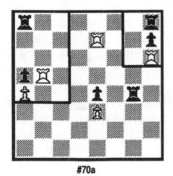

#70a

#70b

In each case in the above diagrams, the White Rook has the aggressive position, the Black Rook the passive position

pawns remaining on the King's wing, the position of the White Rook can be made the basis of an advance on the Kingside. Still more is this the case in the configuration shown on Diagram 70b. White can by means of 1.h4 followed when convenient by h5 and hxg6 lay bare Black's g-pawn to attacks. And whereas the White Rook is the very soul of this new set of operations, the Black Rook cannot muster up sufficient elasticity to get over to the Kingside to offer a defense against

---

the former's attack. And so we formulate the matter thus: The weakness of the defending Rook lies in its deficient elasticity in the direction of the other wing, and further, in this too, that the enemy King wins greater maneuvering freedom (as a rule he is afraid of Rooks, but when the cat's away, etc!). In Diagram 70b, therefore, the threat of the White King's march to b6 (naturally by slow stages) is on no account to be underestimated.

#70c

It is of daily occurrence in games between masters that one of the parties will undertake extended maneuvers and go to immense trouble, simply in order, as a reward for all his pains, to get for himself the aggressive Rook position, to force a passive role on the enemy Rook. On the other hand we must expect the passive Rook sometimes to go on strike, as happens in the following example. Diagram 70c. Black with the move begs to be excused from the passive role intended for his Rook (1...Ra7) and plays instead **1...Rb2 2.Rxa5 Ra2**. The Black Rook is now very mobile and the draw ought to be assured, whereas 1...Ra7 would probably have lost. We may then say, that if faced with the choice of protecting a pawn with a Rook and of thus condemning him to a passive, indeed meditative existence, or of sacrificing the pawn without further to-do, in order to employ the Rook in some active capacity, we should decide on the latter alternative.

#71 White to play should make the aggressive Rook move. Black with the move should find the most enterprising Rook position

When is a Rook's position, taken in regard to his own or an enemy passed pawn, to be considered as aggressive?

This question has already been answered by Dr. Tarrasch, whose excellent formula runs: The Rook's proper place is behind the passed pawn, whether it be his own or an enemy one. In Diagram 71, White with the move plays **1.Ra3** taking up his position behind the passed pawn. The Rook's influence is enormous for he breathes into the passed pawn some of his own life. On the other hand, if it were Black's move, he must not post his Rook in front of the pawn, not 1...Ra8? 2.Ra3! and White wins, but on the contrary behind it, and this he can do by **1...Rd2+ 2.Kf3 Ra2**. The Rook position thus gained is aggressive (1) with regard to the White g-pawn, who, if the opportunity arises, may be gobbled up (2) having regard to a possible journey of the White King. For instance, should the King reach a6 Black can shut him in by ...Rb2, or should he venture to b8 or c8, subject him to a series of checks from behind.

It is not only in the case of Rooks but also in that of minor pieces that the difference in value between an attacking or defending piece weighs heavily in the balance. The weakness of a defending Knight lies in the fact that he is uni-operative, he cannot move about and still keep up the defense of the point under his charge. This characteristic favors the *Zugzwang*. In Diagram 72 Black with the move will succumb under *Zugzwang*. White with the move, on the other hand, suffers only in appearance from a similar disease, for the agile White Knight can develop all manner of threats. White plays **1.Ne3** (or 1.Kd5 with the threat of 2.Ne5) and the *Zugzwang* weapon is again at Black's throat. If the whole position were moved back one rank, White would still win.

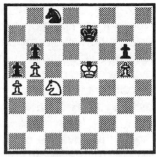

#72 The weakness of the Knight as a defender often leads to *Zugzwang*

In a defending Bishop, one characteristic stands out, that in the capacity to change fronts quickly he cannot compete with his attacking colleague. This is brought out in the delightful winning attack in the position on Diagram 73.

The Black Bishop is here defending, and the White Bishop threatens to get to b8 via h4, f2, and a7. It looks indeed as if this threat can be comfortably parried by a timely ...Ka6. Thus: **1.Bh4 Kb5! 2.Bf2 Ka6!** and if now 3.Bh4 with the threat of Bd8 followed by Bc7, the Black King can get back to c6 in plenty of time. White, however, plays **3.Bc5** (in order to cause the Black Bishop to make a move, and at the same time to prevent 3...Bd6). **3...Bg3** Now White's Bishop goes back to get within range of c7, thus **4.Be7 Kb6! 5.Bd8+ Kc6 6.Bh4!** and Black will no longer have time for the saving maneuver ...Kb5-a6 which he used before, for White has managed to gain a tempo. **6...Bh2 7.Bf2** and White wins by Ba7 followed by Bb8. **7...Bf4 8.Ba7 Bh2 9.Bb8 Bg1 10.Bf4 Ba7 11.Be3!** A lovely ending.

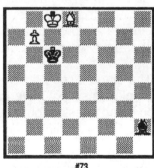

#73

♦ *3. The rallying of isolated detachments and the general advance.*

Since these two maneuvers are very closely connected, so that the one often merges insensibly into the other, they will here be considered together. To bring single scattered detachments into contact with one another cannot be difficult, one has only to know the bearing one piece has on the other. We know several things,

---

for instance that a Knight is able cunningly to construct a shelter for the King by building a bridge. We know, too, that this officer does not despise the hospitality of a private soldier (Knight protected by a pawn), and in gratitude is ready to draw his sword if it comes to defending his humble friend from one of his own class, or to an onslaught on an enemy pawn. See in this connection the White Knight at f5 in game Number 10 (38th move). We know further that a King stops the holes made by the advance of his own pawns. And we must not forget that a centrally posted Queen can gather far off pawns into her net. The contact between the White pieces in the position Kf3, Rf4, pawns g3, a4 would be by no means bad.

Again the advance must be a collective one. For a passed pawn suddenly to run wild and rush away from his protectors and friends, is an absolute exception to the rule, which may be stated thus: The advancing pawn must stay in close contact with his own people. The place vacated by the advance of a pawn must be as quickly as possible taken by a "hole stopper". Thus the square e4 left vacant by the move e5 should speedily be occupied by playing the Knight or King to e4.

It happens sometimes that an enemy Rook by annoying checks seeks to disturb a combined play, in which case he must be reduced to impotency or driven home (see the game Post-Alekhine, Diagram 78).

Combined play forms 80 per cent of the whole of endgame technique, and the details which we have treated, such an centralization, bridge building, the shelter, hole stopping, are all subordinate to one end, combined play. Like a ratchet wheel in a piece of clockwork they see to it that the mechanism gets into motion, they intend to insure a slow, but safe forward movement of the serried ranks of the army. A general advance is the order of the day.

The student should note that "centralization" is possible even on a remote flank. The pieces simply have to group themselves around a pawn as center, and there can be no question but that "centralization" is effectively carried out. (see again the game Post-Alekhine, Diagram 78).

♦ 4. *"Materialization" of the abstract conception of file or rank. An important difference between operations in a file in the middle and endgame.*

A curious and by no means obvious difference must now be noted. In the middlegame the exploitation of a file involves the expenditure of a great deal of energy, in other words is wholly active. We have only to remember the complicated apparatus used: for instance, in particular, the outpost Knight. In the endgame, on the other hand, such operations run on simple lines, are in fact of the meditative order. Far and near not a trace of a Knight outpost. The lucky possessor of the file takes his time. At the most he sends forward a handful of men to clean up some

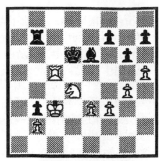

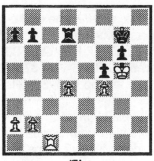

#74 Nimzowitsch-Jacobsen
1923
Materialization of the 5th rank

#74a

position for his advancing Rook. And so we can say that operations in a file are in the middlegame active, in the endgame meditative, even contemplative. And the same applies to a rank. We will illustrate this by some examples. In Diagram 74, White holds the clear 5th rank, and by the following simple series of moves manages to materialize the rather abstract effect of his possession of this rank, to condense it to a concrete point. The game proceeded **42.Rc6+ Kd7 43.hxg6! hxg6 44.Nxe6! fxe6** (44...Kxc6 45.Nd8+) **45.Rc5** to be followed by Rg5 and f4. The occupation of the point g5 is decisive, the more since the passive Black Rook will be forced to move to g7.

The course of the game in Diagram 74a is also typical. White calmly goes for a "walk" with the moves b4, a4, b5, a5, b6 and finally Rc7. If this threat is parried by ...b6, then the move Rc6 is made possible. So, too, reverting to Diagram 70b, after the advance of the h-pawn, the 6th rank was condensed into the concrete point g6.

In the position shown on Diagram 75, in which White commands the f-file, and Black tries to defend his 1st and 2nd ranks, Capablanca won almost automatically by the mere deadweight of the file. **27.Ref1 Rhe8 28.e4 Qb5 29.Ra1!** White takes

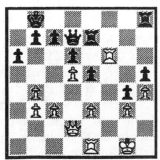

#75 Capablanca-Martinez
Argentina 1914

Elements of endgame strategy   65

his time, the f-file must in the end crush the opposition by its own weight. **29...Qd7** (the threat was 30.c4 Qb6+ 31.c5 with an uncomfortable position for Black) **30.c4 Rf7 31.Rxf7 Qxf7 32.Rf1 Qg7 33.Rf5 Rf8 34.Qg5!** winning a pawn. **34...Qh8 35.Qxh5 Qxh5 36.Rxh5 Rf3 37.Kg2 Rxb3 38.Rf5** and Black resigned since the h-pawn cannot be stopped. (38...Rb2+ 39.Rf2!)

The moral application of this for the student may be thus formulated. If in the endgame a file is in your permanent possession, do not worry about an eventual breakthrough point, this will come of itself, almost without any assistance on your part.

We will now give a few endgames exemplifying the four elements of endgame strategy.

1st example. Diagram 76. With **20.Bf5! Nxd4 21.Bxc8 Rxc8 22.cxd4 0-0 23.dxe5 fxe5 24.Qxd5+ Qf7 25.Qxf7+ Rxf7 26.Bxe5**, White passed into the endgame. He has a temporary pawn majority, and more important, a Bishop permanently posted in the center. There followed **26...Rf5 27.f4 Rxh5 28.Rab1 Be7**. (Spielmann defends himself with his customary ingenuity). **29.Kf2** (progressive centralization) **29...b6 30.Kf3 Rh6 31.Rfd1 Rc4 32.Rd7 Kf7 33.a5 b5 34.Re1 Rcc6 35.Bd4 Rhe6 36.Rh1 h6 37.Rb7 Red6 38.Be5 Re6 39.Ke4**. After the preparatory Rook maneuvers (notice that the Rb7 is in close contact with the

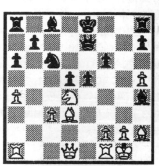

#76 Nimzowitsch-Spielmann
San Sebastian 1911

protected point b6, and that the 7th rank is to be materialized) the Black Rooks prove themselves to be "passive" enough actually to invite a further advance of the White King. Bishop, King, and pawn now form a central island; the Bishop is the bridge builder, the point e4 is our shelter. **39...Rc4+ 40.Kf5 Rc5 41.Rd1 b4.** (The game cannot be saved). **42.Rd8 Rxa5 43.Rf8+! Kxf8 44.Kxe6** and Black Resigned.

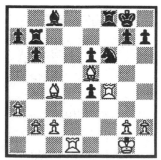

#77 Thomas-Nimzowitsch

The 2nd example again shows centralization. Diagram 77. In his difficult situation, Black tried **20...Kf7** there followed **21.Re1?** (the right move was 21.g4) **21...Ke7 22.Bc3 Nd5**, and after the further moves **23.Rxf8 Kxf8 24.Be5**, the second player had overcome the worst of his difficulties. **24...b5 25.Bb3 Nf6 26.Kf1 Ke7.** Now Sir George could not resist any longer the temptation to win back the pawn and played **27.Bxf6+ gxf6 28.Rxe4**. Furthermore, since after **28...e5**, he exposed his Rook by **29.Rh4**, Black got the upper hand, and by forceful centralization won as follows: **29... Bf5 30.Ke2 Bg6 31.Bd5 Rb8 32.c3 f5 33.Bb3 Kf6.**

Observe the collective advance of Black's central forces. **34.Bc2 a5!** Played because White's majority on this side is really a minority, or better stated, a majority forsaken by all of its patron saints (King and Rook). **35.Rh3 e4 36.Rh4 b4 37.axb4 axb4 38.Rf4 Ke5 39.Rf1 b3 40.Bd1 f4 41.Ke1 Bf7 42.g3 f3.** White is all sewn up. There followed the sacrifice **43.Bxf3 exf3 44.Rxf3**, and after a stubborn fight Black won through his superiority in material.

The 3rd example. An ending rich in combinations. The gifted, imaginative Franco-Russian seems in this game as if he wished to sweep away the rules of my system with the hurricane of his bubbling inspiration. This, however, is only apparently the case. In reality everything is done in the spirit of the system and of centralization. Diagram 78. **40...g4+.** The "candidate" (pawn on f5) stops behind, but we are here concerned with a sacrificial combination. **41.Kg2** (41.Kf4? Kf6 with mating threats). **41...Kf7 42.Nxa6 Re1 43.h4 Kg6 44.Nb4 f4! 45.gxf4 Rg1+ 46.Kh2 g3+ 47.Kh3 Bf2.** Now pawn, Bishop, and Rook are united into one

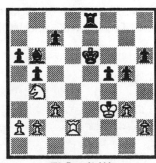

#78 Post-Alekhine
Mannheim 1914

whole, but this whole has, at any rate for the moment, small possibility of expansion. **48.Kg4** (the threat was 48...Rh1+ 49.Kg4 Rxh4+!) **48...Rh1 49.f5+ Kf6 50.Nd5+ Ke5 51.Kf3 Kxf5 52.Nxc7 Rxh4 53.Nxb5.** Black has given up his whole Queenside. With what justification? Because with the fall of White's h-pawn the capacity for expansion which was somewhat lacking before (see note to the 47th move) is now present in rich measure: the two united passed pawns, with the King there to stop the holes, demolish all resistance. **53...Rf4+ 54.Kg2 h5! 55.Rd8 h4! 56.Rf8+** (the Rook wants to stop the combined attack) **56...Kg5 57.Rg8+** (57.Rxf4? Kxf4 followed by Kg4) **57...Kh5 58.Rh8+ Kg6 59.Re8** (in order after Bc5 to safeguard his base which would be threatened by Rf2) **59...Bc5 60.Re2 Kf5** (the hole stopper draws near!) **61.b4 Bb6 62.Kh3 Rf2 63.Nd6+ Kf4 64.Re4+ Kf3 65.Kxh4 Bd8+!! 66.Kh5 Rh2+ 67.Kg6.** The White pieces are all "away," and the house stands deserted and desolate. **67...g2** and White resigned.

The 4th example lets us follow a King in his wanderings, which interests us inasmuch as it takes place under the watchful eye of a centrally placed Queen. Diagram 79. The game proceeded: **39.Qe5 Qd1+ 40.Kf2 Qd5.** The fight for the midpoint of the board. **41.Qf4+ Kg6.** (The beginning of the wandering. 42...Qf5 is now threatened). **42.Ke1 Qf5! 43.Qg3+ Kh5 44.Qg7 Qe4!** (The Black King is making preparations to go either to h2 or to e3). **45.Qf7+ Kg4 46.Qg7+** (or 46.Qd7+ Kh4!) **46...Qg6 47.Qd7+ Kf3 48.Qh3+ Ke4.**

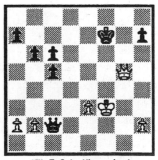

#79 E. Cohn-Nimzowitsch

(Our ideal frontal position). **49.Ke2 Ke5!** (After the King has gone to great pains and trouble to get to the point e4, he retires with the threat of 50...Qc2+. This is the point of the maneuver, namely to get time for the move ...c4, which forces the White Queen perpetually to protect the point d3. The manner in which the Black King, in order to be free of checks, now flees to e7, and the Queenside pawns carry out their irresistible advance, is as interesting as it is instructive). **50.Kd2 c4 51.Qf1 Qe4 52.Qe2 Ke6 53.Qf1 Ke7! 54.Qe2 b5 55.Qf1 a5 56.Qg1 Qe5 57.Kc2 b4 58.Qf2 Qe4+ 59.Kc1 a4 60.Qg3 b3 61.axb3 cxb3 62.Qc7+ Ke6 63.Qc8+ Kd5 64.Qd7+ Kc4 65.Qf7+ Kd3** and White Resigned.

CHAPTER 7

THE PIN

♦ *1. Introductory and General. Tactics or Strategy. On the possibility of reintroducing a pinning motif which has had to be abandoned.*

After the difficult sixth chapter, difficult at any rate in the positional sense, the present one may appear very easy. And the question may perhaps be asked, whether the pinned piece can really be spoken of as an element in our sense, since a game may be laid out on the basis of an open file or a passed pawn, but surely never on a pin! This point of view I cannot share. True, pins as a rule occur in purely tactical moments as, for instance, in the pursuit of the fleeing enemy, on the other hand, however, a pin foreseen in the planning of a game may quite logically influence its whole course. In connection with this possibility game No. 5, Haken-Giese is of special interest. The move 25...Bg6 signifies a resuscitation of the pin motif which had been dead since the 7th move, for now an advance is threatened, when occasion serves, against the objective, the square h3 by ...h5 and ...g4. The original White move h3 was in its turn, however, conceived as a parry to the threatening pin, and therefore stands in logical connection with that motif. Consequently the attack on White's h-pawn should also be considered a logical variation on the same theme, the pin motif. This despite the fact that in the game as played Black did not pursue the adventure involved in or rather restarted by the move 25...Bg6, but contritely returned to the e-file, when virtue found its reward. But this is quite immaterial, for it could easily have happened otherwise. What is of importance is that we should have learned the great strategic range of the pin motif.

♦ *2. The conception of the totally, and half pinned piece. The defense a pinned piece can give is but imaginary. Exchange combinations on the pinning square (the square on which the pinned piece stands), and the two distinct motives for such combinations.*

To a pin belong three actors, (1) the pinning piece, (2) the pinned enemy piece, and (3) the piece standing behind the pinned piece. The first attacks the third across the second, that is to say the pinned piece stands in the way of the capture of the piece behind it by the pinning piece, and for short we shall call them the "pinning," the "pinned," and the "screened" piece. The screened piece is usually of noble blood, that is King or Queen, for otherwise it would not be likely to hide itself behind another piece. All three actors stand either on the same file or the same diagonal. (See Diagram 80). The pinned piece dare not move since if he did the piece behind him would be exposed to the attack from which it had previously been screened. If this immobility is absolute, that is, if the pinned piece dare make no move whatever, he is said to be totally pinned. If on the other hand the pinned piece has any squares

---

#80

White's Rh4 half pins the pawn on h6;
The Bishop on g1 totally pins the
Black Nc5.

at his disposal in the line of the pin to which he can move, he is said to be only half pinned. In Diagram 80, the pin by the Rook is only a half pin since the move ...h5 is possible. A pinned Knight is always totally pinned. Of other pieces we may say that a piece can only half pin one of its own kind. For instance, White: Bh1, Black: Bc6, Kb7. Here the Black Bc6 is only half pinned. He can move anywhere on the diagonal c6 to h1. A pawn can only be totally pinned by a diagonally moving piece. If the pin is in a column the pinning piece must block the pinned pawn (e.g., White: Rg6, Black: pawn g7, Kg8), in order to enforce complete immobility. But such immobility has really no connection to the pin: it could equally be the result of the blockade.

A pinned piece's defensive power is only imaginary. He only makes a gesture as if he would defend, but in reality he is crippled and immobile. We may therefore confidently place our piece en prise to a pinned piece, for he dare not lay hands on it. An example will be found in Diagram 81. The winning moves **1.Qxg3+** or **1.Qxa6+** are easy to find. All we have to be sure of is that the Black Bf4 or pawn b7 is pinned, if this be the case the points (g3, a6) which seem to be protected are really at our mercy. And so we may seek out such points which make a pretense of being protected, and at once rightly declare them to be free as air. How simple! And yet the less experienced amateur would rather put his head in a lion's jaws than put his Queen *en prise!*

It is very often profitable to play for the win of the pinned piece. To us, who know that every immobile, or even weakly restrained piece tends to become a weakness, this fact will not appear surprising. But parallel with the problem of winning the pinned piece is that of preventing its unpinning, for on this its mobility would be restored, and with that all its strength also. Apart from the fact that the possibility of an unpinning must always be kept in view, the fight to win a pinned piece proceeds on the usual lines, namely by multiplying attacks, and in the case of adequate protection by thinning the ranks of the defenders. A clear profit may, however, sometimes be recorded,

#81

Right: 1.Qxg3+ and wins.
Left: 1.Qxa6+ with mate next move

namely in the case when a pinned piece can be attacked by a pawn, for then this attack will be decisive. That this must be so follows from the consideration that a piece can only evade a pawn attack by flight. If, however, the piece is pinned, he is defenseless against an attacking pawn, since flight is denied him. Diagram 82. On

the right, the course would be **1.Rh1 g6** and then up
will come the pawn **2.g4**. On the left things are not
made quite so easy for the pawns, there are one or two
interferences to brush aside, and this is done by **1.Rxa5
bxa5 2.b6** and wins.

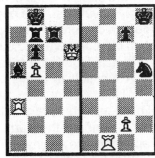

In general, the plan of attack against a pinned piece
calls for a great effort to secure that preponderance in
material which we have on various occasions noted,
meaning a majority of attackers over the defenders of
our objective which in this case is the pinned piece.
The ideal to be aimed at is the pawn attack, which not
infrequently will crown the whole enterprise. For

#82 Two elementary examples
of the win of a pinned piece
by a pawn attack

example: In Diagram 83 (left) it is plainly visible that a close investment of the pinned
Black pawn on b6 has been undertaken. We may add that the ideal result of this
siege may be observed in the passive state to which the Black defenders are
reduced. But now the a-pawn moves forward, and this advance leads to a tangible

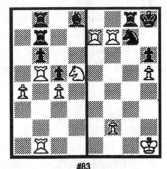

#83
Pawn attack after anterior investment
carried out by pieces

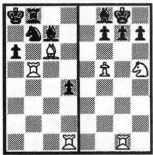

#84   The exchange combination
Right: the 1st motive
Left: the second motive

result. In the same diagram (right) the Black Ng7 is in a pitiful state of pin. The
screened piece is represented here by the mating threat at h7. By the advance of
the h-pawn White has prevented any unpinning of the Knight by ...Kh7-g6. The
pressure exerted on the pinned Knight by the pieces alone is here almost
unbearable, yet does not lead to any immediate result. But now the f-pawn comes
up with a dagger under his cloak, and decides matters. And so while the officers
may put on pressure, the proper person to execute the death sentence will always
be the private soldier.

♦ *3. The exchange combination on the pinning square.*

The first motive. See Diagram 84 (right). In this position the capture of the pinned
Black pawn on g7 may be our object. We pile up attacks (the preponderance 3:2

has here already been achieved), and then find to our disappointment that the pawn jauntily advances. The beggar was not even pinned, or at best only half pinned, for though a capture by the g-pawn would not be feasible, ...g6 is. The problem of how to win our objective, is, nevertheless, easy of solution, and this by **1.Nxg7 Bxg7 2.f6**. The idea is that White substitutes the totally pinned Bishop for the half-pinned pawn g7. A substitution of this kind is our first motive.

There is, however, still a knotty question to answer, namely how White, notwithstanding the surrender of one of his attacking pieces, can maintain his preponderance against the point g7. The answer of course lies in the fact that though Black still has two of his original defenders (King and Bishop) on the board, the Bishop can no longer be regarded as a defender of the threatened point, but has himself become the pinned object of our attack at that point, whereas White still has his Rook and the f-pawn which, close at hand, is ready to plunge into the fray so that the operation 1.Nxg7 Bxg7 puts a piece on each side out of action and the relative preponderance of White is unchanged.

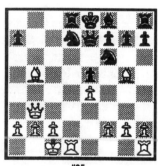

#85
The 2nd motive

The 2nd Motive. In the famous game, Morphy-Duke of Brunswick and Count Isouard, after the moves **1.e4 e5 2.Nf3 d6 3.d4 Bg4? 4.dxe5 Bxf3 5.Qxf3 dxe5 6.Bc4 Nf6 7.Qb3 Qe7 8.Nc3 c6 9.Bg5 b5 10.Nxb5 cxb5 11.Bxb5+ Nbd7**, the position of the pinned Black Nd7 was a very critical one. There followed **12.0-0-0** (the quickest way to unite the Rooks for an attack on the d-file against the point d7). **12...Rd8** (Diagram 85). In this position the simple doubling of the Rooks on the d-file would win the Knight, 13.Rd2 Qe6 14.Rhd1 Be7 15.Bxf6, but Morphy has a much stronger maneuver at his command. There followed: **13.Rxd7 Rxd7 14.Rd1.** This exchange combination on the pinning square deserves our notice. Did it take place in order to substitute a totally pinned piece or one which is half pinned? No, for the Nd7 as it was, was totally pinned. Would it have taken place if the White Rook had already stood at d2? No, for in that case doubling the Rooks would have sufficed. The exchange combination was evidently carried out in order, in the struggle for the point d7, to gain a tempo.

Let us dispassionately consider the state of affairs before and after Rxd7. Before this capture White had two attackers against two real defenders, for the Nf6 is half dead, and the Queen is too great a personage, and does not fare well in rough and tumble with minor pieces. After 13.Rxd7, White loses one attacker, whom he, however, at once replaces with a fresh Rook, whereas the defending Rook which previously stood at d8 is irrevocably lost to Black. (see the "knotty question" above). Accordingly White has profited to the extent of a fighting unit, and has thus a preponderance of forces in his fight for the pinned piece. The 2nd motive, therefore, is the gain of a tempo. After **14...Qe6**, 15.Bxf6 would have won easily, but Morphy preferred the prettier method **15.Bxd7+ Nxd7**, and now the Knight is in its turn pinned because of the mating threat at d8. The Knight is, however, forced to move whereupon mate follows: **16.Qb8+! Nxb8 17.Rd8** mate.

#86 The 1st and 2nd
motives appear together

In the position back in Diagram 84 (left) the pinning Rook is attacked. To withdraw him would mean giving the enemy the tempo he needs to get rid of the pin. For instance, 1.Rb2 Ka7 2.Rdb1 Nd6. The correct play is **1.Rxb7 Rxb7** and now **2.Rb1** wins. Since the sacrifice at b7 was made only to avoid the loss of a tempo, our 2nd motive is obviously present.

The two motives can also appear together in one combination. Diagram 86. Here a general exchange is clearly indicated. However after 1.Bxf6+ Rxf6 2.Rxf6 Kxf6 3.b4 Ke5, the Black King would arrive on the scene just at the right moment. We must therefore bring about the exchanges more cleverly. This we can do by **1.Rxf6! Rxf6 2.b4**, for now Black will have to lose a tempo with a King move. Thus **2...Kf7 3.Bxf6 Kxf6 4.b5** and now the pawn cannot be caught. A tempo-winning combination, you will say. Quite true, but the gain of a tempo was only attained because we were able to replace the half-pinned Bishop by the fully pinned Rook. Taking one thing with another, we see that in this case we have a combination of the two motives.

We will close this section with an example which will show us the utilization of the pin combined with the justly popular *Zugzwang* motif. That a pin may easily lead to a dearth of available moves is obvious, for often enough the elasticity of the defending pieces is very small. In fact, it not infrequently happens that the defense is uni-operative. By uni operative we mean that the defenders cannot shift their ground and still maintain the protection of the threatened point(s). In Diagram 87, after the initial sacrifice which we have so often discussed (1st motive), **1.Rxe5! Rxe5**, there followed **2.g3!** Were it not for 2.g3, Black could have given his King air by means of f4, but now this move

#87 From a game at odds by Dr. Tarrasch. The pin exploited by means of
Zugzwang

would fail after 3.g4 and Black succumbs owing to the uni-operative quality of his defense of the Rook on e4. After 2...g4 Black is equally "in hot water," and for the same reason. *(Editor's note - 2...Kg6! 3.Bxe5 Kh5 [threat of 4...f4!] with a draw).*

We have now, in essentials at any rate, exhausted the subject of play against a pinned piece and will go on to the subject of unpinning.

♦ *4. The problem of unpinning: (a) The "question," its character and the dangers involved. (b) Ignoring the pin. (c) Unpinning by bringing up the reserves. (d) Maneuvering and holding choice of policy in suspense. (e) The "corridor" and the defensive alliance of the beleaguered.*

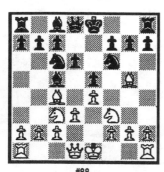

#88
The problem of unpinning

After the moves **1.e4 e5 2.Nf3 Nc6 3.Bc4 Bc5 4.Nc3 Nf6 5.d3 d6,** White can set up a pin by **6.Bg5,** and curiously enough this simple little pin evokes a forest of possibilities. Diagram 88. Should Black immediately put the "question" to the bold Bishop by 6...h6 7.Bh4 g5 8.Bg3, or should he even risk a counter-pin with 6...Bg4? Again may he not consider it reasonable to ignore the threat involved in the pinning move 6.Bg5 (namely 7.Nd5, with consequent disorganization of his Kingside pawn position by a Bishop or Knight capture on f6), in order with 6...Nd4 quietly to "centralize"? There is further 6...Na5 to be considered, while 6...0-0 must not be dismissed with a mere shrug of the shoulders.

(a) The "Question."

It will be clear without further remark that the premature advance of the wing pawns must have compromising effect. In the Scotch game, to give an example, after **1.e4 e5 2.Nf3 Nc6 3.d4 exd4 4.Nxd4 Nf6 5.Nc3 Bb4 6.Nxc6 bxc6 7.Bd3 d5 8.exd5 cxd5 9.0-0 0-0 10.Bg5 c6 11.Ne2,** there can follow **11...h6 12.Bh4 g5?,** but now after **13.Bg3,** White has at his command the attacking move f4, and also the possibility of occupying the squares f5 and h5 which have been weakened by the advance of the g-pawn, as neither point can ever be attacked by ...g6. The "question" was therefore ill-timed.

On the other hand, there are occasions when the "question" is very opportune. For instance, in the following opening of a tournament game, E. Cohen-Nimzowitsch **1.e4 e5 2.Nc3 Bc5 3.Nf3 d6 4.d4 exd4 5.Nxd4 Nf6 6.Be2 0-0 7.0-0 Re8.** Black has given up the center, but has pressure on the e-pawn. **8.Bg5?** 8.Bf3 was the right move. **8...h6! 9.Bh4 g5! 10.Bg3 Nxe4.** It was to win this important pawn that Black puts up with the disorganization of his own position (See Chapter 1). The continuation was **11.Nxe4 Rxe4 12.Nb3 Bb6 13.Bd3 Bg4 14.Qd2 Re8,** and after ...Nc6 and ...Qf6, Black's position was consolidated. The pawn on d6 has in particular a stabilizing effect. Black won easily.

We have purposely taken two extreme cases in order to see what is at stake if the "question" is put, and we have found that the "question" is disorganizing, and therefore should not be put unless there is compensation in another direction. Such compensation usually lies in the fact that the Bishop which has been driven off finds himself in a "desert". Such a desert will, however, at once be changed into a flowering garden if the center can be opened. The following examples will make this point clear:

After the moves **1.e4 e5 2.Nf3 Nc6 3.Nc3 Nf6 4.Bb5 Bb4 5.0-0 0-0 6.Bxc6 dxc6 7.d3 Bg4 8.h3 Bh5 9.Bg5** (9.g4 at once would be bad because of 9...Nxg4 10.hxg4 Bxg4 followed by ...f5). **9...Qd6 10.Bxf6 Qxf6**, it is perfectly correct to play **11.g4**, for the Black Bishop upon arrival at g6 will find nothing to "bite on" but the unshakable mass of center pawns.

It should be noted that if Black still had his d-pawn (a pawn at d6 instead of c6), this "desert" could have been given life by ...d5. True the Black Bishop can eventually be brought to f7 after ...f6, but that costs time. White on the other hand has nothing to suffer, for with a compact center a disorganized Kingside is easily defensible. Also, these disorganized Kingside pawns, will become a slowly but surely advancing instrument of attack (of the "tank" order), especially with a Knight to help out at f5. (See game No. 16, Nimzowitsch-Leonhardt, of which the above are the opening moves).

And now, having shown more or less definitely the logical connection between a "desert" and the "center," it will be profitable to analyze the position referred to at the beginning of this section. (Diagram 89). After the moves: **1.e4 e5 2.Nf3 Nc6 3.Bc4 Bc5 4.Nc3 Nf6 5.d3 d6 6.Bg5 h6 7.Bh4 g5 8.Bg3**, it will be interesting to see whether the desert into which the Bishop has been forced can be made hospitable or not. To this end we must minutely examine White's possibilities of attack in the center.

#89 The "question" and
its "consequences"

There are, as will be seen, two such possibilities, the one Bb5 followed by d4, the other Nd5 with c3 and d4 to follow. (It may be remarked in passing that the position of the Nd5, as a diagonal outpost in the diagonal of the Bc4, is analogous to that of an outpost in a file). After 8...a6 (to remove the first possibility), White could play 9.Nd5. For example, 9...Be6 10.c3 Bxd5 11.exd5 Ne7 12.d4 exd4 13.Nxd4, and now Black can pocket a pawn, but after 13...Nfxd5 14.0-0, White's game is to be preferred, for the Bg3, now having come alive, will by no means have to kick his heels in idleness any longer.

After 8.Bg3 (Diagram 89) Black can also play **8...Bg4** in order in some measure to curb White's aspirations in the center. In a game (see No. 17, Nimzowitsch-Fluss) the continuation was **9.h4 Nh5** (9...Rg8 or even 9...Nd7 were possible here. 9...Nh5 takes too many troops from the middle of the board). **10.hxg5** (as tempting as this move looks (for is it not the natural consequence of the pawn advance?), it is not good here. The right move was 10.Nd5. The argument is this: 9.h4 has had 9...Nh5 as a result, by which White has attained a preponderance in the center which he can exploit by 10.Nd5), **10...Nd4.** This transposition of moves loses, since White has a surprising combination in reserve. With 10...Nxg3 11.fxg3 Nd4, Black could have launched a lovely attack. Thus: 12.Rxh6 Rxh6 13.gxh6 Bxf3 14.gxf3 Qg5. Or 12.Nd5 (this attempt to exploit the center comes too late), 12...Bxf3 13.gxf3 Qxg5 14.g4 c6 15.Rh5 cxd5! and wins, since the Queen has all of White's pieces as her traveling companions to the next world.

It is therefore of the utmost importance for the student to realize that the "question," though seemingly only a matter concerning the wing, is fundamentally a problem affecting the center. Later under (c) we shall demonstrate the reality of this connection by another example.

(b) Ignoring the threat, or, in other words, permitting our pawn position to be broken up.

This method may be chosen if we can in return secure greater freedom of action in the center, and by this we mean not merely a passive security such as was considered under (a) above, we must here have a guarantee that we will get active security. For instance, after the same opening moves, **1.e4 e5 2.Nf3 Nc6 3.Bc4 Bc5 4.Nc3 Nf6 5.d3 d6 6.Bg5.** See again Diagram 88. The threat of 7.Nd5 is unpleasant for Black. Nevertheless the threat can be ignored, thus **6...0-0 7.Nd5 Be6.** Now the breakup of the Kingside by **8.Nxf6+ gxf6 9.Bh6 Re8 10.Nh4 Kh8,** would yield a game with chances and counter chances, yet white can by no means claim any striking advantage, for Black has the desired freedom of action in the center (the possibility of ...d5), and there is no more effective response to an operation on a flank than a counterthrust in the center. White has let his troops create a diversion, which has in fact made them lose contact with the center. This diversion would only find real justification if it led to the permanent possession of the point f5, and this seems questionable. After 8.Bxf6 (instead of 8.Nxf6+) 8...gxf6 9.Nh4, the outcome would also be uncertain.

Best for White, after 6...0-0 7.Nd5 Be6, would be 8.Qd2, which keeps up the pressure. After the further moves 8...Bxd5 9.Bxd5, the unpinning by means of the "question" is impracticable (9...h6 10.Bh4 g5? 11.Bxc6 bxc6 12.Nxg5 and White stands clearly better.

(c) Bringing up reserves in order to effect the unpinning by peaceful means.

For all who love the quiet life, this is a very commendable continuation. We have excellent examples of it in the Metger defense to the Four Knights Game, and in Tarrasch's match game (a Petroff) against Marshall.

The Metger defense is this: **1.e4 e5 2.Nf3 Nc6 3.Nc3 Nf6 4.Bb5 Bb4 5.0-0 0-0 6.d3 d6 7.Bg5,** and now Metger would play **7...Bxc3 8.bxc3 Qe7,** intending Nd8-e6, and if the White Bishop then goes to h4, Black persistently follows him up by ...Nf4-g6 on which if the Bishop goes back to g5, Black plays ...h6 at last. It is again evident that such a lengthy time-wasting maneuver is only feasible if the position in the center is solid. In reply to 8...Qe7 the usual continuation is **9.Re1 Nd8 10.d4 Ne6 11.Bc1 c5** (or ...c6) with about even chances.

In the Petroff, Tarrasch, after the moves **1.e4 e5 2.Nf3 Nf6 3.Nxe5 d6 4.Nf3 Nxe4 5.d4 Be7 6.Bd3 Nf6 7.0-0 Bg4,** would get out of the pin by the quiet maneuver Re1, Nbd2-f1-g3 and then h3. (Occasionally he played h3 first, and won some fine games thus). The logical framework, which seems to justify him in a maneuver taking up so much time as this does, is based on the two following postulates: (1) the unpinning must be brought about as quickly as possible, (2) to the troops thus hurried up in support, there is offered, as a kind of reward for the aid they bring, a favorable position with possibilities of getting contact with the enemy (by Nf5). I would like to add the remark that, incidentally, the moderns don't mind putting up with the unpleasantness of a pin for some considerable time. We are no longer quite convinced that a pin must be shaken off without any delay. Our plan of action may be seen from (d).

(d) Maneuvering and holding the choice of (a), (b), or (c) in reserve.

Such a line of action is difficult, and makes great demands on our technical skill. As an example, in the position shown on Diagram 88, Capablanca played **6...Be6 ,** and the continuation was **7.Bb5 h6 8.Bh4 Bb4! 9.d4 Bd7.** This advance of the d-pawn which Capablanca provoked leaves White's e-pawn lacking protection. **10.0-0 Bxc3 11.bxc3** (11.Bxf6 could have been played first here), **11...g5 12.Bg3 Nxe4** (Black had postponed the unpinning until a suitable moment occurred). **13.Bxc6 Bxc6 14.dxe5 dxe5 15.Bxe5** (15.Nxe5 perhaps was better) **15...Qxd1 16.Raxd1 f6 17.Bd4 Kf7 18.Nd2 Rhe8** with a favorable endgame for Black. His opponent, the author of this book, had to lay down his arms on the 64th move.

(e) The corridor and the need for the defenders to maintain effective contact.

#90 Unpinning by occupying one of the points in the "corridor", Here by ...Nb6 or ...Nb4

In an advanced stage of the game, particularly in tactical operations, the process of unpinning presents an entirely different aspect. In Diagram 90, for instance, Black plays **1....Nb4** or **1...Nb6**. We call the space between pinning and pinned pieces and that between the pinned and the screened pieces the "corridor." By placing a protected piece in such a corridor the pin can be raised. Another possibility lies in the removal of the screened piece out of the line of the pin. Thus in Diagram 90 either **1...Kc6** or **1...Kc7** would also put an end to the pin. If the screened piece is not too valuable, we may achieve the same end by giving it adequate protection, but in this case we must be careful to maintain contact between the pieces concerned in the pin, whether directly, or as defenders indirectly.

Diagram 91. White intends with 1.Rab2 followed by Bd3 to make the threat a4 a reality. How can Black anticipate this maneuver? By transferring his Rook from b6 to b7 and then safeguarding it by ...Bc6, after which for all he cares the pawn may be played to a4 at any time. Notice too, how the unpinning is effected in Diagram 92 by **1...Rb1+ 2.King moves Rb2+** followed by **3...Bd4.** In this position by establishing contact between the Bishop and Rook, the Bishop, which otherwise would have been lost, is saved.

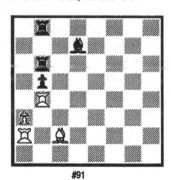

#91

#92

The Beleaguered troops get in touch
Black releases the pin

Another example of the pin. (Diagram 93). In the game White played 22.Rb1, which Black countered by 22...Re8, but as I afterwards showed, **22.Re4** would have won. The main variation runs: **22...Bc6 23.Nf6+ gxf6** (if 23...Kh8 24.Rh4 Qxc2 25.Nxh7!) and now we come to a direct pursuit of the Black King, who will be driven to flight, but by no means to an untroubled flight, rather in one which some disagreeable pins lie in wait for him, for, as we observed at the beginning of this chapter, the pin is characteristic of a pursuit. There follows **24.Rg4+ Kf8 25.Qxf6 Bd7! 26.Rg7 Be6 27.Rxh7 Ke8** and now comes pin No. 1, namely **28.Re1** threatening 29.Qxf7+! To escape this Black must play **28...Kd7**, but now the f-pawn is pinned (No. 2) and **29.Qxe6+** wins easily. Let us for the sake of practice, dwell a moment on the position after 25.Qxf6 Bd7. Here 26.Rf4 would also win, for 26...Be6 will not do because of 27.Qxe6. 26...Be8 fails against 27.Re1, and on 26...Kg8, then 27.Qxf7+ Kh8 28.Qf6+ Kg8 29.Rf3 decides matters.

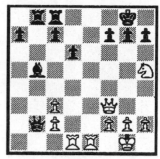

#93
From the game Nimzowitsch-Vidmar
Carlsbad 1911

The reader is advised to study now Games 16, 17, and 18, which illustrate the connection between the pin and the center.

CHAPTER 8

DISCOVERED CHECK

A short chapter, but rich in dramatic complications.

♦ *1. The degree of relationship between the pin and the discovered check is more closely defined. Where should the piece which discovers the check move to?*

Diagram 94 gives a clear picture of the degree of relationship between the pin and discovered check, and we see from it that the pinned piece, tired of eternal persecution, has changed his color. This change has had the effect of transferring the once sickly youth into a valiant warrior. We can describe a discovered check as a pin in which the pinned piece has passed over with flying colors into the enemy camp. Further, in the discovered check, as in the pin, we have three actors, (1) the piece threatening a check which is now masked by one of its own pieces. (2) the masking piece (3) the piece standing behind the masking piece. These pieces will, for short, be referred to as **(1) the threatening piece, (2) the masking piece, (3) the threatened piece.**

#94 The Rook is the "threatening" piece, the Knight the "masking" piece, and the King the "threatened" piece

In the pin the immobility of the pinned (masking) piece is the source of all his troubles, but in the discovered check the masking piece enjoys quite astonishing mobility. Any and every square within his reach is open to him. He can even seize a point subject to multiple enemy attacks, for his opponent cannot touch him, since he is in check.

If we examine the possible moves open to such a masking piece, we find that he can do three things:

(a) He can take anything within reach with impunity since the enemy cannot recapture him.

(b) He can attack any major enemy piece, not letting himself for one moment be disturbed by the thought that the square on which he lands by right belongs to the enemy.

(c) He can change from one square to another, if for any reason this appears more favorable to him than the one he has just vacated.

#95

Thus in Diagram 95, (a) could be carried out by **1.Rxa5+** or **1.Rxh5+**. Notice that the Rook can make either capture without fear. If he chooses to follow the course outlined in (b), he will play **1.Re5+** or **1.Rd3+**, while the use of method (c) would find **1.Rd1+ King any 2.Bxe3.**

The (c) method naturally has a very wide range, but no purpose would be served by further elaboration, for the reasons why a piece is more effectively placed here or there are manifold. We may refer, however, to yet another example in the *See-saw.*

♦ *2. The See-saw. The long range masking piece can move to any square in his line of motion without spending a tempo, free of charge.*

In Diagram 96, White plays **1.Bh7+**, whereupon the Black King has only one move, **1...Kh8**, and now the terrible weapon concealed in the discovered check is revealed. If White now plays **2.Bb1+**, Black with **2...Kg8** escapes the discovered check, but with **3.Bh7+**, White forces him back again to the fatal square, since the Black King has only this move at his disposal, and only has this because the Bishop by moving to h7 has masked the attack of the threatening piece. This stalemate position which we have described gives us thus a kind of see-saw, with the great advantage that the masking piece can occupy any square in the line of his withdrawal (here the diagonal b1-h7), without the maneuver costing him a tempo, for White again has the move.

#96 The See-saw. White can, of course mate here, but (as an example), after 1.Bh7+ Kh8 2.Be4+ Kg8 White has altered the position of his Bishop while retaining the move. The Bishop is able to take any square on the diagonal without loss of tempo.

#97 The See-saw
Great slaughter, the conciliatory sacrifice, and finally, mate.

The See-saw can be the cause of frightful devastation. In Diagram 97 the game would proceed as follows, **1.Bh7+ Kh8 2.Bxf5+ Kg8 3.Bh7+ Kh8 4.Bxe4+ Kg8 5.Bh7+ Kh8 6.Bxd3+ Kg8 7.Bh7+ Kh8 8.Bxc2+ Kg8 9.Bh7+ Kh8 10.Bxb1+ Kg8** and now White gives back of his superfluity, somewhat like a loan shark who has grown very rich and in his old age at a small outlay turns benefactor. So comes **11.Rg6+ fxg6 12.Bxa2+** and mate follows. The Bishop has gobbled his way to b1 in order, after the preparatory Rook sacrifice, to seize the diagonal a2-g8.

#98
White to play and win

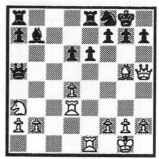

#99 Torre-Lasker
Moscow, 1925

A similar but finer picture is shown in Diagram 98. Here the problem is to entice Black's Bd5 from the defense of his f-pawn. This is accomplished by **1.Bh7+ Kh8 2.Bc2+!** (the "better square" in the sense of (c) as mentioned earlier), **2...Kg8 3.Rg2+! Bxg2,** and now again **4.Bh7+ Kh8 5.Bg6+ Kg8 6.Qh7+ Kf8 7.Qxf7 mate.**

Another example of the see-saw is seen in the game (Diagram 99) which Torre won against Dr. Lasker. In this threatening position (White's Re1 is directly, and his Bg5 indirectly, attacked), Torre hit upon the move **21.b4!** There followed **21...Qf5** (and not 21...Qxb4 22.Rb1. Better than the text move, however, was 21...Qd5) **22.Rg3 h6 23.Nc4** (this intervention of the Knight would have been impossible had the Black Queen been at d5), **23...Qd5 24.Ne3** (Torre fights to break the pin, but without a point for his Bishop to fall back on, he could not have succeeded), **24...Qb5 25.Bf6!!** (That this might have real effect it was necessary to entice the Queen on to an unprotected square, which was the object of 24.Ne3), **25...Qxh5 26.Rxg7+ Kh8** (now we have the see-saw), **27.Rxf7+ Kg8 28.Rg7+ Kh8 29.Rxb7+ Kg8 30.Rg7+ Kh8 31.Rg5+ Kh7 32.Rxh5 Kg6 33.Rh3 Kxf6 34.Rxh6+** and White won easily.

♦ *3. Double check. This is brought about by the masking piece also giving check. The effectiveness of a double check lies in the fact that of the three possible parries to a check, two are in this case unavailable, namely the capture of the piece giving check and the interposition of a piece. Flight is the one and only resource.*

See Diagram 100. Here the choice lies between 1.Qh7+ and 1.Qh8+. The former yields only an ordinary discovered check (1.Qh7+ Kxh7 2.Bf6+) and allows the parry 2...Qxh1 or 2...Qh5. The second move leads, however, to a double check, and these parries are now automatically ruled out. Therefore **1.Qh8+! Kxh8**

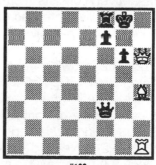

#100
An example of double check

#100a

#101 Black to move wins

2.Bf6+ (double check) **2...Kg8 3.Rh8 mate.** In Diagram 100a, White mates in three moves; **1.Qh8+! Kxh8 2.Nxf7+** (double check) **2...Kg8 3.Nh6+ mate.**

The double check is a weapon of a purely tactical nature, but of terrible driving effect. Even the laziest King flees wildly in the face of a double check.

We close this chapter with three fitting examples:

(1) In a game played many years ago between v. Bardeleben and Nisniewitsch there occurred the amusing position shown in Diagram 101. White's last move was Rook from b7 to c7 (obviously not 1.Rb8+? because of 1...Rf8+ followed by 2...Rxb8). In answer Black played 1...Qxc7 and the game was drawn. I subsequently pointed out the following win for Black. **1...Rf1+! 2.Kxf1 Ng3+ 3.Ke1 Qe3+ 4.Kd1** (observe the driving effect; the King is already at d1 and only a move or two ago he was sitting comfortably at home!) **4...Qe2+! 5.Kc1 Qe1+ 6.Kc2 Qxe4+ 7.Kc1 Ne2+!** winning the Queen and the game. Note that on the double check there was built a line of play which is well-known, and only strikes us as unusual because it takes place on a diagonal and not on a file as is usual. This line of play (a tactical maneuver) consists in breaking a link in the defense by forcing a third piece between two mutually protecting pieces. In the position under consideration the King was enticed on to c2 between the Qb1 and the Be4.

(2) The following well known little game was played between Reti (White) and Dr. Tartakower. **1.e4 c6 2.d4 d5 3.Nc3 dxe4 4.Nxe4 Nf6 5.Qd3** (a most unnatural move) **5...e5?** (the theatrical gesture of the first player (5.Qd3) has worked; Black has in mind a brilliant refutation of it, but his idea proves impossible of execution. 5.Qd3 was not *that* bad! White now gets the better game. The proper move was 5...Nxe4 6.Qxe4 Nd7 followed by ...Nf6 with a solid game). **6.dxe5 Qa5+ 7.Bd2 Qxe5 8.0-0-0 Nxe4?** (a mistake - Black should have played 8...Be7) **9.Qd8+! Kxd8 10.Bg5+ Kc7 11.Bd8 mate.**

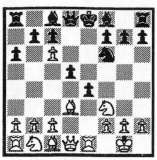

#101a

(3) In December of 1910, I gave a simultaneous display in Pernau (on the Baltic), in which the following pretty little game was played. Nimzowitsch-Ryckhoff **1.e4 e5 2.Nf3 Nc6 3.Bb5 Nf6 4.0-0 d6 5.d4 Nxe4? 6.d5 a6 7.Bd3 Nf6** (7...Ne7 would have saved the piece but not the game. For example 8.Bxe4 f5 9.Bd3 e4 10.Re1 exd3 [or exf3] 11.Qxd3 [or f3] with a strong attack). **8.dxc6 e4 9.Re1 d5** (Diagram 101a) **10.Be2!!** (By forcing Black to protect his e-pawn, White got time to remove his pieces from the fork unhurt; but he plays his Bishop to a square which allows the capture of the Knight!). **10...exf3** (Black sees no danger and unconcernedly pockets the piece). **11.cxb7 Bxb7** (if 11...fxe2 White simply moves 12.bxa8=Q for the e-pawn is pinned again!) **12.Bb5+** double check and mate.

CHAPTER 9

THE PAWN CHAIN

♦ *1. General remarks and definitions. The base of the pawn chain. The conception of the two distinct theatres of war.*

After **1.e4 e6 2.d4 d5 3.e5**, a Black and a White pawn chain have been formed. The pawns at d4, e5, d5, and e6 are the links in the chain. The d4 pawn is the base of the White chain, while the e6 pawn is the Base of the Black one. Accordingly we call the bottommost link of the chain, on which all the other links depend, the base.

Every Black and White pawn chain divides the board diagonally into two halves. For convenience we shall call such a Black and White pawn chain simply the pawn chain. (See Diagrams 102a and 102b)

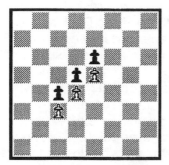 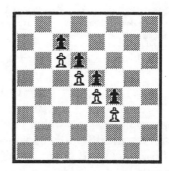

#102a and #102b
Pawn chains

Before the student tackles what now follows, he should make perfectly sure that he has grasped the principles of the open file and the blockade of the passed pawn. If he has not, he should read through Chapters 2 and 4 again, for they are indispensable to a proper understanding of what we have now to consider.

The situation is this: After **1.e4 e6 2.d4 d5**, as long as White's pawn remains at e4, he can if he wishes, open the e-file with exd5, in order to start permanent operations on the file, by perhaps planting an outpost Knight at e5. By playing **3.e5** he renounces this chance, and in addition he relieves the tension in the center and this for no visible reason. Why then does he do it? I do not believe that the attacking energy latent in White's position before the move e5 can suddenly disappear as a

---

consequence of 3.e5. It must be present as before, though in a modified form, for 3.e5 above all things checks the movement of the Black pawns, and therefore implies a blockade. We know already that pawns, especially those in the center are consumed by an enormous desire for expansion to press forward, and we have consequently inflicted on the enemy not inconsiderable pain. Moreover, thanks to 3.e5 there are now two theatres of war on the board, the center and Black's Kingside.

On the Kingside.

#103 The Kingside as a theater of war. The pieces engaged are Queen, Bishop, and Knight. The Rook is held in reserve ready for the counter ...f5, when White will play exf6 e.p. ...Rxf6. The Rook will then go to the e-file to attack the Black e-pawn

See Diagram 103. The pawn on e5 may here be described as a detachment which has been pushed forward to form a wedge in enemy territory, and to act as a demobilizing force. This pawn robs a Black Knight of the square f6, and thus allows an easy approach of the White storm troops (Qg4). Black's Kingside which is cramped by the same pawn is also a target for bombardment by other pieces (the Bd3, Nf3, and Bc1). If Black seeks to defend himself by opening communications in his 2nd rank, by a timely advance ...f5, and eventually posting a Rook on a7, our e5 pawn will prove himself an excellent wedge driver. We mean by this that when White attacks the point g7, Black will play ...f5 in order to use his second rank for the defense of the threatened point This otherwise excellent defensive idea would, however, fail because the e5 pawn would protest violently. The reply to ...f5 would be exf6 e.p. and White, after the recapture ...Rxf6 would use the e-file, including the point e5, for bringing pressure on the now backward pawn on e6. In the first case (Kingside as theatre of war) a White pawn at f4 would be a hindrance to White, since its negative effect (as an obstruction to the dark-squared Bishop and to any other of his pieces wishing to use the square) would overshadow any positive advantage it might have.

In the center.

Beside that of cramping the enemy Kingside, the White e5 pawn pursues other and quite different ends. White, in fact, intends by the move e5 to fix the Black e6 pawn at his post in order later to open fire on him with f4-f5, for ...exf5 would then imply the surrender of the base of Black's pawn chain. Should Black abstain from this move, White can either form a wedge by f6 or play fxe6 and after ...fxe6 build a piece attack against the now weak Black e-pawn.

In order to understand the association of ideas, it will be good to examine more closely the germcell of a flank, or an enveloping attack. In Diagram 104 (left side) we see the Rook in a frontal attack, in which the objective is bombarded at White's leisure. On the right a frontal attack is out of the question. The maneuver Rg6-Rxf6 or Rg7-Rf7-Rxf6 is planned. It is important for our purpose to emphasize the fact that the White f-pawn in this position is a necessary element of the problem, for if it were absent, a frontal attack against the Black f-pawn would not only be possible, but by far our easiest course. Moreover, the attack against the point f6 if it had not been pinned down, would have no

#104
Left: frontal attack
Right: flank or enveloping attack

strategic sense, in conformity with the principle: the objective must first be reduced to immobility. It follows that the position shown in Diagram 104 (right side) represents the true prelude to the flank or enveloping attack.

This being established, the plan of action shown in Diagram 105 is seen to be logically justified. Its end is a preparation for such an attack as we have seen in the making on the right side of Diagram 104, and if this operation can be called an attack, as indeed it is, we can with good conscience ascribe to the maneuver e5 (chain building) followed by f4-f5 an attack as well. In this vein we can say that the Black pawn on e6 may be considered a second theater of war.

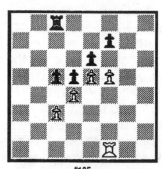

#105
A representation of the central theater of war. Both players attack the respective bases of the pawn chain. Rooks are on alert ready for the breakthrough

To recapitulate: By White's move e5, the formation of a pawn chain, always creates two theaters of war, of which the enemy wing, cramped by the advance, forms one, and the base of the enemy pawn chain the other. Furthermore, e5 is inspired by the desire to attack. The attack on the Black d5 pawn (present before the pawn moved to e5) has been transferred to the Black e6 pawn, which has been reduced to immobility by our pawn on e5, so as to be exposed to a flank attack by f4-f5.

♦ *2. The attack against the pawn chain. The pawn chain as a blockade problem. The attack against the "base".*

There was a time, before 1913, when it was the firm conviction that a pawn chain, with the disappearance of one of its links, must give up all pretension to a happy existence. To have shown this conviction was based on pure prejudice is a service for which I may take credit, since as early as the year 1911 I had proved by some

---

games (against Salwe, Carlsbad 1911, Game No. 46, against Levenfish, and against Dr. Tarrasch, in 1912, Game No. 20) that I was inclined to conceive of the pawn chain as a purely cramping problem. The question is not whether the links of the chain are complete, but simply and solely whether the enemy pawns remain cramped. Whether we effect this by pawns or pieces, or by Rooks and Bishops at long range, is immaterial. The main thing is that the enemy pawns should be cramped. This conception of mine, to which I had arrived through an intensive study of the blockade problem, did not fail, in those days, to arouse a storm of protest. Today, however, everyone knows that all the things which I then said about the pawn chain are incontestable truths.

It was disputed at that time that after **1.e4 e6 2.d4 d5**, any attack on Black's d-pawn existed at all. The friendly readers of this book know well that such an attack does very much exist. We know from his article in the *Wiener Schachzeitung*, in 1913, that Alapin did not know it, since he was not acquainted with the theory of the open file, which I originated. To take another disputed point, everyone now recognizes that in positions characterized by the advance **3.e5** (at the third move or later), the thrust f4-f5 may well be, and often is, the logical sequence. We can learn much by a closer investigation of the question, why after 1.e4 e6 2.d4 d5 the Black attack **3...c5** should hold the field rather than an immediate White attack by f4-f5. As we have already insisted, the disposition of both the White and Black links in the chain is directed towards cramping the opponent. The White pawns wish to blockade the Black and vice-versa. Now after 1.e4 e6 2.d4 d5 3.e5, it is the Black pawns who are held up on their road to the center, whereas the corresponding White pawns have already outstripped the middle of the board (compare the relative positions of the two e-pawns). We are justified in regarding the White as the cramping and the Black as the cramped pawns. Since the pawns' desire to expand is naturally greatest when directed towards the center, we see that Black is more justified in the attack ...c5 than White is in the corresponding thrust on the other wing (f4-f5). The threat of the advance of the f-pawn exists, however, in spite of all this, and when Black's attack has burned itself out, White's turn then comes for the thrust with his f-pawn.

That this threat fails in many games to be translated into action only goes to prove that White has plenty on his hands in meeting the attack ...c5, or else that he has chosen the first of the two theaters of war (Black's cramped Kingside) for his operations.

Concerning the transfer of our attack from d5 to e6, the student will soon see how wide is the bearing of this proposition of mine. But let us proceed systematically.

♦ *3. Attack on the "base" a strategic necessity. The clearing away of the links in the enemy chain is only undertaken with the idea of freeing our pawns which they had been cramping. The problem of the chain is essentially reduced to one of blockade.*

To recognize an enemy pawn chain as an enemy and to go for it is one and the same thing. We may thus formulate: Freeing operations in the region of a pawn chain can never be started soon enough.

This war of liberation will, however, be conducted thus - We first direct our operations against the base, which we attack with a pawn, and, by threats or otherwise, seek to cut off the base from its associates in the chain. This done, we turn our attention to the next opponent, namely the link which has now become the new base. For instance, after **1.e4 e6 2.d4 d5 3.e5**, the Black pawns (e6, d5) are cramped. The attack on the cramping White chain should, by our rule, be launched without any delay, by **3...c5** rather than 3...f6, for the White e-pawn corresponds to an architectural adornment to our building (the chain), whereas the White d-pawn is the very foundation of the whole structure. If we wished to destroy a building, we would not begin with its architectural ornaments, but we would blow up its foundations, for then the destruction of the ornaments with all the rest will follow automatically.

White has several replies to 3...c5. The plan of the second player will stand out clearest if White plays ingeniously, as if he had no conception of the problem of the pawn chain. For example, **4.dxc5 Bxc5 5.Nc3? f6!** Events have taken their logical course. The base, the d4 pawn was first put out of action, and then the e5 pawn got it in the neck. We must always begin with the base of the pawn chain. To continue our game: after 5...f6! there would follow **6.exf6?** (as artless as ever. 6.Nf3 was certainly better). **6...Nxf6 7.Nf3 Nc6 8.Bd3 e5!** Thanks to White's faulty strategy, Black's freeing operations which as a rule take up to 20-25 moves have already been completed. Black first caused the links in White's chain voluntarily to disappear one after the other, beginning with the base (by the captures 4.dxc5 and 6.exf6) and thereupon let his own pawns advance in triumph with 8...e5! This advance, so eagerly sought after, affords the explanation of the energetic measures taken by Black with his 3rd and following moves, namely the recovery of mobility for his cramped pawns. This was all that Black sought or desired. It often happens that pawns so advanced are filled with a particularly war-like spirit. We get the impression that they wish to take bitter vengeance for the humiliation they have suffered by being hemmed in.

#106
Correct for Black is to attack the chain by ...b5-b4 in order to provoke cxb4. The immediate...f6 would be wrong in this position

Diagram 106 shows another example. Here White's c-pawn and not his b-pawn, is the base of the chain, be it well noted, for this pawn has not yet been attached to the association in the Black and White pawn chain, since a Black colleague is lacking at b3. Against this base Black sends forward his b-pawn to storm it

---

(...b5-b4). Having provoked White's cxb4, the d4 pawn is now promoted to the base, but, unlike his predecessor, is not protected. The unprotected base (unprotected by a pawn) is a weakness, and therefore gives occasion for a lasting siege, such as we will propose in ♦ 5. In the above example ...f6 (instead of the correct ...b5-b4) would have to be labeled a mistake, for after the fall of the e-pawn, White's pawn chain would remain intact.

We are now on the road to a true understanding of the matter. The freeing operations in the domain of the pawn chain are analogous to the fight against a troublesome blockader (Chapter 4) and accordingly our present problem is reduced to one of blockade.

♦ *4. The transfer of the blockade rules from the "passed pawn" to the "chain." The exchange maneuver (to bring about the substitution of a more amenable enemy blockader for a strong one) applied to the pawn chain.*

It is clear to us, after studying Chapter 4, that every enemy piece which holds a pawn in check which would otherwise be mobile must be conceived of as a blockader. Nevertheless it must cause surprise that after the moves 1.e4 e6 2.d4 d5 3.e5, we should agree to regard the d4 and e5 pawns as proper blockaders in our sense. The surprise lies in seeing a pawn so described, for in general we think of pawns as being blockaded, and the role of a blockader we imagine to be reserved for an officer. In general this is true, but the pawns in a chain are pawns of a higher order, and in their functions differ from the common herd. To conceive of the pawns in a chain as blockaders would then appear to be quite correct.

Recognizing this, let us now try to apply the "exchange maneuver on the blockading square," with which we became acquainted in Chapter 4, to the chain. The exchange, as we there said, could only be justified if the new blockader proved himself to be weaker than his predecessor. The same applies to the chain.

An example: After **1.e4 e6 2.d4 d5 3.e5 c5! 4.Nc3**, Black can get the blockader (the d4 pawn) replaced by another (the Queen). In fact after the further moves **4...cxd4 5.Qxd4 Nc6**, the Queen turns out to be a blockader whom it will be difficult to maintain at her post, and the exchange is proven to be correct. If now 6.Bb5, after 6...Bd7 7.Bxc6 bxc6, Black has two Bishops and a mobile mass of pawns in the center, and has the advantage.

This exchange maneuver, on the other hand, would be weak after **1.e4 e6 2.d4 d5 3.e5 c5 4.c3 Nc6 5.Be3**, for after **5...cxd4** (5...Qb6 would be better) **6.Bxd4**, the Bishop would be a tough customer to deal with, and a further exchange to be rid of him by **6...Nxd4 7.Qxd4 Ne7 8.Nf3 Nc6 9.Qf4** (Diagram106a) would lead to the driving off of the blockading troops, but only at the cost of loss of time caused by the moves of the Black King Knight.

#106a

In Diagram 106a White stands quite well. his pieces are placed as they would be for a Kingside attack, but also have a sufficient bearing on the center. For example: **9...f6** (to roll up White's chain) **10.Bb5 a6 11.Bxc6+ bxc6 12.0-0** and Black will never succeed in making his e6 pawn mobile, for if 12...fxe5 13.Nxe5 and the establishment of the Knight at e5 follows.

With this we have gotten further towards an understanding of the pawn chain. All exchange operations in the region of a chain only take place with the object of replacing a strong enemy blockader by a weaker one, and the experience we have gotten from Chapter 4 will be of great help to us here.

#107

We have to decide in a given case whether the blockader in question is strong or weak, elastic or inelastic, and the faculty of discriminating correctly in such cases will be of enormous service to us. See for example Diagram 107. Here 1.Qc2 would be a weak move in spite of the sharp threat of 2.Bxf6 to be followed by 3.Bxh7. The mistake lies in the fact that White would have done much better in doing something towards the defense of his blockading wall. **1.Nd2 0-0 2.Nf3** is the right course. On the other hand if 1.Qc2?, the continuation might be 1...0-0 2.Bxf6 Rxf6 3.Bxh7+ Kh8 4.Bg6 (or Bd3) 4...e5! White has won a pawn, but Black has overcome the blockade, and now stands ready to march in the center. White should lose.

In Diagram 108, the maneuver 15.Bd4 Qc7 16.Qe2 might be considered, with the intention of following with 17.Ne5. This plan to widen the blockading ring is, however, impracticable, for after 16.Qe2 Ng4!! 17.h3 e5!, the Black pawns assert themselves. The right move is **15.Qe2** and there follows **15...Rac8** (or 15...Bxe5 16.Nxe5 Rac8 17.c4) **16.Bd4! Qc7 17.Ne5**, and Black is seriously blockaded. We may say that the line of play 15.Bd4 Qc7 16.Qe2 was bad because the reserve blockader who was keeping watch (the Nf3) would have but slight blockading effect (would never succeed in reaching e5). In the notes to my game

#108

against Salwe (no. 46, from which this example is taken) we shall prove our theory of exchanges by further examples.

◆ *5. The conception of a war of movement and that of siege-warfare applied to the region of the chain. The attacking party at the parting of the ways.*

If the attacking party has played in the spirit of the explanations given in this chapter (attack on the "base" and the correct application of the exchange operation of the blockading point), it will often happen that the full freedom of his hampered pawns will be his reward. There will be times, however, when the fight he has waged with the measures indicated here will reach a dead end, and in such cases the use of some new plan becomes necessary. As an example we will take the following position. The opening moves of the game were: **1.e4 e6 2.d4 d5 3.e5 c5 4.c3 Nc6 5.Nf3 Qb6** (Black seeks by hook or by crook to induce White to give up his base, the d4 pawn. An attack with the purpose of rolling up a pawn chain, we class as a war of movement, of which the move 5...Qb6 must be a part. Queen moves in the opening are as a rule out of place. Here, however, the state of the pawn chain dictates all of our actions). **6.Bd3** (Diagram 109) **6...Bd7**. A very plausible move, and since White still hesitates to make the capture dxc5, Black proposes to make his decision easier by 7...Rc8. The right move is 6...cxd4 7.cxd4 and with it to adopt other methods, namely siege or positional warfare. These were the opening moves of the game No. 46, Nimzowitsch-Salwe, played at Carlsbad in 1911. From first move to last it is highly instructive. I regard it as the first game to be played in the spirit of the new philosophy of the center, which I originated. The student is advised to play through this game before proceeding further.

#109

We have already said, and the course of the game shows, that at his sixth move (Diagram 109) Black could, and should have sought a quieter channel by playing 6...cxd4 7.cxd4 Bd7, with an eventual Ne7-f5. He preferred to play instead for the complete capitulation of his opponent (in the region of the chain). His plan was (1) to force White to play dxc5 and exf6, (2) to drive off any blockading pieces that might take their place, (3) triumphantly to advance his center pawns, now freed. His plan failed because the substitute blockaders were not to be driven away. The two following postulates are here of importance: (a) It makes no difference whatever to the strangled (hemmed in) pawns whether they are strangled by pawns or by officers. It follows that (b) the destruction of the cramping pawns in the chain does not in itself imply a more or less complete liberating operation, for the substitute blockaders, the pieces still have to be driven away. How and in what measure this last is possible is the question of really decisive importance.

The following, taken from my article, "The surrender of the center - a prejudice," written in 1913, may serve to throw light on the relations between pawns and pieces. "True, the pawns are best fitted for building up the center, since they are the most stable; on the other hand pieces stationed in the center can very well take the place of pawns." As we shall see later, the center can often be effectively held at long range by Bishops and Rooks, so that the actual occupation of the center by a pawn or pawns does not necessarily mean its control. We are inclined to regard as most dangerous any liberating operation which is begun but not completed (as in Salwe's attempt in the game under consideration), dangerous that is to say, to the one ostensibly freeing himself. We return now to the position in Diagram 109.

♦ *5a. Positional warfare, in other words, the slow siege of the unprotected base. Repeated bombardment. The defending pieces get in each other's way. How can we maintain the pressure? The genesis of new weaknesses. The base as a weakness in the endgame.*

Since in the position shown in Diagram 109 the move 6...Bd7 seems to give little promise of profit, Black, as we have several times insisted, would have been better off to have played 6...cxd4. What does this move signify? The White base (d4) has thereby been made immobile, has been fixed at d4. Before 6...cxd4 took place White's d-pawn could, whether for good or evil, at any rate leave his place (by dxc5). Now this is no longer possible. We must be quite clear on one point, that by playing 6...cxd4 Black has had to resign himself to renounce his ambitious dreams of forcing his opponent into complete capitulation in the chain area, these have now gone to their grave. Black does retain certain small yet real possibilities. For instance: d4 will be attacked by several pieces, not so much for the reason that the conquest of White's base is likely, but rather in order to force upon the defending enemy pieces a passive, because purely defensive, role. Black's aim is, in fact, an ideal one, the advantage of the aggressive position for his pieces. The continuation could be

6...cxd4 7.cxd4 Bd7 (threatening 8...Nxd4, which could not have been played the move before because of 7...Nxd4?? 8.Nxd4 Qxd4 9.Bb5+ winning the Queen). **8.Bo2** (If 8.Bo2 Blaok with 8...Nb1 oould obtain tho advantage of the two Bishops) **8...Nge7!** Whether it be slow or quick, Black chooses the development which puts pressure on the base. This is correct, for in close games, those characterized by the presence of pawn chains, the chain is the one true guidepost. **9.b3 Nf5 10.Bb2** (see Diagram 110a) **10...Bb4+!** This check shows up, and in the most glaring light. The defending pieces are in each other's way. **11.Kf1** (11.Nc3 or Nbd2 would rob the base of a defender). **11...Be7.** Tarrasch's idea, the student should ponder the argument on which this move is based. If he is to keep

#110a
White's base, the d4 pawn is under pressure. The typical siege of an "unprotected" base

---

The pawn chain 95

up the pressure on d4 Black must never allow the equilibrium of attack and defense (now 3:3) to be disturbed to his disadvantage. The attacking pieces must strive to maintain their attacking positions. To effect this 11...h5 could be played (to prevent the pawn push g4). The text move attains the same end by other means. If now 12.g4 the answer would be 12...Nh4, an attacker and a defender would disappear together and the *status quo* would be maintained.

The typical strategy appropriate to the various cases which may arise is made clear by the following postulates:

(a) The enemy base being fixed to one spot, should be attacked by several pieces.

(b) By these means we shall at least obtain the ideal advantage of the aggressive position for our pieces. Worth mentioning in this connection is the slight elasticity or capacity for maneuvering possessed by the defending pieces. For instance, in the case of a sudden attack on another wing, they will not be able to equal the attacking pieces and will lag behind.

(c) We must seek to keep up the pressure on the base for as long as possible or until the appearance of new weakness in the enemy camp, which will follow as the logical consequence of his difficulties in development.

(d) When this occurs our plan of action will be modified. The original weakness, the base, will be left alone and the new one attacked with the greatest of energy. Only much later, perhaps not again until the endgame, will the weak enemy base be again "promoted" to the dignity of being our objective.

(e) The weak base, when all is said and done, is to be regarded in particular, as an endgame weakness. The specific attacking instrument, the open adjoining file (in this case the c-file) only comes completely into its rights in the endgame. (...Rc4 followed by ...Rxd4, or ...Rc2-d2 follow by ...Rxd4).

(f) The attacking party must never forget that he has a base of his own to defend. If his opponent succeeds in making his part of the chain region healthy (shaking off the pressure on his base (d4 in our case), an entirely new and disagreeable turn may be given to the game by his playing f4-f5, with attack on the base (e6), or on the other hand launching an attack with his pieces on the Kingside which is still cramped by the pawn at e5.

The application of (a) will hardly present any difficulties to the student. Take for instance Diagram 110b. The chain we are interested in is formed with the d and e-pawns on both sides. Black's base is the d6 pawn. Play goes **1.cxd6 cxd6 2.Rc6 Nf7 3.Nc4 Rd8** (if 3...Rc8 4.b5 Rxc6 5.dxc6 with the superior ending) **4.a4!** (played to maintain the attacking Knight on c4). White has now put the base d6 under pressure, and consequently has the advantage referred to of the more aggressive position for his pieces. The Nc4 is more aggressively placed than Black's Nf7. This advantage could be exploited either by 5.b5 followed perhaps by Kc3 and a5, or by play on the Kingside. For instance h4, and then Ke3-f3-g4-h5 followed by the advance of the g-pawn to g5. In this case the parry ...h6 would allow the King's entry at g6.

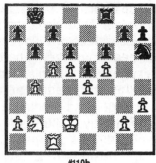

#110b

It is much more difficult for the student to assimilate the points made in (c) and (d). The direct exploitation of a pawn weakness is not, in general, a matter for the middle game (see point (f)). All that we may hope to attain is to cause our opponent to suffer for a considerable time under the disadvantage of the duties of defense which have been forced on him. If as a result of these difficulties, a new weakness is induced in the enemy camp (as is by no means improbable), it is not merely permissible for the attacking party to release the base from pressure, in order to devote his attention to the new weakness, such a course is absolutely indicated. The further removed (geographically and logically) the two weaknesses are from each other, the better for us! This connection of ideas was more or less unknown to the pseudo-classical school. Tarrasch, for instance, was relentless in keeping under continual attack the base which he had once selected as his objective, or at least remain true to the wing of his first choice. (See game No. 19, Paulsen - Tarrasch).

In opposition to this we lay stress on the principle that the weakness of the enemy base cannot be completely exploited until the endgame, or more accurately, in the endgame our aim is the direct conquest of the base which serves as our objective. In the middlegame the bombardment of this base can and should only help to yield us indirect advantages. For example, suppose Black is attacking the enemy base in the middlegame. White's pieces will get in each other's way, difficulties of development will arise, and White will find himself forced to create a new weakness in his own camp in order to remove those difficulties. Black now concentrates his attack on these new weaknesses. Only in the endgame may he find it profitable to again take up the attack on his first objective, the enemy base.

As an example of this indirect exploitation of a weakened enemy base we may take the position shown on Diagram 110c, taken from the game Paulsen-Tarrasch (see illustrative game No. 19). After the moves **1.e4 e6 2.d4 d5 3.e5 c5 4.c3 Nc6 5.Nf3 Qb6 6.Bd3 cxd4 7.cxd4 Bd7 8.Be2 Nge7 9.b3 Nf5 10.Bb2 Bb4+**, White saw himself forced to forego castling by having to play his King to f1, thus the pressure on d4 has taken tangible shape. Black's problem no longer consists in keeping up the pressure on the d-pawn (which can be done by 11...h5 or 11...Be7 as we have already indicated), he should instead give up the attack on White's base and do everything he can to expose and exploit the weakness of White's uncastled King. This is only possible by means of a hidden sacrifice of the exchange. In this position in reply to **11.Kf1** (Diagram 110c) I play **11...0-0!** If then 12.Bd3 to lessen the pressure on the d-pawn, there would follow 12...f6 13.Bxf5 exf5 with advantage to Black due to his two Bishops. The main variation after 11.Kf1 0-0! lies in the

#110c

continuation **12.g4 Nh6 13.Rg1 f6 14.exf6 Rxf6! 15.g5 Rxf3! 16.Bxf3** (or 16.gxh6 Rf7) **16...Nf5 17.Rg4** (Diagram 110d). White's desolate Kingside and the weakly defended points on the f-file ought, in my opinion, to lead to a lost game. I give one possible continuation: **17...Be8** (17...Rf8 would also suffice) **18.Qe2 Ncxd4**

#110d

19.Rxd4! Nxd4 20.Qe5 (the last chance) **20...Bb5+ 21.Kg2 Nf5 22.Bxd5** (if 22.Nc3 Bxc3 23.Bxc3 d4) **22...exd5 23.Qxf5 Rf8 24.Qxd5+ Rf7** (a self-pin for the safeguarding of g7 against a possible Qd4) **25.Qd4 Bc5** and White must resign. The decision took place, as was logical, on the Kingside. Black was able to exploit fully the new weakness (uncastled King) without regard to the old one. The student will do well to note most carefully the transfer of the attack from the center (d4, the base) to the Kingside which had been weakened by the move Kf1.

As an antithesis to the maneuver we have just demonstrated, we would emphasize the fact (see Diagram 110c) that 11...Be7, after 12.g3 followed by Kg2, with the subsequent safeguarding and relieving of the d4 pawn would give White good chances, for after his position becomes consolidated White would well be able to turn the tables on his opponent as outlined in (f), by an attack on Black's Kingside which is cramped by the pawn on e5. (See Game No. 20, Nimzowitsch-Tarrasch).

Before we proceed further, we would impress upon the student that he should practice in order to be able to take advantage of a weak enemy base in the endgame. We recommend the study of Game No. 15 and further the application of the following method. Using the pawn setup of Diagram 110e, try to take advantage of the weakness of White's d4 pawn in an endgame. Try it with a Rook or Rooks on each side of the board. Then practice with a Rook and minor piece on each side.

♦ *6. The transfer of the attack.*

In the position in Diagram 109 Black had the choice, as we have often pointed out already, of two different lines of play, namely between 6...Bd7 with a war of movement, or 6...cxd4 with positional or siege warfare directed against White's fixed base, the pawn at d4. It will be granted that a moment must come when Black will be forced to make his choice. It is not possible to keep open at will the choice between two lines of play, least of all when we are concerned with a pawn chain, for the simple reason that the defending party, relying on the state of suspense in the position, and the possibilities arising out of it, can threaten an attack to

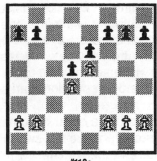

#110e
Practice Position

free himself. Once this enemy threat becomes actual, we are forced to make an immediate decision. Another crisis which compels a decision occurs when our opponent threatens us on another wing, when we shall have to decide on as sharp a counter as possible, since any further flirting with two different plans would no longer be favorable.

We have up to now considered only the choice between two methods of attack. The objective (White's d4 pawn) in the previous example remained fixed, and was therefore not in doubt. We will show in what follows how painful even the choice of an objective can sometimes be. We are concerned with a pawn chain which is to be attacked. "What can there be doubtful in such a case?" the reader will ask. "We must of course direct our attack against its base." But what if the base is not to be shaken? Would it not be better to direct our attack against a new base? How this is done will be seen from the stratagem of the transference of the attack which will now be outlined.

Let us consider the following chain resulting after **1.e4 e5 2.Nf3 Nc6 3.Bc4 Be7 4.d4 d6 5.d5 Nb8**. White now chooses the center as the theater of war, and plays 6.Bd3 followed by 7.c4 with the idea of eventually pushing the pawn to c5. (He could as an alternative have decided on an attack with his pieces without playing c4, on the Queenside which is cramped by the d5 pawn). Black tries to make ...f5 possible in order to shake White's base, the pawn on e4. The pseudo-classical school held ...f5 to be a refutation of White's d5. This is however, not the case, as I proved in my revolutionary article on Dr. Tarrasch's *Moderne Schachpartie*. The move ...f5 is only a natural reaction to White's d5, and as such every bit as endurable as c4-c5. The position (in essentials) arrived at could be that of Diagram 111. Black's attack on the base e4 does not look as if it promised much, for if at

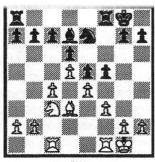

#111

any time ...fxe4, the answer would be either fxe4, and the base is well defended, or recapturing with either the Knight or Bishop on e4 with a good "substitute center". Black therefore plays ...f4, changing White's base from e4 to f3. True the latter can be sufficiently defended (against ...g5-g4-gxf3 which Black plans), but White's King position seems then to be threatened and is certainly cramped. In other words the White King position marks f3 as a weaker base than e4.

There are other circumstances which may make one base appear weaker than another, hence the switching over of the attack from one base to the next is not a mere matter of chance (as Alapin and other masters seemed to think before the appearance of my essay to which reference has just been made). It is in fact an additional weapon in the fight against a pawn chain. A judgment on the strength of a pawn chain as a whole must run something like this: "The base e4 is difficult to attack, the base f3 (after ...f4) is for such and such reasons sensitive to attack, therefore it will pay to transfer the attack to the new base, f3". This formulation of the case I may claim as my discovery.

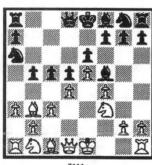

#111a

We must content ourselves with the above concise suggestions, otherwise this chapter would stretch to too great a length. The transference of attack is typical, and we could give endless examples from games. We will, however, only show the following opening here. **1.e4 Nc6 2.d4 d5 3.e5 Bf5 4.f4 e6 5.Nf3 Nb4 6.Bb5+ c6 7.Ba4 b5 8.a3! Na6 9.Bb3 c5 10.c3** (Diagram 111a). Since the White base, the pawn at d4, seemed actually overdefended, Black quite rightly played here **10...c4**, transferring the attack from d4 to c3. After the further moves **11.Bc2 Bxc2 12.Qxc2 Ne7**, Black put White's Kingside under restraint, which was ready to start an attack, by making the natural advance f5 impossible, and eventually by means of ...a5 and ...b4 launched the attack on the new objective, White's base at c3.

Before closing this chapter and with it the discussion of the "elements," we would like to point out quite briefly how difficult it is to conduct the game in the pawn chain correctly. Very soon after the formation of the chain, we have to choose whether a wing or the base shall be our objective. Later, incidental to an attack on the base, we have to make the difficult decision between a war of movement and siege warfare, and as if that were not enough, we have always to deal with a possible transfer of the attack to the next link of the chain. And in addition to all of this, we must never forget, in spite of all of these possibilities of attack, that we may also have our own vulnerable base.

A difficult chapter, but one in which the inherent obscurity of its subject matter will, we hope, now have largely disappeared, thanks to our treatment of it.

It will have been seen that my laws governing pawn chains have grown logically from those applying to "open files" and "play against the blockader." The reader will find a further discussion of the subject in Part 2 on the "center" and "restraint". He is urged at this point to play over the following illustrative games - Nos. 19 through 24 and No. 46, all of which illustrate the subject of the pawn chain.

PART TWO

POSITIONAL PLAY

CHAPTER 10

THE CONCEPTION OF POSITIONAL PLAY AS CONCERNS THE CENTER

Sets forth an introduction to my conception of positional play and carries the treatment of the problem of the center further.

♦ *1. The mutual relations between the treatment of the elements and of positional play.*

As the reader will soon see, my conception of positional play is based for the greater part on the knowledge we have laboriously squeezed from our consideration of the elements. This is especially true of the devices of centralization and of restraint which we have outlined. The connection which thus exists has the advantage, that it must give to this book a certain unity of structure, which can only be of benefit to the reader. It would, however, be an error on his part to indulge in the expectation that the exploration of the spirit of positional play cannot now afford him any further difficulties worth mentioning. Primarily, positional play contains other ideas than those we have met so far, as for instance the law of "overprotection," which I discovered, or the very difficult strategy of the center. Secondly, the actual transference of the ideas which we have learned from the elements on to a new field, that of positional play, is difficult enough. The degree of difficulty is much the same as that which faces a composer who wishes to adapt a violin sonata for a full orchestra. However unchanged the theme, the motives, the whole must gain in depth and breadth. Let us explain this by a concrete case in chess, for instance "restraint," In the "elements," this touches a comparatively small field. A passed pawn is to be checked, or an enemy pawn chain which has become free to move is to be prevented from advancing. In positional play on the other hand the restraint theme makes a much more impressive appearance. Now it is often a whole wing which must be held in check. In games in which the player who is putting restraint on his opponent is "scoring" his theme very heavily (I have in mind for instance my game against Johner, No. 35), we have the whole board, both wings, every corner taking up the theme, and blaring it forth.

The second case is even worse for the student, for here the theme appears in epic breadth, with a series of seemingly purposeless moves, back and forth, mixed with it. This kind of maneuvering corresponds in a way to the accompaniment in music. Many people feel this accompaniment and maneuvering as things which may be dispensed with. Many lovers of chess go so far as to characterize this moving to and fro as a fruit of decadence. In reality, however, this maneuvering often enough provides the only strategic - be it noted strategic, not merely psychological - way of throwing in the scale a slight advantage in terrain and the consequent capacity of moving our troops more quickly from one side of the board to the other.

♦ *2. On certain toxic weeds which choke a proper understanding of positional play, namely (a) the obsession to be forever doing something, which haunts so many amateurs, and (b) the overrating of the principle of the accumulation of small advantages which may inspire the master.*

There are, it would seem, a number of amateurs to whom positional play appears to mean nothing. Twenty years' experience in teaching chess has, however, convinced me that this trouble can be easily removed, since it results from a faulty presentation of the subject. I maintain that there is nothing inherently mysterious in positional play, and that every single amateur who has studied my "elements" in the first nine chapters of this book, must find it an easy matter to penetrate into the spirit of this style of play. He has only (1) to destroy the weeds which perhaps choke his understanding, and (2) to carry out the precepts laid down in the rest of the book.

A typical and very widespread misconception is the assumption of many amateurs that each single move must accomplish something directly, so that such a player will only look for moves which threaten something, or for a threat to be parried, and will disregard all other possible moves such as waiting moves, or moves calculated to put his house in order, etc. Positional moves as I conceive them, are in general neither threatening nor defensive ones, but rather moves designed to give our position security in the wider sense, and to this end it is necessary for our pieces to establish contact with the enemy's strategically important points or our own. This will be brought out later when we are considering "overprotection," and the fight against enemy freeing moves.

When a positional player, one who understands how to safeguard his position in the wider sense, engages one who is a purely combinational player, the latter who has only attack in his thoughts, is preoccupied with but two kinds of countermoves, and looks only for a defensive move from his opponent, or calculates on the possibility of a counterattack; and now the positional player dumbfounds him by choosing a move which will not fit into either of these categories. The move somehow or other brings his pieces into contact with some key point, and this contact has miraculous effects. His position is thereby permeated with strength, and the attack on it comes to nothing. The positional player protects a point not only for the sake of that point, but also because he knows that the piece which he uses for its defense must gain in strength by mere contact with the point in question. This will be considered further under "overprotection".

Now we will take a game which is an admirable illustration of the very widespread misconception to which I have referred. I had the White pieces against a very well known and by no means weak amateur, who, however, was under the impression that a "correct" chess game must take some such course as this: One side castles on the Kingside, the other on the Queenside, a violent pawn attack is launched on both sides against the respective castled positions, and he who gets in first wins! We shall see how this amateurish conception was reduced *ad absurdum*.

The game was played in Riga in 1910. **1.e4 e5 2.Nf3 Nc6 3.d4 exd4 4.Nxd4 d6** (this move is quite playable but only in conjunction with a strong defensive structure, attainable by perhaps ...Nf6, ...Be7, ...0-0, and ...Re8 with pressure on White's e-pawn), **5.Nc3 Nf6 6.Be2 Be7 7.Be3 Bd7 8.Qd2 9.a6? 9.f3 0-0 10.0-0-0 b5**. The attack seems hardly in place here, so that my opponent's expression, "Now we're in for it," charged as it was with the lust of battle, struck one as even prettier. I understood him at once. He clearly expected the answer 11.g4 with a consequent race between the pawns on both sides, according to the motto "he who gets there first wins". See Diagram 112. What I did play however was **11.Nd5**. With this move, by which an outpost station on the d-file is occupied, White obeys another principle of positional play, namely that the premature flank attack should be punished by play in the center. There followed **11...Nxd5 12.exd5 Nxd4 13.Bxd4** and White has much the better of it. He has a centralized position which cannot possibly be taken away from him by, for example 13...Bf6 14.f4 Re8 15.Bf3 followed by Rhe1. Black has a disorganized Queenside which exposes weaknesses for the endgame. The moral of the story is: Do not be always thinking of attack! Safeguarding moves, indicated by the demands made on us by the position, are often much more prudent.

#112
Black's attempt at attack by ...b5? is
defeated by a positional move

Another erroneous conception may be found among masters. Many of these and numbers of strong amateurs are under the impression that positional play above all is concerned with the accumulation of small advantages, in order to exploit them in the ending. This type of play is said to be the most esthetically satisfying.

In contradiction to this we would remark that the accumulation of small advantages is by no means the most important constituent of positional play. We are inclined rather to assign to this plan of operation a very subordinate role. The difficulty of this method is very much overestimated. It is not easy to see how the petty storing up of values can be called beautiful. Does not this procedure remind one in some sense of the activities of some old miser, and who would think them beautiful? We note here the fact that there are other matters to which the attention of the positional player must be directed, and which place this "accumulation" completely in the shade.

What are these things, and in what do I see the idea of true positional play? The answer is short and to the point - in "prophylaxis".

♦ *3. My original conception of positional play as such: the well known idea of the accumulation of small advantages is only of second or third significance. Of much greater importance is a prophylactic applied both externally and internally. My new principle of overprotection, its definition and meaning.*

As I have several times observed, neither the attack nor defense is, in my opinion, a matter properly pertaining to positional play, which is instead an energetic and systematic application of prophylactic measures. What is important above all else is to blunt the edge of certain possibilities which in a positional sense would be undesirable. Of such possibilities, apart from the mishaps to which the less experienced player is exposed, there are two kinds only. One of these is the possibility of the opponent making a "freeing" pawn move. The positional player must accordingly arrange his pieces in order to prevent the freeing moves. In connection with this we should notice that we must examine every case that arises to see whether the freeing move in question is really freeing, for as I pointed out in my article on Dr. Tarrasch's *Die moderne Schachpartie,* the true saying, "*Not all that glitters is gold,*" applies to freeing moves. There are many which only lead to an unfavorable, premature opening up of the game, whereas other freeing moves should be considered normal reactions, and as such must be calmly accepted, for it would be a presumption to wish to fight against natural phenomena! In spite of the fact that freeing moves will be considered in detail in another place under "restraint," it will not be improper to give here two illustrations.

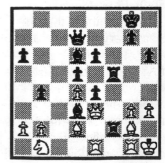

#112a
White (a piece up) to play. A drastic example of a lack of "freeing" moves. The ultimate "*Zugzwang.*" See Illustrative game No. 8

For an example of an incorrect freeing move see Diagram 113. In similar positions the move ...e5 would be classed under the heading of "freeing moves". It opens up Black's otherwise cramped game, and in addition stands for the action in the center, and is positionally indicated as a countermeasure to the encircling movement which White is striving for on the Queenside. White, nevertheless, plays correctly **1.b4!** (instead of 1.Re1) **1...e5? 2.dxe5 Nxe5 3.Bf4! Nxf3+ 4.Qxf3 Qd8 5.h3** followed by 6.Rad1 and the occupation of the square d4 (the blockading point) by a Bishop or Knight with the superior game for White. Black was initially behind in development and his freeing maneuver therefore failed.

#113
White plays b4 allowing his opponent to make the freeing move ...e5. Is this correct?

#114

Our second example, Diagram 114, shows us that it is not possible permanently to hold up a freeing advance for which the time is ripe. Our object must therefore in similar cases be limited to making the freeing maneuver as difficult as possible to execute. We must not under any circumstances persist in the attempt to stop such a maneuver when it is clearly impossible to achieve this. The position in Diagram 114 was reached after the moves **1.e4 e5 2.Nf3 Nc6 3.Bc4 Be7 4.d4 d6 5.d5 Nb8.** The pawn chain made up of the d and e-pawns will make White strive for c4-c5, Black for ...f5. Forcible measures, such as 6.Bd3 Nf6 7.h3 0-0 8.g4? would not be in keeping with the position. On the other hand **6.Bd3 Nf6 7.c4 0-0 8.Nc3 Ne8 9.Qe2** would seem indicated, in order in reply to **9...f5** to undertake the operation **10.exf5 Bxf5 11.Bxf5 Rxf5 12.Ne4**.

We note then, that the prevention of freeing pawn moves (as far as this appears necessary and feasible) is of great importance in positional play. Such prevention is what we wish to be understood as an exterior prophylactic. It is much more difficult to grasp the idea of interior prophylactic, for here we are speaking of an entirely new conception. We are in fact now concerned with the warding off of an evil, which has really never been understood as one, yet which can, and in general does, have a most disturbing effect on our game. The evil consists in this: Our pieces are out of, or in insufficient contact with their own strategically important points. Since I conceived of this condition as an evil, I was led to advance the strategic proposition that one must overprotect his own strategically important points, by providing defense in excess of attack, to lay up a reserve of defense. My formulation of this argument runs as follows - weak points, still more strong points, in short everything that we can include in the conception of strategically important points, should be overprotected. If the pieces are so engaged, they get their reward in the fact that they will then find themselves well posted in every respect.

There are two explanatory remarks to be made here. First, that as we have incidentally shown in our discussion of the passed pawn, we have the puzzling circumstance that blockading squares prove themselves as a rule to be in every respect good squares, and the pieces detailed for dull blockade duty find quite unexpectedly their reward in the possibility of a heightened activity from their blockading station.

#115
Nimzowitsch-Giese
White to move. What point
must be overprotected?

The idea of overprotection is in a certain sense no other than that above sketched though in an expanded form, as we may see from the following example (see Diagram 115). Here we overprotect the strong e5 pawn which has been pushed forward. The defense afforded by the d-pawn is insufficient, since White plans to reply to ...c5 by dxc5 (surrendering the base pawn in order to occupy d4 with pieces). White will then overprotect the e-pawn with pieces, thus **9.Nd2** and the game Nimzowitsch-Giese continued **9...Ne7 10.Nf3! Ng6 11.Re1! Bb4** (to eventually get the Bishop to c7, and finally, despite the overprotection of White's e-pawn, to play ...f6) **12.c3 Ba5 13.Bf4!** (the third overprotection) **13...0-0 14.Bg3 Bc7 15.Ng5** (and now the inner strength of overprotection is manifested in a drastic manner. The seemingly lifeless overprotectors, the Nf3, the Bf4, and the Re1 suddenly make themselves felt) **15...Rfe8 16.Nf4 Nh8 17.Qg4 Nf8 18.Re3** (the old soldier sniffs a fight and rejoices) **18...b6** (better was 18...Bd8) **19.Nh5 Nhg6 20.Rf3 Re7** (Diagram 115a) **21.Nf6+ Kh8** and now White could win immediately by **22.Nfxh7 Nxh7 23.Nxf7+ Rxf7 24.Rxf7**. The idea was the following: It was a good deed to overprotect a strategically important point, the reward came in the form of a large radius of activity for the pieces engaged on that service.

#115a
Career of the "overprotector"

Just one more example, for later on a whole chapter will be devoted to overprotection in all of its aspects. (Diagram 116). After **15.Rad1 Rae8** there followed a maneuver which seemed most unlikely, 16.Rd2 followed by 17.Rfd1. Why? Because the Queen on d3 (and also perhaps the d4 pawn) is the keystone of White's position, and therefore overprotection is indicated. In fact, after a few moves the two Rooks prove to be most serviceable combatants (they protect their own King admirably). **16.Rd2 Qg5 17.Rfd1 Ba7!! 18.Nf4 Nf5 19.Nb5 Bb8** and now Re2 and Rde1 should have been played, when the overprotectors would have reaped their due reward.

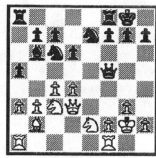

#116
Nimzowitsch-Alekhine
Baden-Baden, 1925
After 15.Rad1 Rae8, what point
needs overprotection by White?

Second, the rule for overprotection applies as is natural most particularly to strong points, to important squares in the center which are likely to come under heavy fire, to strong blockading squares, or to strong passed pawns. Ordinary weak points should under no circumstances by overprotected, for this might very well lead to the defenders getting into passive positions. No matter how weak, a pawn that forms the base of an important pawn chain may and should be well overprotected. To illustrate this let us return to our old friend the pawn chain made of the d and e-pawns on each side. See Diagram 117a and compare it with Diagram 117b. In the first the Rooks protect the weak base of the pawn chain (every such base is in a certain sense to be classed as weak since the one sure defense, by a pawn, is lacking). Yet this protection makes all the stronger the e5 pawn, for as we know, the strengthening of the base involves at the same time a strengthening

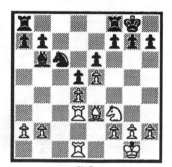

#117a
The safeguarded base at d4
increases the importance of
the attacking pawn at e5. The Rooks
act as overprotectors.

#117b
Here the doubled Rooks do not have
the effect of overprotection, but are
instead a prime example of the
passive defense of a weak point.

throughout the whole chain. The reader is encouraged to play over again my game (No. 20) against Dr. Tarrasch, in which after first overprotecting the point d4, I, having achieved my purpose got a strong attack which led to victory. The soul of that attack was however the e5 pawn, which could trustfully lean on the d4 pawn, which by that time was thoroughly healthy. On the other hand in the position shown on Diagram 117b, a pawn at e5 is missing, and therefore the role which the Rooks would otherwise have had to play, is much restricted. In fact, of the once so responsible role, nothing remains but the tedious obligation of preventing the d4 pawn from being lost. In other words, the disposition of the overprotection in the case of Diagram 117b does not carry with it any sort of plan of attack for the future (in noteworthy contrast to the case of Diagram 117a), and consequently we get nothing but that passive disposition of defending pieces, against which we had to register so emphatic a warning. To recapitulate - The law of overprotection applies in general only to strong points. Weak points can only lay claim to overprotection in such cases where they help to support other strong points.

♦ *4. Side by side with the idea of prophylaxis, that of the collective mobility of a pawn mass is a main postulate of my teaching on positional play.*

In the last resort positional play is nothing more than a fight between mobility (of the pawn mass) on one side and efforts to restrain this on the other. In this all-embracing struggle the essentially very important device of the prophylactic is merely a means to an end.

It is of the greatest importance to strive for the mobility of our pawn mass, for a mobile mass can in its lust to expand exercise a crushing effect. This mobility is not always injured by the presence of a pawn that has possibly remained behind in the general advance, for example a backward pawn, which can be used as a nurse to tend to his friends on the front lines. In the case of a mobile pawn mass we must

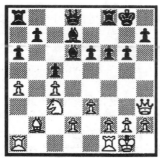

#118a
White establishes a mobile pawn
mass and leaves one of them at
home to serve as a nurse. How
is this accomplished?

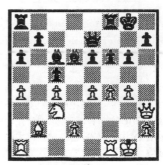

#118b
The White e, f, and g-pawns, along
with the diagonal a1-h8 lurking in the
rear, form the storm troops. By playing d3, White safeguards c4 and e4.

therefore look for collective and not individual mobility, each pawn for itself. For instance in Diagram 118a we should expect sooner or later the leveling advance d4, in order to be rid of the backward pawn. In the game, however, there was played more correctly **17.f4 Qe7 18.e4! Bc6 19.g4** (Diagram 118b), and White won easily. See game No. 25.

In the game Nimzowitsch-Rubinstein, Dresden, 1926 (Illustrative game No.33), I was in no hurry to get rid of my backward pawn. Thus after the opening moves **1.c4 c5 2.Nf3 Nf6 3.Nc3 d5 4.cxd5 Nxd5 5.e4 Nb4 6.Bc4 e6 7.0-0** (Diagram 118c), if Black had played 7...a6, I would not have been in any hurry to advance the backward d-pawn, for 8.d4 cxd4 9.Qxd4 Qxd4 10.Nxd4 Bc5 11.Be3 Bxd4 12.Bxd4 Nc2! 13.Rad1 Nxd4 14.Rxd4 Nc6 15.Rd2 b5, followed by ...Bb7 and ...Ke7 would have only lead to an equal game. I would rather after 8.a3 N4c6 have chosen 9.d3 and after

#118c

playing my Bishop to e3 and marshaling my major pieces I would have been well prepared to attack. In the game he played **7...N8c6** (instead of 7...a6) and after **8.d3 Nd4** (otherwise 9.a3) **9.Nxd4 cxd4 10.Ne2**, White got, after f4, a mobile pawn mass, effectively supported by the Bc4.

We will now turn our attention to that terrible region in which the amateur (and on occasion also the master) only too often trip up, the center.

♦ *5. The center. Insufficient watch kept on the central territory as a typical and ever recurring error. The center as the Balkans of the chessboard. On the popular, but strategically doubtful diversion of the attack from the center to the wings. On the invasion of the center. The occupation of central squares.*

It may be taken as common knowledge that in certain positions it is necessary to direct our pieces against the enemy center. For instance in positions characterized by the presence of White pawns at e4 and f4, Black at d6 and f7 (or White at d4 and c4 vs. Black at c7 and e6). On the other hand it is not so well known that it is a strategic necessity to keep the center under observation even if it is fairly well barricaded. The center is the Balkans of the chessboard; fighting may at any time break out there. Take the position already discussed under Diagram 89, which from the point of view of the center seems harmless enough, yet after the moves **1.e4 e5 2.Nf3 Nc6 3.Bc4 Bc5 4.Nc3 Nf6 5.d3 d6 6.Bg5 h6 7.Bh4 g5 8.Bg3**, Black's center is threatened by two raids, (1) Bb5 followed by d4, and (2) Nd5 followed by c3 and d4. Another example is furnished by the opening of the game Capablanca-Martinez (1914). After **1.e4 e5 2.Bc4 Bc5 3.Nc3 Nf6 4.d3 Nc6 5.Bg5 h6 6.Bh4 g5** (6...d6 7.Nd5 g5 8.Bg3 Be6 with the threat of 9...Bxd5 10.exd5 Ne7 11.Bb5+ c6 12.dxc6 bxc6 and Black dominates the center). **7.Bg3 h5 8.h4 g4 9.Qd2 d6 10.Nge2 Qe7 11.0-0.** Black thought that he could treat himself to a move like **11...a6**. See Diagram 119. The loss of time involved is more serious since the position is only in appearance closed, and can be opened at any time. (The same applies to 90% of all closed central positions). There followed **12.Nd5 Nxd5 13.exd5 Nd4 14.Nxd4 Bxd4 15.c3 Bb6 16.d4 f6!** and as I pointed out White could get a

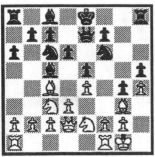

decisive advantage by **17.Rfe1** (Capablanca played the weaker 17.Rae1) **17...Bd7** (17...0-0 18.dxe5 fxe5 19.Rxe5 Bxf2+ 20.Qxf2 Qxe5 21.Bxe5 Rxf2 22.Kxf2 dxe5 23.Re1 winning. But not 23.d6+? Kg7 24.dxc7 b5 followed by ...Ra7). **18.a4 0-0-0 19.a5 Ba7 20.b4**, followed by Reb1 and b5 with a winning attack.

These examples teach us that the function of a Knight at c3 does not only consist in holding up a pawn advance to d5. No, the Knight so posted is under obligation, the moment the enemy gives him a chance, of undertaking an invasion of the center by going to d5. Such a chance is often given by amateurs, who show a preference for starting a maneuver on a wing before it is justified, without unfortunately giving much thought to the question of whether they may perhaps be taking too many troops away from the center. How could such a line of play as the following otherwise persist for so many years, yes, even in master tournaments!

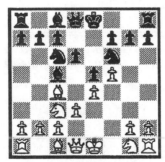

#120
White has just played his pawn to f5. As this move does nothing toward observation of the center, how might this strategy be punished by Black?

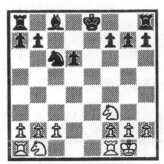

#121
The game went 1.Re1+ Be6 2.Ng5. Instead of this change of front what central strategy was indicated in this position?

1.e4 e5 2.Nc3 Nf6 3.Bc4 Bc5 4.d3 Nc6 5.f4 d6 6.f5? (Diagram 120). Naturally 6.Nf3 is the proper move, and now by 6...Nd4 followed by ...c6, ...b5, ...a5, ...Qb6, and when the opportunity comes, ...d5, Black gets a strong game in the center and on the Queenside which yields him a pronounced advantage.

Another example, though this time a milder one, of the evils which follow an unwarranted change of front from center to flank, against which the student cannot be sufficiently warned. **1.e4 e5 2.Nf3 d6 3.d4 Nf6 4.dxe5 Nxe4 5.Bd3 Nc5 6.Bf4 Nxd3+** (Black had the opportunity here, by 6...Ne6 followed by ...d5, to build up his position on scientific principles. The Knight at e6 would have been our strong, elastic blockader). **7.Qxd3 Nc6 8.0-0** (8.Nc3 followed by 9.0-0-0 would have been better).

8...Be7 9.exd6 Bxd6 10.Bxd6 Qxd6 11.Qxd6 cxd6 (Diagram 121). There followed: **12.Re1+? Be6 13.Ng5** (the change of front characteristic of non-positional players) **13...Kd7 14.c3** and White's game is not to be envied. The right course was 12.Nc3, and after 13.Nb5 and 14.Nd4 he would be centralized and have the superior game.

It will be instructive to give an example here characteristic of the disregard so often shown even by strong players for central strategy. It is from a game played in 1920 in a Swedish tournament between K. Berntsson (White) and S.J. Bjurulf. **1.d4 d5 2.Nf3 Nf6 3.Bf4 e6 4.e3 c5 5.c3 b6** (the following line of play seems best here. 5...Nc6! and if now 6.Nbd2 Be7 7.h3 [anticipating ...Nh5] 7...Bd6! 8.Ne5 Bxe5 9.dxe5 Nd7 10.Nf3 and now a fierce fight will be waged around the e5 square. Diagram 122a). We strongly recommend the would-be positional player to exercise himself in such central fights. In the present position a good plan would be 10...a6! 11.Bd3 f6! (not 11...Qc7 because of 12.0-0 Ndxe5 13.Nxe5 Nxe5 14.Qh5 and wins), in order after 12.exf6 Qxf6 to seize the hotly disputed square e5 by ...e5. We counsel our readers to study this position. The move 5...b6 is a typical error in that it seems to disregard the fact that there is such a thing as a central theater of war). **6.Nbd2 Bd6 7.Ne5** (this move is pleasing, although there is here a tactical possibility which is perhaps objectively preferable, 7.Bb5+ Bd7? 8.Bxd6 Bxb5 9.dxc5. The move 7.Ne5 is the more logical move, since owing to the loss of time involved in Black's 5...b6, the center was ripe for an invasion). **7...Bxe5 8.dxe5 Nfd7 9.Qg4 Rg8 10.Nf3 Nc6 11.Bd3 Nf8** (Diagram 122b). **12.Ng5** (White commits the strategic error of

#122a
Black's move.
A typical example of a fight for a central point. Here the square e5.

#122b
White's move. The point e5 is in his undisputed possession.. But should the attack be directed on the Kingside, the Queenside, or the center?

underestimating the importance of the point e5, the key point in his entire position. Under no circumstances should the attack be conducted in a manner which would endanger its safety. Overprotection of this point would here be indicated. The right course was to remain passive on the Kingside, to advance e4 in the center and then on the Queenside play b4 and a4. A sample variation: 12.0-0 Bb7 13.b4! c4 [and not 13...cxb4 14.cxb4 Nxb4 because of 15.Bg5 winning a piece or causing some

---

other similar unpleasantness]. 14.Bc2 Qd7 15.a4 a6! [if 15...0-0-0, then 16.a5 bxa5 17.b5! with a winning attack]. 16.e4! 0-0-0 17.Be3 Kc7 18.a5! with a decisive attack). **12...Qc7! 13.Bxh7 Rh8 14.Bc2** (Diagram 122c). **14...Bb7?** (Black must here seek to conquer the point e5, dangerous as this might appear. Simply 14...Nxe5! and he would have gotten the better game. For instance, 15.Qg3 f6 16.Nf3 Nxf3+ 17.Qxf3 e5! 18.Qxd5 Bb7 19.Ba4+ Ke7 and Black wins a piece. Or 14...Nxe5 15.Ba4+ Ke7 with the threat of 16...Nd3+. On the other hand the reply 15...Bd7 would have been bad, for White, by means of 16.Bd7+ N8xd7 17.Nxe6! fxe6 18.Qxe6+ Kd8 19.Qxd5 would get a strong attack, with three pawns for his sacrificed Knight. But, as indicated with the idea of ...Nxe5 followed by ...Ke7 on the Bishop check at a4, Black could have gotten an excellent game. The strategic events in this game present

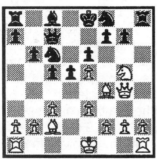

#122c Black plays. How should
he punish White's neglect of
keeping the point e5 under
control in his last moves?

#122d
White is able and obligated to
win back the square e5.
How is he to accomplish this?

themselves as follows: 5...b6 had no bearing on the center, and in consequence White was strong and mighty there (Ne5), but at his 12th move he did not pay sufficient regard to this key point (e5) and this, if Black had made the correct reply, could have led to his losing all of his advantage. We see then what a dominating influence central strategy exercises). **15.Nf3 g6 16.Bg5?** (barely had he by luck escaped the dangers in the center, than the leader of the White forces, always on the lookout for a combination, again sacrifices his chief possession from a strategic point of view, the point e5. The overprotectors, the Nf3 and the Bf4 should have remained at their posts. His proper course was indicated in the note to move 12). **16..Nxe5!** (now he shows courage!) **17.Nxe5 Qxe5** (Diagram 122d) **18.h4** (it is absolutely essential for White to play to recover the point e5. He must play 18.Bf4! and if in reply 18...Qh5, then 19.Qg3 f6 20.Bd6, and Black could hardly succeed in consolidating his position, which is threatened on all sides. After the text move Black, on the contrary could make himself fully secure). **18...b5?** (not only spells loss of time but also weakens the c5 pawn and allows a4. The right move was 18...Nd7 and if 19.Ba4, then 19...f6 20.Bf4 Qe4! 21.Bb5 g5, or 21...0-0-0 and Black stands well). **19.0-0 Nh7 20.Bf4 Qh5 21.Qxh5 gxh5 22.a4**, and White won a skillfully conducted endgame.

The moral of this game runs as follows. (1) Watch the center (see Black's 5th move, White's 12th and following moves, Black's 14th move). (2) Overprotect the key point (see White's 12th and 16th moves). (3) Do not divert your attack prematurely. (see White's 12th and 16th moves). (4) After the pawns are gone the key point must be occupied by pieces (see White's 18th move).

♦ *6. The leitmotif of correct strategy is the overprotection of the center, with, further, a systematically carried out centralization of our forces. Wing attack must be met by play in the center.*

In the very characteristic game which has just been quoted we saw how the diversion of the attack from the center to a wing, and, what is in principle the equivalent, the disregard of the central key points, led to some curious situations. This "diversion" sometimes appears also in the games of masters. We need only remind the reader of Game No. 22, Opocensky - Nimzowitsch, which in the position shown in Diagram 123 there occurred the following moves: **13.Ne2? Nh5 14.Qd2 g6 15.g4 Ng7 16.Ng3 c6!** The diversion of the Knight, now completed has so altered the situation that Black, though much cramped on the Queenside, can venture to proceed to the attack!

#123 White commits the error of maneuvering the Nc3 to the Kingside

Centralization is ever characteristic of master play. The talented Czech master Opocensky was of course no exception. Alekhine made use of this strategy with special predilection, and this (with play against enemy squares of a particular color) formed the leitmotif of all of his games. Even when the knife seemed actually to be at his King's throat in a Kingside attack, he always found time to mass troops in the center. A typical example is furnished by the game Nimzowitsch - Alekhine, Semmering, 1926, in which after the moves **1.e4 Nf6 2.Nc3 d5 3.e5 Nfd7 4.f4 e6 5.Nf3 c5 6.g3 Nc6 7.Bg2 Be7 8.0-0 0-0 9.d3 Nb6**, he got into some trouble by having omitted 9...f6. There followed **10.Ne2 d4 11.g4** (the beginning of a violent attack) **11...f6 12.exf6 gxf6** (otherwise the centralization of the Knight by Ng3-e4 would follow). **13.Ng3 Nd5! 14.Qe2 Bd6! 15.Nh4** (see Diagram 124) **15...Nce7! 16.Bd2 Qc7 17.Qf2**, and now the inner strength of the centralized

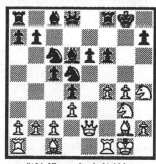

#124 Nimzowitsch-Alekhine Semmering, 1926

structure of Black's position was made clear by the surprising continuation **17...c4!**
18.dxc4 Ne3! and Alekhine had equalized the game.

#125
Yates-Nimzowitsch
Semmering, 1926
Possession of the open e-file, the d4
pawn, and the centralized Qe4 stamp
Black's position as very centralized

I too, both theoretically and in practice, am absolutely on the side of centralization. Examine my game against Yates (Semmering, 1926), in which I had the Black pieces. **1.e4 e6 2.d4 d5 3.Nc3 Bb4 4.exd5 exd5 5.Bd3 Ne7 6.Nge2 0-0 7.0-0 Bg4 8.f3 Bh5 9.Nf4 Bg6 10.Nce2 Bd6 11.Qe1** (here 11.Bxg6 followed by 12.Nd3 would have been in the spirit of centralization, and the squares c5 and e5 would have been kept under perpetual observation) **11...c5! 12.dxc5 Bxc5+ 13.Kh1 Nbc6 14.Bd2 Re8 15.Nxg6 hxg6!** (creates a central point at f5) **16.f4** (the normal development of things would have been 16.Qh4 Nf5 17.Qxd8 Raxd8 and Black has a slight advantage in the ending) **16...Nf5 17.c3 d4! 18.c4 Qb6 19.Rf3 Bb4** (to clean up the central point e3) **20.a3 Bxd2 21.Qxd2 a5 22.Ng1 Re3 23.Qf2 Rae8 24.Rd1 Qb3 25.Rd2 Nd6 26.c5 Nc4! 27.Bxc4 Qxc4** (White's c-pawn is weak, the blockading Bd3 has been removed, and the central pressure is more arduous to White than ever) **28.Rc2 Qd5! 29.Rc1 Qe4!** (Diagram 125). With this move centralization has been completed. White sacrificed a pawn by **30.f5** in order to defend himself against the ever increasing pressure on the e-file , but lost the ending after **30...Rxf3 31.Qxf3 Qxf5.** Further striking examples of centralization will be found in abundance in the games of the masters.

We now proceed to the analysis of play in the center vs. play on a wing. The game Nimzowitsch-Alekhine, just given, furnishes an example of how such a struggle usually proceeds. The "central" player always has the better prospects, especially in the frequently recurring positions which we are about to outline. One side has undertaken a diversion against his opponent's Kingside which in itself promises a reward. All would be in the most perfect order, but that (there's always a "but"!) his opponent holds an open center file, and with astounding regularity the flank attack is shipwrecked on this rock.

We will first note (see Diagram 126) the plan of such a situation. In the position shown Black's attack must always fail, because his Rooks are under the unpleasant obligation to guard their base (here their first and second ranks) against an inroad of the White Rooks which are all ready for the adventure. In addition, e5 is insufficiently protected, and this again is not accidental, since the White Nf3 is centralized in harmony with the rest of the White structure. As the whole matter is of extraordinary importance to an understanding of the spirit of the dogma of the center, we will illustrate it by a complete game, Rubinstein-Nimzowitsch, San

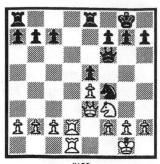

#126

Illustrates the theme "center file vs. flank attack". The Nf4 is the mainstay of Black's so-called "attack".

#127

Rubinstein, playing the White pieces demonstrated the weakness of Black's diversion on the Kingside

Sebastian, 1912. **1.d4 Nf6 2.c4 d6 3.Nf3 Nbd7 4.Nc3 e5 5.e4 Be7** (the immediate fianchetto of the King Bishop is also a possibility here) **6.Be2 0-0 7.0-0 Re8 8.Qc2 Bf8 9.b3 c6** (here, as Lasker very rightly pointed out, the sounder line was ...g6, ...Bg7 followed by ...exd4 and ...Ne5) **10.Bb2 Nh5? 11.g3 Nb8 12.Rad1** (the center file looms up) **12...Qf6 13.Nb1! Bh3 14.Rfe1 Nf4** (that I should be able to get the Knight to f4 under any circumstances, I had foreseen when I played 10...Nh5, a misfortune, for otherwise I would have withstood the temptation to undertake this diversion). Diagram 127. **15.dxe5 dxe5 16.Nxe5 Rxe5 17.Bf1** (after 17.Bxe5 Nxe2+ 18.Qxe2 Qxe5 19.Rd8 - the center file!, White would also have the advantage) **17...Nd7 18.Qd2** (now the Black pieces embarked on their Kingside diversion are in the air) **18...Bxf1 19.Rxf1 Nh3+ 20.Kg2 Ng5** (threatens mate in two moves) **21.f4 Qg6 22.fxg5 Rxe4** (22...Qxe4+ 23.Kh3 Re7 24.Rde1 and White wins a piece. Best was 22...Re7, but White would still have won). **23.Qxd7 Re2+ 24.Rf2** and White won. See also Game No. 28, Kline - Capablanca for another variation on the same theme.

♦ *7. The surrender of the Center.*

As early as 1911 and 1912 I had published some notes on games in which I put forward what was then an entirely new idea, that the center need not necessarily be occupied by pawns; that centrally posted pieces or even lines bearing on the center could, as I maintained, take the place of pawns, the main point being to place the enemy center pawns under restraint. I represented this idea in 1913 in an article which, by the courtesy of G. Marco, Editor of the *Weiner Schachzietung*, I am allowed to reproduce here, and do so because in this the age of the "neo-romantic school" it is in a high degree pertinent. The article ran as follows -

When Black in the much disputed variation of the French Defense 1.e4 e6 2.d4 d5 3.Nc3, plays 3...dxe4, he gives up, according to the current opinion, the center.

This view seems to me to rest upon an incomplete grasp, in fact a misconception, of what the center really is. In what follows the attempt will be made, (1) to show that this view is based on a prejudice, (2) to set out its historical development.

First the definition of the concept "center." Here we have simply to abide by the meaning of the word. The center consists of the squares in the middle of the board, SQUARES, not pawns. This is a fundamental and must never under any circumstances be forgotten.

The importance of the center, the complex of squares in the middle of the board, as a base for further operations, is beyond question. A note of Dr. Emanuel Lasker's to a game is worth remembering. "White," he wrote, "does not stand well enough in the center to undertake an operation on the wing." This is finely conceived, and at the same time illustrates the close relationship between center and the wings, the center being the dominating principle, the wings subordinate to it.

That the control of the center is of great significance, is, other considerations apart, clear from one thing, that if we have built up our game in the center, we have from then on the possibility of exercising influence on both wings at the same time, and of embarking on a diversion should opportunity offer. Without healthy conditions in the center, a healthy position is definitely unthinkable.

We spoke of control of the center. What are we to understand by this? How is this conditioned?

Current opinion holds that the center should be occupied by pawns. e4 and d4 (for Black e5 and d5) is the ideal, but in fact the presence of one of these two presumes occupation of the center, provided the corresponding enemy pawn is lacking.

But is this really the case? Is the d4 pawn, after the moves 1.e4 e6 2.d4 d5 3.Nc3 dxe4 justified in speaking of a conquest of the center?

If in a battle, I seize a bit of debatable land with a handful of soldiers, without having done anything to prevent an enemy bombardment of the position, would it ever occur to me to speak of a conquest of the terrain in question? Obviously not. Then why should I do so in chess?

It dawns upon us then, that control of the center depends not on a mere occupation, (placing of pawns), but rather on our general effectiveness there, and this is determined by quite other factors.

This thought I have formulated thus - With the disappearance of a pawn from the center (as referenced above after 3...dxe4 4.Nxe4) the center is a long way from being surrendered. The true conception of the center is a far wider one. Certainly, pawns as being the most stable, are best suited to building a center, nevertheless centrally posted pieces can perfectly well take their place. Pressure, also, exerted on the enemy center by the long range action of Rooks or Bishops directed on it can well be of corresponding importance.

We meet this last case in the variation with 3...dxe4. This move, so wrongly described as a surrender of the center, as a matter of fact increases Black's effective influence in the center very considerably, for with the removal of the pawn from d5 (it was also an obstruction!), Black gets a free hand on the d-file and the long diagonal a8-h1 which he will open for himself with the move ...b6. Obstruction! that is the dark side of the occupation of the center by pawns. A pawn is by nature, by his stability, a good center builder, but alas, he is also an obstruction.

That effective influence in the center is independent of the number of pawns occupying it, appears from many examples and of their abundance we will take one or two.

Pieces in the center. (1) Black's pawns at d5 and e6 held in restraint by the White Ne5 and pawn at c3. Diagram 128, a position from the game Nimzowitsch-Levenfish, Carlsbad, 1911. (2) The isolated pawn couple at d5 and c6 rigidly blockaded by White pieces as in Diagram 129. The two cases quoted show us a blockade. But blockade is an elastic term and often slight restraint induced by an annoying Rook whose primary function was to hold up the advance of the enemy center may be the prelude to a complete crippling, which concludes in its mechanical stoppage.

#128

#129

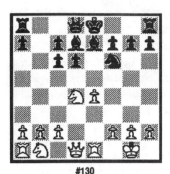

#130

The cases in which pressure is exerted on the enemy center are without number. In Diagram 130 the course of events will lead either to a blockade with consequent destruction of the e-pawn (for movement is life), or to uncomfortable positions for the defending pieces, which will lead to the downfall of the "lucky possessor" of the center.

All of this teaches us that by counting the heads of the pawns in the center, nothing, literally nothing, is gained. To make mere arithmetic the starting point of a philosophy of the center can only be characterized as a mistaken proceeding. I am sure that in very few years no one will regard 3...dxe4 as a "surrender" of the center, and with the disappearance of such a prepossession, the way will be clear for a new and brilliant development in chess philosophy - and strategy.

A word on the genesis of this prejudice, which is closely bound up with the history of positional play. First came Steinitz, but what he had to say was so unfamiliar, and he himself was so towering a figure, that his "modern principles" could not immediately become popular. There followed Tarrasch who took hold of Steinitz's ideas and served them up diluted to the public taste. And now to consider the application to our case. Steinitz was, we repeat, deep and great, but deepest and greatest in his conception of the center. When in his defense to the Ruy Lopez (...d6) he was able to transmute the enemy e4 pawn which was to all appearances so healthy, into one whose weakness was patent to every eye, this was an unsurpassable achievement. Nothing lay further from his thoughts than a formalistic, arithmetical conception of the center....

For illustrations we would recommend for study before continuing on, illustrative games 25-30 inclusive, (and in particular No.26), which bear on this chapter's theme.

CHAPTER 11

THE DOUBLED PAWN AND RESTRAINT

♦1. The affinity between a "doubled pawn" and restraint; the former should favor the execution of enemy plans for restraint. What does laboring under the disadvantage of a doubled pawn mean? The conception of passive (static) and active (dynamic) weaknesses. When does the dissolution of an enemy doubled pawn seem to be indicated? The one real strength of a doubled pawn.

Restraint is conceivable without the presence of enemy doubled pawns, but a really complete restraint, which extends over large tracts of the board and makes it difficult for the enemy to breathe, is only possible under the disadvantage of a doubled pawn. What do we mean exactly by laboring under this disadvantage? Mainly this, that in the event of an advance in close formation certain paralyzing phenomena may intervene. See for example, Diagram 131. If a White pawn had been at b2 instead of c2 the advance d4-d5, followed by c4, b4, and c5 would have been possible. In the diagramed position, however there is no b-pawn and therefore any attempt of a transference of attack (see Chapter on the "Pawn Chain") will be in vain. On d4-d5 and c4 the answer would be ...b6, and the further advance c5 we had planned is shown to be impossible of execution. What we have just learned about the chief weakness of compact (easily defendable) doubled pawns (which we would class as active, or dynamic, weaknesses) enables us to formulate this rule, that it pays to incite the possessor of a pawn mass whose attacking value is lessened by the presence of doubled pawns to an advance. Acting in this spirit Black in the case under consideration should, if White has played d4, try to induce his opponent to continue his action in the center. As long as he can stop at d4, the defect of the doubled pawn will not be in great evidence. It is only in the advance that the weakness will appear.

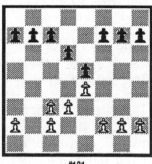

#131

We must differentiate an active and a passive (static) weakness. The latter is, in contrast to that in our last example, revealed when we send our own pawns forward in a storming party against the doubled pawn. Let us imagine in Diagram 131 that the White d-pawn is at d5 instead of d3, the White King at g1, and White Rook at e2. Black's King at f8 and Rook c8. Here the static weakness of the doubled pawn is great, for after 1...c6 2.dxc6 Rxc6, or 1...c6 2.c4 cxd5 3.cxd5 Rc3, followed by ...Ra3, Black will in either case get the advantage. The rule therefore is: Given a passive weakness in a doubled pawn an advance against this pawn is indicated, whereby the dissolution or undoubling of the enemy pawn need cause us no fear.

The evil is in fact only half dissipated. Part of the weakness has been gotten rid of, but for what remains behind the player has to suffer more intense remorse.

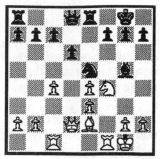

#132
Black strives to exchange the d6 pawn for White's e4 pawn

Let us now turn to Diagram 132. Black, the author of this book, allowed his opponent (E. Cohn) to take the initiative in the hope that the resulting play would in the end lead to a simplification, after which in the ending it could not be very difficult to take advantage of the doubled pawn. The game proceeded: **16...Qd7 17.Qe1 Ng6 18.Bd3 Bf6 19.Qf2 Be5** (Black relies on the solid strength of the point e5) **20.Rc2 Rf8 21.Kh1 b6 22.Qf3 Rae8 23.Rcf2 Nh8 24.Qh5 c6 25.g4 f6.** And now Cohn let himself be carried away by the idea of an interesting attack, which in the end only resulted in the simplification of the game, and the exposure of the hopelessness of his pawn position (e3, e4). He played **26.c5** and after **26...Bxf4 27.Rxf4 dxc5 28.Bc4+ Nf7 29.g5 Re5 30.Rf5 Rxf5 31.exf5** the win could be forced by 31...Kh8, for the answer to 32.g6 would have been 32...Nh6, and to 32.Bxf7 it would be 32...Qxf7 33.g6 Qd5+ followed by h6. Black was therefore right in choosing a waiting strategy for the wing attack must fail against the center file, with Black's strong point, e5, and the endgame is hopeless for White. Although the waiting strategy was correct, the advance was also possible, for White's e3 and e4 pawns constitute a static weakness. This advance could be executed somewhat as follows 16...Nd7 (instead of 16...Qd7) 17.Bf3 Nf6 18.Qc2 c6! He "sacrifices" the d-pawn in order at once to get the White e4 pawn. After 19.Rcd1 Qe7 we get our "exchange of pawns" and then White's e3 pawn can be bombarded in comfort.

The full rule, therefore runs: To isolated doubled pawns, and to "compact" doubled pawns, or those which are advancing, the "question" should be put (attacked by pawns). An enemy doubled pawn complex which has not started its advance, should, before the "question" is put to it, first be incited to action.

♦ *1a. The one real strength of the doubled pawn.*

As we have seen, a pawn mass which is afflicted with a doubled pawn has in it a certain latent weakness, which makes itself felt when the time comes to make use of that mass by advancing it. We characterize this as we have said, as a dynamic weakness. This mass if at rest, holding its configuration, may be very strong. Turn back to Diagram 131. After White has played d4, a position is reached out of which he can be driven only with the greatest trouble. We mean by this that Black hardly possesses the positional means to be able to force his opponent to a decision to play dxe5 or d5. On the other hand this would be much easier if White's pawn were at b2 instead of c2. The doubled pawn in fact makes holding out easier. Why this should be true it is difficult to explain. Perhaps it is due to an equalizing act of justice, an attempt to compensate for dynamic weakness by static strength. It may be perhaps that the b-file enters into the question. At any rate experience has shown that the doubled c-pawn does favor holding out.

In this tenacity we see the one real strength of the doubled pawn. See my game against Haakanson in the next section and further those against Rosselli and Johner (Illustrative games Nos. 34 and 35).

♦ *2. The most familiar doubled pawn complexes (for short double-complexes) are passed in review. The double complex as an instrument of attack.*

See again Diagram 131. The strongest formation for White is the one reached after he has played d4. This formation should be preserved for as long as possible. After d5, however, White's weakness will make itself felt, so that it is a strategic necessity for Black to force White to this move, and if possible without the aid of c5. For after ...c5, d5 the possibility of putting the question by ...c6 will have gone, and also the chance of occupying the point c5 with a Knight.

In the same position (Diagram 131) many players, having Black, make the mistake of letting loose at once with ...d5, a course which runs counter to our rule, according to which an enemy double complex must first be incited to action. Then and only then may the active (dynamic) weakness of the doubled complex be exploited.

We shall now give some examples which will illustrate the struggle between a defense which is trying to hold out in its position and an attacking force which is seeking to force a decision. First, one in which the defending party (in this case White) by one careless move throws away all of the trumps in his hand.

Haakanson-Nimzowitsch, 1921. **1.d4 Nf6 2.c4 e6 3.Nf3 b6 4.Bg5 h6 5.Bxf6 Qxf6 6.e4 Bb7 7.Nc3 Bb4 8.Qd3 Bxc3+ 9.bxc3 d6** (and now after ...e5 the double complex we have been discussing will have arisen) **10.Qe3 Nd7 11.Bd3 e5 12.0-0 0-0 13.a4 a5 14.Ne1** White stood well, for it is improbable that Black would have been able to force him to a decision (d5). The better plan was 14.Nd2 followed by 15.f3. This would have given the somewhat exposed Qe3 a retreat at f2. There followed **14...Rae8 15.f3 Qe6!** and now White should have gritted his teeth and played 16.d5, but instead he played **16.Nc2** and after **16...exd4! 17.cxd4 f5! 18.d5 Qe5 19.Qd4 Nc5 20.Rad1 fxe4 21.fxe4 Nxd3 22.Rxd3 Qxe4** lost a pawn and with it the game.

The next example is of much heavier metal and is taken from the game Janowsky-Nimzowitsch, Petrograd, 1914. **1.d4 Nf6 2.c4 e6 3.Nc3 Bb4 4.e3 b6**

#133 Janowsky-Nimzowitsch Black
on the move fights against White's
effort to maintain his pawn position.

5.Bd3 Bb7 6.Nf3 Bxc3+ 7.bxc3 d6 8.Qc2 Nbd7 9.e4 e5 10.0-0 0-0 11.Bg5 h6 12.Bd2 Re8 13.Rae1 (Diagram 133) How can Black force White to take action in the center? **13...Nh7** Another possibility was: 13...Nf8 14.h3 Ng6 15.Nh2 Re7! and if now 16.f4 exf4 17.Bxf4 Qe8 and White has no way of comfortably defending the e4 pawn. **14.h3 Nhf8 15.Nh2 Ne6! 16.Be3** (holding on!) **16...c5** (he sees no other way of breaking his opponent's obstinacy) **17.d5 Nf4! 18.Be2 Nf8** and the weakness of c4 and Black's possession of the point f4 offer him chances of attack on both wings.

Since, as we have seen, it is often very difficult to induce an opponent who is hanging on to this "crouching" position to take action in our sense, it is obvious that we ought only to bring about an enemy double complex if it seems likely that we shall succeed in forcing him out of it. In this connection the following opening will be found extremely instructive.

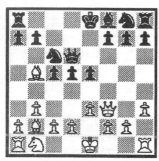

#134
Nimzowitsch-Rosselli
White to move refrains from bringing
about 1.Bxc6+ bxc6, a double
complex in Black's position, as he
recognizes the impossibility of
inducing him to advance his d-pawn,
for in reply to e4, Black would simply
leave the pawn at d5

Nimzowitsch-Rosselli, Baden-Baden, 1925. After the moves **1.Nf3 d5 2.b3 c5 3.e3 Nc6 4.Bb2 Bg4? 5.h3! Bxf3 6.Qxf3 e5 7.Bb5 Qd6** (see Diagram 134). White could here give his opponent a doubled pawn by 8.Bxc6+ bxc6 9.e4. But what would he have gained? How can Black be forced into playing ...d4? White played **8.e4** renouncing the idea for the time being. **8...d4** but now with the advance ...d4 already made, the doubled complex is highly desirable for White to force. To this end White played **9.Na3** (threatening 10.Nc4 Qc7 11.Bxc6+ bxc6), and the game proceeded: **9...f6! 10.Nc4 Qd7 11.Qh5+ g6 12.Qf3 Qc7** (12...0-0-0 13.Na5 Nge7 14.Qxf6) **13.Qg4**, and the diagonal c8-h3 soon led to Black's resigning himself to the doubled pawn in order to be rid of other unpleasantness. For the entire game see Illustrative game No. 34.

If saddled with a double complex, the player has to take into account the fact that its mobility is very limited, and therefore must suit his moves to the occasion, artfully formulated to bear on both sides. What is meant by this will appear from the following examples.

Nimzowitsch-Samisch, Dresden 1926. After the moves **1.c4 e5 2.Nc3 Nf6 3.Nf3 Nc6 4.e4 Bb4 5.d3 d6 6.g3 Bg4 7.Be2 h6 8.Be3 Bxc3+ 9.bxc3 Qd7**. White was fully conscious of the dynamic weakness of his double complex, and accordingly he made his plan to let the d-pawn persist at d3 or at most d4. Observe the artful little moves of the White pieces, which suit the conditions created by the pawn configuration in the center. With small working capital (and the slight mobility of White's pawns is analogous to this), the greatest economy is necessary. The continuation was **10.Qc2! O-O 11.Qd2!** If he had at once played 10.Qd2 the answer would have been 10...0-0-0, and the White Queen would have been very awkwardly placed at d2. After 10.Qc2 the answer 10...0-0-0 would have been met by 11.0-0 followed by Rfb1 and White would have had a fine ensemble, the Qc2 being not the least contributing factor, **11...Nh7 12.h3! Bxh3** (12...Bxf3!, but White with the Bishops is better) **13.Ng1 Bg4 14.f3 Be6 15.d4** and White won a piece and the game.

We have now submitted the doubled pawn complex to a very searching analysis. Viewed in the light of this analysis many incidents of daily occurrence appear under a new aspect. In the position in Diagram 135, reached after the moves **1.e4 e5 2.Nf3 Nc6 3.Nc3 Nf6 4.Bb5 Bb4 5.O-O O-O 6.d3 d6 7.Bg5 Bxc3 8.bxc3 Qe7 9.Re1 Nd8 10.d4**, White is said to have the attacking position in the center. This is not true in my view. It would be true if a White pawn were at b2 instead of c2. As it is, the apparently attacking position of the d4 pawn has only the deep purpose of hiding the weakness in his own camp, namely the doubled c-pawns. Once d5 has taken place this (dynamic) weakness would be evident. Therefore the pawn configuration we have in Diagram 135 will be regarded by one who has thought the matter out as a crouching position. The game proceeded **10...Ne6 11.Bc1 c6** (11...c5 was correct here. After 12.dxe5 dxe5 13.Nxe5? Nc7) **12.Bf1 Rd8 13.g3 Qc7 14.Nh4** (and White intends to play 15.f4. So did White have the initiative in the center?! No, the situation is this - since Black at his 11th move did not take the opportunity to bother his opponent, White could, out of his crouching position, build up an attack, but originally

#135
White's attacking position in the center has here helped conceal his own dynamic weaknesses (c2 and c3). His position must therefore be regarded as a "crouching" one.

it was in fact such a position. The continuation was: (we are following the excellent game Spielmann-Rubinstein, Carlsbad, 1911) **14...d5 15.f4! exf4 16.e5 Ne4 17.gxf4 f5 18.exf6 e.p. Nxf6 19.f5 Nf8 20.Qf3** and Spielmann won in brilliant style - **20...Qf7 21.Bd3 Bd7 22.Bf4 Re8 23.Be5 c5 24.Kh1 c4 25.Be2 Bc6 26.Qf4 N8d7 27.Bf3 Re7 28.Re2 Rf8 29.Rg1 Qe8 30.Reg2 Rff7 31.Qh6! Kf8 32.Ng6+.** Breaking through brilliantly. **32...hxg6 33.Qh8+ Ng8 34.Bd6.** Black, hemmed in and pinned all over, has nothing left to oppose an invasion at g8 via the g-file. **34...Qd8 35.Rxg6 Ndf6 36.Rxf6! Rxf6 37.Rxg7!** and Black resigned.

We now pass to a consideration of the next species of double complex. See Diagrams 136a and 136b. These positions are very similar, the White center pawn

#136a

#136b

being on e4 or d4 according to Black's double complex on the Queenside or Kingside. The importance of this pawn configuration lies in the fact that Black may regard his c6 pawn (or f6 pawn) as compensation for his lost center, since either pawn has an action towards the center. This action finds expression in the fact that White, (in Diagram 136b) cannot use e5 as an outpost station. Furthermore, Black has the threat of ...e5, and also the possibility of ...f5 ...f4 ...Rg8 (White would here play g3), ...h5, ...f4 and ...h4. In other words, the pawn mass e6, f6, and f7, which in the first instance is defensive in its action, can deploy and be thrown forward to the attack. Its weakness lies in the isolated h-pawn. White will seek to neutralize the attack we have outlined (Black's ...Rg8, ...f5, etc.) by posting his pawns at f4, g3, and h2 with perhaps Knights at f3 and g2. The game would then be equal. It is, however, extremely difficult for Black to decide the fitting moment when to emerge from the defensive with ...f5. We give here an example -

Nimzowitsch-Dr. Perlis, Ostend, 1907. **1.e4 e6 2.d4 d5 3.Nc3 Nf6 4.Bg5 dxe4 5.Nxe4 Be7 6.Bxf6 gxf6 7.Nf3 Nd7 8.Qd2 Rg8.** This move could have been postponed **9.0-0-0 Nf8** (protects the weak, isolated h-pawn) **10.c4 c6 11.g3 Qc7 12.Bg2 b6 13.Rhe1 Bb7 14.Kb1 0-0-0.** Dr. Perlis has very skillfully turned the defensive strength of his "complex" to good use, and will soon see the moment ripe to let his double complex appear as an attacking weapon. **15.Nc3 Kb8.** See Diagram 137. **16.Qe3** (White feels the lack of an outpost station on e5 painfully) **16...Ng6** (already ...f5-f4 is threatened, for the Knight is now watching e5) **17.h4 f5 18.Ne5** (finally!) **18...f4! 19.Qf3 Nxe5 20.dxe5 fxg3 21.fxg3 Bb4** with an equal game. **22.a3 Bxc3 23.Qxc3 c5 24.Bxb7 Qxb7 25.Rd6 Rxd6 26.exd6 Rd8 27.Rd1 Qe4+ 28.Ka2 Rd7** and the game was abandoned as a draw two moves later.

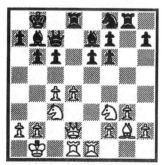

#137
Black has exploited his pawn complex defensively. White cannot use the square e5 as an outpost station

The treatment of the problem was less convincing in the game Yates-Dr. Olland, Scheveningen, 1913. **1.e4 e6 2.d4 d5 3.Nc3 Nf6 4.Bg5 dxe4 5.Bxf6?** (5.Nxe4 should have been played first) **5...gxf6 6.Nxe4 f5?** (the moment for the advance seems premature. The construction of the characteristic position [pawn skeleton] by means of ...b6 ...c6 ...Nd7 ...Qc7 ...Bb7, and ...0-0-0, similar to the previous game, was a better plan). **7.Nc3 Bg7** (the Bg7 now undertakes the protection of the point e5, but the f-pawn [now pushed] would have made a better watchman) **8.Nf3 0-0** (if 8...Nc6 [my recommendation] 9.Bb5 0-0 10.Bxc6 bxc6 11.Qd3! Rb8 12.0-0-0, and any Black attempt at attack would probably fail because of a White invasion of e5. For example 12...Qe7 13.Ne5 Qb4 14.b3, etc) **9.Bc4?** (9.Qd2 followed by 10.0-0-0 was better) **9...b6?** (9...Nc6 10.Ne2 e5! 11.dxe5 Nxe5 would have given the Black Bishops maneuvering space. i.e. 12.Nxe5 Bxe5 13.c3 Be6 and Black stands well. The important point is that the chance of playing ...e5 arose. See introductory remarks to Diagrams 136a, 136b). **10.Qd3 Bb7 11.0-0-0 Nd7 12.Rhe1 Qf6 13.Kb1 Rad8 14.Qe3 c5?** (14...c6 seems better, in order to hold White's d-pawn in check, while at the same time preparing ...b5 followed by ...Nb6. The move 6...f5? has not turned out well. Black's pawn mass came to nothing, and the pawn push g4 is in the air for White). **15.d5 e5 16.g4** (White should have been happy with the passed d-pawn in this position. Best would have been maneuvering to restrain the Black e-pawn by Nd2 and f3. White would then stand well. The move 16.g4 leads to great complications) **16...fxg4 17.Ng5 Bh6 18.Nce4 Qg6 19.f4 exf4 20.Qxf4** and after further mistakes on Black's part White won in 44 moves.

In the game just given Black's double complex did not make itself felt as an instrument of attack. The case is quite otherwise in the following game, in which it is true we have to do with the complex of pawns c7, c6, d6 vs. c2, e4. We may regard this position as wholly identical in characteristics to the skeleton positions of Diagrams 136a and 136b.

Teichmann-Bernstein, Petrograd, 1914. **1.e4 e5 2.Nf3 Nc6 3.Nc3 Nf6 4.Bb5 d6 5.d4 Bd7 6.0-0 Be7 7.Re1 exd4 8.Nxd4 0-0 9.Bxc6 bxc6 10.b3 Re8** (Diagram 137a. In addition to the problem of how to take proper advantage of his double complex, Black has another problem to solve, the restraint of the free enemy center) **11.Bb2 Bf8 12.Qd3 g6 13.Rad1 Bg7 14.f3** (forgoing the chance of attaining, by the move f4, the aggressive development of his center, he strives for a secure position) **14...Qb8** (the final measures are taken to make the effect of the intended ...f5 a powerful one) **15.Bc1 Qb6** (better, according to Dr. Lasker was 15...a5, [threatening 16...a4!] 16.Na4! c5. If 16.a4, comes 16...c5 17.Ndb5 Bc6 followed by ...Nd7 with a

#137a
Teichmann-Bernstein
Petrograd, 1914

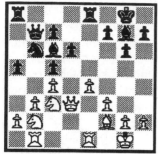

#138 Aggressive utilization of the complex. White can get his outpost station at d5.. Observe the appropriate measures taken in support of and against ...a4

good game for the second player). **16.Na4 Qb7 17.Nb2! c5 18.Ne2 Bb5 19.c4 Bc6 20.Nc3** The text aims at stopping ...a5-a4. White is unable to play a4 as the b-pawn, a sick, weak child would rob him of any winning chances. **20...Nd7 21.Be3 Nb6 22.Rb1 a5 23.Bf2.** (Diagram 138). Now 23...Qc8 should be played, for then 24...a4 is threatened. The reply to 24.Nd5 would be 24...Nxd5 25.cxd5 Bd7 followed by ...a4. Other trumps, besides 24.Nd5, White hardly possesses. The impression we gain is this. Black's ...c5 frees the square for White to play Nd5 at some point, as is therefore somewhat two-edged. If however, the primary condition to be satisfied is to keep the White e-pawn under restraint, and if an effective parry is in readiness to meet a possible Nd5, then the thrust ...c5 may be justified. The counter structure chosen in this game, White's pawns at c4, b3, a2, with Knights at b2 and c3, I consider sound, but insufficient to win. Games by the strongest players in these lines have recently all lead to draws.

On the other hand we hold the development ...d5 to be bad, since it may easily provoke menacing restraints. The following instructive game illustrates this. Billecard-Dr. Bernstein, Ostend, 1907. **1.e4 e5 2.Nf3 Nc6 3.Nc3 Nf6 4.Bb5 d6 5.d4 exd4 6.Nxd4 Bd7 7.0-0 Be7 8.Bxc6 bxc6 9.b3 0-0 10.Bb2 d5 11.e5 Ne8 12.Qd2!** (White correctly thinks that the doubled Black pawns will get no stronger by advancing) **12...c5 13.Nde2 c6 14.Rad1 Qc7 15.Nf4 Qb7** (a Knight capture on d5 was threatened). **16.Na4** (Diagram 138a. This move ushers in a blockade by the occupation of the point c5. The effect of a White Knight on c5 would be very unpleasant. It would be crippling for Black were his pawns still on c7, c6, d5) **16...c4 17.Bd4 cxb3 18.axb3?** (more logical seems 18.cxb3) **18...Nc7 19.Nd3 Ne6 20.Ndc5 Qc7 21.Nxd7 Qxd7 22.Qe3 Nxd4 23.Qxd4 Rab8 24.Nc5 Qf5 25.Nd3.** White dominates the point c5, but had he played 18.cxb3, the pressure on the open c-file would have been appreciably strengthened. With this 10...d5 seems to be refuted. The student who is interested in the deeper logical connections will now say to himself: "How easy

#138a

the complex c7, c6, d5 must be to blockade, for Black succeeded in undoubling the pawns, in addition White made a serious mistake (18.axb3? instead of cxb3), and yet the mobility of Black's c6 and d5 pawns remained as slight as it was before!" This calculation is in fact correct. The pawns c7, c6, d5 are very susceptible indeed to blockade. In other words the "affinity" between the doubled pawn and restraint which we emphasized at the beginning of this Chapter may already be accepted as probable. As we go on the probability is likely to be turned into a certainty. See game No. 12, Leonhardt-Nimzowitsch.

♦ *3. Restraint. The "mysterious" Rook moves. On true and imitation freeing moves, and how they are to be combated.*

#139
Blackburne-Nimzowitsch, 1914
Black makes the "mysterious"
Rook move ...Re8.

#139a

In Diagram 139 White clearly intends to play d4 at any moment when this move seems feasible. Black's moving his Rook to e8 is intended to help make this freeing move difficult to execute for all time. We have here therefore an interest in preventive action. It is only the outer form of the move which is mysterious (a Rook seizing a file which is still closed). Its strategic purpose is more clear. To demand of a piece only direct attacking activity is the stamp of the mere "woodpusher". The sharper chess mind quite rightly demands of the pieces that they also undertake preventive action. The following situation is typical: A freeing action (usually a pawn advance) planned by the opponent would give us an open file. The potential of the opening of this file, which is not in our power, we nevertheless seize, and in advance, with the idea of giving our opponent a distaste for the freeing action. The "mysterious" Rook move is an indisputable ingredient of a rational strategy. See Diagram 139a. The position is a constructed one, in the opening stage of a game, and White plays 1.Rfd1. He expects ...c5 to be played at an opportune moment, and intends in this case after dxc5 and ...bxc5, to take advantage of the c and d-files, bringing pressure on the resulting hanging pawns (on c5 and d5).

The "mysterious" Rook move is generally an affair of the opening, though in the early stages of the middlegame it also plays an important role. In Diagram 140 Black calmly plays 1...Ra7. If White now plays 2.a3 then 2...Rfa8. Now White can only realize his plan to play b4 and c5 at the cost of certain concessions to his opponent.

#140

Black tries by ...Ra7 and ...Rfa8
to prevent or reduce the effect of
White's intended plan of a3, followed
by b4 and c5

#141

Black (Capablanca) starts a preventive action against g4, and carries it
out with great virtuosity

The line might run as follows: **1...Ra7 2.a3 Rfa8 3.Qb2 Qd8 4.b4 axb4 5.axb4 Qb8 6.Rfb1** (6.Rxa7? Qxa7, and Black keeps control of the a-file) **6...Kf8 7.c5 bxc5 8.Rxa7 Rxa7 9.bxc5 Qxb2 10.Rxb2 Ra3 11.Rc2 Bc8! 12.c6!** (Best. Not 12.cxd6 cxd6 13.Nb5 Ra1+ 14.Kf2 Ba6 and the game is about equal) **12...Ne8** followed by ...f5 with some counterplay.

A further example (Diagram 141) is taken from an actual game, Kupchik-Capablanca, Lake Hopatcong, 1926. After White's 19th move the position shown in the diagram was reached. The pawn chain calls for a Black attack on its base, the White c3 pawn, by the moves ...a6, ...b5, ...a5, and ...b4. Black must, however guard himself against the possibility of White playing the move g4. With this idea in mind, Black played **19...h5! 20.Ref1 Rh6!!** (the "mysterious" Rook move, for Black sees White's h3 and g4 coming, and he wants to be ready to attack on the h-file when this happens) **21.Be1 g6 22.Bh4 Kf7! 23.Qe1 a6** (the right moment!) **24.Ba4 b5 25.Bd1 Bc6 26.Rh3** (a defensive move on the Queenside was indicated here) **26...a5 27.Bg5 Rhh8 28.Qh4 b4 29.Qe1** (or 29.Bf6 Be7) **29...Rb8 30.Rhf3 a4** and Black pushed his attack home. **31.R3f2 a3 32.b3 cxb3 33.Bxb3 Bb5 34.Rg1 Qxc3**. The Rook maneuver in this game (Rf6-h6-h8) stands out with plastic effect and must give pleasure to anyone who plays through the game.

In Diagram 141a (from the Game Gottschall-Nimzowitsch, Hanover, 1926), Black wanted to take advantage of his majority on the Kingside by the maneuver ...Kg6-f5 followed by ...e5. On Black's ...Kg6, however, White would play g4. I therefore chose the "mysterious" Rook move (even in an endgame this is possible!) **28...Rh8!** and after the further moves **29.Rd1 Kg6 30.Rd4 Kf5 31.Bd2**, there again followed a "mysterious" Rook move **31...Rf8**, which we might more accurately call "semi-mysterious," for while ...Rh8 followed merely preventive ends, ...Rf8 has this essential difference, that its nature is purely active, there followed **32.Be1 e5 33.fxe5**

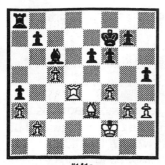

#141a
Gottschall-Nimzowitsch
Hanover, 1926

fxe5 34.Rh4 g5 35.Rb4 (35.Rxh5?? Kg6+) **35...Ke6+ 36.Ke2 e4 37.Bf2 Rf3.** The passed pawn, the penetration of the Rook into the enemy position, and a certain weakness in White's c-pawn slowly wrought the destruction of White's game.

The "mysterious" Rook move, places our Rook on a closed file, which can only be opened by the enemy himself (and if he does not our Rook is left standing there with nothing to do). Such a move must never be played, except consciously and with the intention of sacrificing some of the Rook's effective strength. This sacrifice is made in order to prevent an enemy freeing maneuver, or at any rate to render it difficult. If we, however, recognize a freeing move planned by our opponent as illusory, and not really having a freeing effect, then it would be in the most uneconomical to make such a sacrifice. In the game which was quoted earlier, Blackburne-Nimzowitsch, the difference between a true and illusory freeing move leaps to the eyes, and as it is also pertinent to our conception of prophylactic strategy we give it in full in the Games Section (No. 32). The student is advised to play through it before proceeding further.

The following postulate I regard as of the utmost importance: <u>There is no such thing as an absolute freeing move</u>. A freeing move in a position in which development has not been carried far always proves to be illusory, and vice versa, a move which does not come at all in the category of freeing moves, can, given a surplus of tempi to our credit, lead to a very free game.

Consider for instance the position in Diagram 142. White obviously has a substantial plus in tempi, and in these circumstances the Black freeing move ...f5, only leads to a premature opening of Black's undeveloped game. For example 1...f5 2.exf5 gxf5 3.Nh5 followed by f4 with a strong attack. This association of ideas was unknown to the pseudo-classical school, which knew only absolute freeing moves. Black's ...f5 in a position with the central pawn configuration as in the diagram was reckoned as such by this school, and in 80% of cases was held worthy of commendation. We have reduced the proportion to about 60%, for even after the defensive White move 3.f3 (after 1...f5 2.exf5 gxf5) the strength of the pair of Black pawns at e5 and f5 must not be rated too high. With this we suddenly

#142
Black's "freeing" move ...f5 leads,
owing to his backward development,
to a premature opening of the
game and an unfavorable position for
the second player

find ourselves facing the germcell of restraint action. Because of its importance, a separate section will be devoted.

◆ *4. The germcell of restraint action directed against a pawn majority is developed. The fight against a central majority. The qualitative majority.*

I find it impossible to present the germcell of restraint by means of diagrams, so I will adopt another method. Black, shall we say, has a majority: pawns a5 and b5 against White's pawn a3, or perhaps Black pawns e5, f5 vs. White's f3. In both cases Black threatens to create a passed pawn, and in the second to attack White's castled position by the wedge ...f4 in conjunction with ...Rf5-h5, etc. The idea of the restraint now lies in the plan of neutralizing the enemy's pawn, plus by means of the open e-file and two different blockade points. In the position under consideration, the possessor of the pawn majority has two threats at his disposal. One consists in the advance ...e4, the other in the wedge ...f4, supplemented perhaps by the diversion ...Rf5-h5 or ...Rf5-g5, or possibly ...h5. At the same time the establishment of a Black Knight at e3 will be planned.

In what does the restraint idea now consist? In the case of ...e4, the move f4, followed by an eventual Be3 to blockade Black's e-pawn at that point, and on the other hand if Black should advance ...f4, the idea is to stop any further advance by Ne4. This Knight, thanks to his radius of action, will help make Black's diversion difficult to carry out. It follows that we must look for the germcell of restraint action in an open file combined with a two-fold possibility of setting up a blockade.

A central majority must not be allowed to advance too far, otherwise the wedge threat would have a much too painful effect. For example in the position White: Kg1, pawns f2, g2, h2. Black: pawns e4, f4, g7, h7 (imagine any number of pieces added.) Black with ...f3 (the wedge) threatens to cut the White lines of communication between his h and g pawns along the rest of his 2nd rank, and Black's attack must be reckoned as very strong. It is therefore necessary to fix an enemy central majority on its 4th rank - with the configuration Black: pawns e5, f5. White: pawn f3.

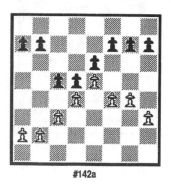

#142a

The conception of the qualitative majority is an easy one to assimilate by anyone who has mastered the pawn chain. In Diagram 142a, White has the qualitative majority on the Kingside, Black on the Queenside. The majority which is the more advanced toward the enemy base is naturally regarded as qualitatively the superior one.

◆ *5. The different forms under which restraint customarily appears are further illustrated. (a) The fight against mobile center pawns. (b) The restraint of a qualitative majority. (c) Restraint of double complexes. (d) My "special variation" and its restraint motif.*

(a) The mobile center pawn. White with an e4 pawn against Black's pawns at d6 and f7. Such a pawn can result from **1.e4 e5 2.Nf3 Nc6 3.Bb5 d6 4.d4 exd4 5.Nxd4 Bd7**. Black's restraint operation will be begun by ...Nf6 ...Be7 ...0-0 ...Re8 and ...Bf8. Another important aid towards the crippling of White's center is the more passive pawn structure with pawns at d6 and f6. The position White: pawn e4. Black: Pawns at d6, f6 is typical and I call it the "sawing" position, since White's e-pawn is to be sawed up between these pawns.

The sequence of events in a maneuver directed against a mobile center is usually: (1) the passive "sawing" position, then (2) the more aggressive hindering action of a Rook exerting pressure on it, (3) making backward or isolated a once mobile center pawn, (4) mechanical stopping of the same by a blockading piece, (5) the winning of the pawn.

The aim of the restraining party in a game may be sufficiently summed up thus: First restrain, next blockade, lastly destroy! To carry this out is difficult but remunerative, and the process is instructive for the student. The analysis, therefore, of the position reached after **1.e4 e5 2.Nf3 d6 3.d4 exd4 4.Nxd4** is excellent training, and as such cannot be too strongly recommended to the aspiring student of chess.

The following illustrative game is apparently complicated, but it is this in its motives only. In reality it is the fight against White's e4 pawn, which dominates. Shoosmith-Nimzowitsch, Ostend, 1907. **1.d4 Nf6 2.c4 d6 3.Nf3 Nbd7 4.Nc3 e5 5.e4 Be7 6.Bd3 0-0 7.0-0 exd4!** (if 7...Re8, then 8.d5 and Black will be cramped for a long time. For example, 7...Re8 8.d5 Nc5 9.Be3 Nxd3 10.Qxd3 Nd7 11.b4 a5 12.a3, etc) **8.Nxd4 Re8 9.b3 Ne5 10.Bc2 a6** (this advance will soon be intelligible) **11.Bb2 Bd7 12.h3 Bf8 13.f4 Ng6 14.Qf3 c6 15.Rae1 b5** (now the situation is clear: Black keeps an eye on White's e-pawn and seeks at the same time to be rid of the disturbing c-pawn, since the latter makes his d6 pawn backward) **16.Qd3 Qc7 17.Kh1 Rad8 18.Bb1 b4!!** (Diagram 142b. This has to do with a chain formation, certainly a rather unusual one. This plan for the links of the chain would be White's pawns on b3, and c4, Black's pawn on b4 and Knight on c5! Why as an exception should we not allow an officer to play the role of a pawn in a chain? The plan consists in the maneuver ...Bc8 ...Nd7-c5 and ...a5-a4 attacking the enemy pawn base at b3. Accordingly 18...b4!! involved the

#142b
Shoosmith-Nimzowitsch
Ostend, 1907

transference of the attack from c4 to b3) **19.Nd1 Bc8 20.Qf3 Nd7 21.Nf5 Nc5 22.g4?** (a mistake which leaves f4 for a moment insufficiently defended, but this short moment is long enough to allow Black to break through brilliantly) **22...Ne6 23.Qg3 Bb7 24.h4 d5 25.e5 c5 26.cxd5 Rxd5 27.Kg1** (27.Be4? Rxd1!) **27...Rd2 28.Nfe3 Qc6** and White resigned.

The reader may here be referred to my games against Teichmann and Blackburne (Nos. 2 and 32).

(b) The fight against a qualitative majority. Let us imagine that in Diagram 140 the Black Knight is at c5 instead of f6. We would then have a typical case of the restraint of a qualitative majority. If now 1.Nxc5, then 1...bxc5 and White's advance is crippled. If however, 1.a3 intending 2.b4, then 1...a4! 2.b4 Nb3! and this strongly posted Knight is compensation for White's possibility of playing c5. The student should notice that the action of Black's a-pawn is made up of equal parts of passive and aggressive effect, for this pawn, or the pawn on h5 in Diagram 143, is the true prop of our whole restraint maneuver. In both positions White's a3 (or h3) will be answered by pushing the flank pawn to the fourth rank (...a4 or ...h4).

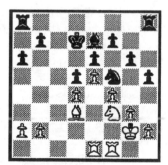

#143
White's qualitative majority appears
to be held in restraint. 1.h3 will be
effectively met by 1...h4, and
on 2.g4 comes 2...Ng3

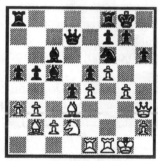

#144
Van Vliet-Nimzowitsch

Another typical example is shown in the following endgame. (Diagram 144). Here the advance in close formation planned by White, namely Qg3, h4, g5, cannot be held up permanently. This advance (let us imagine for a moment that Black's inevitable ...f6 has taken place) would expose the base of Black's pawn chain. Much worse for Black, however, would be the Kingside attack that is involved in this advance. The right plan for Black would be to hold up White's h4 and g5 long enough for his King to escape. With this idea Black played **21...Nh7 22.Nf3 Qe7 23.Qg3 Rfe8 24.h4 f6 25.Ra1** (White has weaknesses, too) **25...Qb7 26.Rfe1 Kf7! 27.Re2** (if 27.g5, then 27...hxg5 28.hxg5 Ke7! with a tenable game) **27...Rh8!** (the "mysterious"

Rook move!) **28.Kf2 Nf8 29.g5 hxg5 30.hxg5 Nd7**
(White's Kingside attack may be said to have spent
itself, for after 31.gxf6 gxf6 32.Qg6+ Ke7 33.Qg7+ Kd6,
Black would have a superb game). The game
proceeded: **31.gxf6 gxf6 32.Nh4 Rag8 33.Ng6 Rh5
34.Rg1 Rg5** with advantage to Black. The resource
demonstrated here is worth the attention of the student.

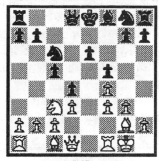

(c) Restraint of double complexes. Side by side with
the dynamic weakness of such a complex, which we
have often emphasized, we have to characterize the
following points as often decisive: (1) the imprisoned
Bishop (2) cramped terrain and consequent difficulties
in finding a defense.

Bird's opening and the English will give us examples of (1) and in both forms of
the opening.

1.f4 d5 2.Nf3 c5 3.d3 Nc6 4.Nc3 Bg4! 5.g3 Bxf3!! 6.exf3 e6 7.Bg2 f5! 8.0-0 d4
(delightful play; the Bishop at g2 is now a prisoner in his own camp. Black's weakness
at e6 is easily defended. See Diagram 145) **9.Nb1 b5 10.a4 b4 11.Nd2 Na5 12.Qe2
Kf7 13.Re1 Qd7 14.Nc4 Nxc4 15.dxc4 Nf6** and Black dictated the tempo.

1.e3 e5 2.c4 Nf6 3.Nc3 Nc6 4.Nf3 Bb4 5.Be2 (if 5.d4 exd4 6.exd4 d5 7.Be2 with
an equal game) **5...0-0 6.0-0 Re8 7.a3 Bxc3 8.bxc3 d6** and White labored the whole
game through under the difficulty of making use of his Queen Bishop. (From the
game Nimzowitsch-Reti, Breslau, 1925).

Diagrams 146 and 147 are given to illustrate (2). The
latter shows us a blockading Knight whose effect on the
double complex is simply enormous. Not only is
Black's majority in its collective value illusory, but each
single component of that majority seems individually to
have its life threatened. Under these conditions
White's majority will unquestionably win. Even with
Rooks present on both sides of the board (White: Rook
on a4, Black: Rook on d8 or b6), the game would be
lost for Black. This shows to what degree a restrained
doubled pawn may cripple a position.

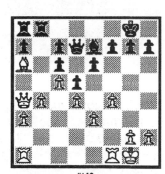

(d) My "special variation" with its restraint motif. The
line of play in question is **1.c4 e5 2.Nc3 Nf6 3.Nf3 Nc6**
and now **4.e4**. As early as 1924 I had tried (after the

#147
The effect of a Knight blockading
an enemy doubled pawn
complex is crushing

moves 1.f4 c5 2.e4 Nc6 3.d3 g6), the move 4.c4, the motive of which I visualized as a blockade spanning half the board, and in a review I made the following note to this move: "Since this move is not inspired by the hope of preventing or even of making ...d5 more difficult, a special explanation is needed. Black wishes to build up the configuration e6-d5. This done, he will consider the extension of his attack formation to the Queenside by ...Nd4 when opportunity offers, in order after Nxd4 ...cxd4, to bring pressure on the c-file to the point c2. The text move is made to forestall this possible extension of play on the Queenside. The hole at d4 does not seem to be a serious matter."

When I today ask myself where I got the moral courage to form a plan running counter to all tradition, I think I may answer that it was only my intense preoccupation with the problem of the blockade which helped me do so. To this problem I was ever seeking to bring out new sides, and so in Dresden, 1926, as Black after the moves 1.e4 c5 2.Nf3 Nc6 3.Nc3, I ventured the move 3...e5, which at that time caused a huge sensation. My special variation given above is to be considered merely a further step on a trail which had already been broken. The able Danish theorist Dr. O. H. Krause, has pursued an original inquiry into the possibility of a combination of e4 and c4, in which, independently of my analysis, he has arrived at much the same conclusions as I did.

The student is advised to study games No. 33-35 at this point.

CHAPTER 12

THE ISOLATED d-PAWN AND ITS DESCENDANTS

♦ *1. Introductory*

The problem of the isolated d-pawn is in my opinion one of the fundamental problems in the whole theory of positional play. We are concerned with the appraisal of a statically weak pawn, which, even though weak, is permeated with dynamic strength. Which is dominant, the static weakness or the dynamic strength? The problem gains in significance, in fact it strays in a sense beyond the circumscribed boundaries of chess.

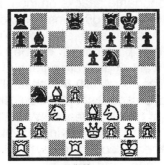

#148
The isolated d-pawn. Notice White's
outpost station at e5, Black's at d5

#149
Skeleton diagram of the isolated
d-pawn. White outposts at c5 and e5.
Black outpost at d5

It is indispensable that the student face this problem himself, meaning that he must experience the problem head-on in actual play. He should try as White to get the so-called normal position in the Queen's Gambit. **1.d4 d5 2.Nf3 Nf6 3.c4 e6 4.e3 c5 5.Nc3 Nc6** and then alternately, in one game **6.Bd3 cxd4 7.exd4 dxc4 8.Bxc4** and White has an "isolani", in the other, **6.cxd5 exd5 7.dxc5 Bxc5**, and White now is fighting against the isolani. It will do him good to realize how dangerous an enemy isolani may be, and how difficult it is to save his own from an untimely end.

♦ *2. The dynamic strength of the isolated d-pawn.*

The strength of an isolani (Diagram 149) lies in its lust to expand (advance). In addition to the circumstance, this pawn protects and indeed creates the White outpost stations at e5 and c5. On the contrary, the Black outpost station at d5 does not have, at any rate in the middlegame, the full equivalent value. Quite apart from any arithmetical preponderance (two outposts to one), White can point to the fact that a Knight on e5 (see Diagram 148) would have a sharper effect than is ever possible to an opposing Knight on d5. It is clear that a Ne5 supported by two powerful Bishop diagonals (b1-h7 and h4-d8) must exert pressure on Black's Kingside, and what can be sharper than an attack on the King? The lineal investigation yields therefore an undoubted plus to White.

Our pawn, on the other hand, as is well known, tends to become weak in the endgame. How are we to understand this? Is the difficulty only this, that the d-pawn is hard to defend, or are there other calamities in store?

♦ *3. The isolani as an endgame weakness.*

Our judgment on the problem, which we have outlined must be influenced by the circumstance that the points e5 and d5 must have a different evaluation in the ending than was the case in the middlegame. In the endgame attacks on the King are not in question, so White's e5 loses much of its glory, while d5 gains in importance for Black. If White has not by the time the ending has come, at least gotten through to c7, or obtained another trump of some sort, his position will not be particularly enviable. White will suffer not only under the want of protection felt by his isolani, but also from the fact that the light squares such as d5, c4, and e4 can easily become weak. Imagine in Diagram 149, a White King at c4 and Bishop at d2; Black with his King at c6 and a Knight d7. Black with a Knight check drives the White King from c4, plays his King to d5, and pushes further forward with his King via c4 or e4. In every pertinent case that may arise d5 must be regarded as the key point of Black's position. With this point as a base he will blockade, centralize, and maneuver. d5 will provide a gate of entry into the enemy position and also a point of junction in all possible troop movements, as for instance (imagine now Diagram 149 enlivened by the presence of Rooks and Knights) the case of Black's Rd8-d5-a5, or Nf6-d5-b4, or finally Nd5-e7-f5xd4. A Black Knight posted at d5 exercises an impressive effect on both wings. A Bishop at d5 not seldom forces a decision even with Bishops of opposite colors (if Rooks remain on both sides). White may obviously have counterbalancing, or even apparently a preponderance of compensation for these trumps of Black's. For instance, one of his Rooks may have penetrated to c7, but such cases can only be considered as exceptions to the rule. To recapitulate: White's weakness in the endgame rests on the fact that d4 seems to be threatened, while d5 is extraordinarily strong for Black. Further, the light squares c4, d5, e4, tend to become weak, while the importance of e5 (from the middlegame) has been spent. White's pawn position was in fact not "compact", (by "not compact" we are describing positions with isolated pawns) and other disadvantages to which we have called attention, such as weakness pervading a complex of squares of a given color, must necessarily attach themselves to a pawn position which is not compact. We earnestly recommend to the student that he sharpen his sense for compact positions and the reverse. He must also bear carefully in mind that it is not only the isolani itself that tends to become weak, but also the complex of squares surrounding it. In this the principal evil is to be found.

♦ *4. The isolani as a weapon of attack in the middlegame.*

Solidity of construction and purpose should at the first sign of neglect on the part of the opponent (if he has withdrawn his pieces from the Kingside) give place to a violent attack. Many players with an isolani proceed much too violently, but it seems to me that there is no objective motive for "plunging" on a desperate attack. At first the utmost solidity is called for. The attack will come of itself in good time, for instance when Black has withdrawn his Nf6, which he will at some time naturally do, since the Knight wants to get to d5. In the development stage (see Diagram 148) we would therefore recommend solid construction, Be3 (not g5), Qe2, Rooks c1 and d1 (not d1 and e1), Bd3 or b1 (not b3); and White cannot be too strongly warned against attempting surprise attacks in the early stages, started by perhaps N(e5)xf7 (with a Bishop at a2), or by a Rook sally (Re1- e3-h3). A solid position aimed at maintaining the security of the d4 pawn is the one and only right course, and it must be ever remembered that the Be3 belongs to the d4 pawn as does a nurse to a suckling child! *(Editor's note - nowadays theory does find instances of placing the Bishop on g5, and placing Rooks on d1 and e1 thereby avoiding exchanges on the c-file).*

It is only when Black has withdrawn his pieces from the Kingside that White may sound the attack, and this he may carry out in sacrificial style. (Diagram 150). White has developed his pieces in the spirit of this section, the text move (19...Ne8) gives him the chance which, as in all similar cases, he avidly hurries to launch a direct attack on the enemy King. The result in the present case is doubtful, but since the whole manner of conducting the attack is characteristic of "isolani positions", we give here a few variations. **19...Ne8 20.Qh5 g6** (20...f5 21.Bg5) **21.Qh6 Ng7** (21...f6 22.Ng4) **22.Bg5** (the pieces now come out of reserve), **22...f6 23.Bxg6 hxg6 24.Nxg6** and now two variations arise according to how the Queen chooses to retreat. If **24...Qd7 25.Bh4!** (or 25.Bxf6 Nxf6 26.Qh8+ Kf7

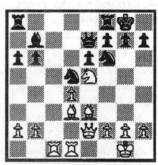

#150 Nimzowitsch-Taubenhaus
Black to move played ...Ne8 (to get to d6). This is the trumpet call for the attack for White. How will the attack be started, and what wll be its course?

27.Ne5+ Ke8 28.Nxd7 Rxh8 29.Nxf6+ with three pawns for the sacrificed piece). If **24...Qd6 25.Qh8+ Kf7 26.Qh7 fxg5 27.Ne5+** and the continuation could be **27...Ke8 28.Qxg7 Qe7 29.Qg6+ Kd8 30.Rc6** with wild complications. So, once more, remember to build up a solid position, support the isolani (Be3) and only attack when the opportunity really is there.

♦ *5. Which cases are favorable for White and which for Black?*

In general it may be said that the two following cases are worth striving for by White:

(i) When White has effected d5, ...exd5; or (after d5) a piece x d5, and White thereby gets the better, because more centralized position (as in the game Rubinstein-Tartakower, Baden-Baden, 1925).

(ii) When White has built up a position on the c-file (see game 36, Nimzowitsch-Taubenhaus).

For Black the following are desirable:

(i) All positions of an endgame character (other things being equal).

(ii) Those positions where Black has played ...N(d5)xN(c3), and White's recapture was bxc3. Black's idea is to pin down the c3 pawn from the start and of laying siege to it (see game 11, Thomas-Alekhine and ♦7 of this chapter on the isolated pawn couple).

♦ *6. On the possible genesis of reflex weaknesses among the Queenside pawns of the player with an isolani.*

#150a

An index of the weakness of the isolani appears in the possibility which is not seldom offered to the opponent, of transferring his attack from the d-pawn to the Queenside. Such a case of "reflex weakness" may be seen in game No. 23 (Rubinstein-Duras). A similar picture as presented in the following game (Rubinstein-Dr. Lasker, Moscow, 1925). After the moves **1.d4 d5 2.c4 c6 3.e3 Nf6 4.Nc3 e6 5.Nf3 Nbd7 6.Bd3 dxc4 7.Bxc4 b5 8.Be2 a6 9.0-0 Bb7 10.b3 Be7 11.Bb2 0-0 12.Ne5 c5 13.Bf3 Qc7 14.Nxd7 Nxd7 15.Ne4 Rad8 16.Rc1 Qb8 17.Qe2 cxd4 18.exd4 Rc8 19.g3 Qa8 20.Kg2 Rfd8 21.Rxc8 Rxc8 22.Rc1 Rxc1 23.Bxc1 h6** Black took advantage strategically of the isolated d4 pawn. The continuation was **24.Bb2 Nb6 25.h3** (since he wants to avoid the exchange of Queens, 25.Qc2 Qc8 would be of no use) **25...Qc8 26.Qd3 Nd5!** (with the idea of 27...Nb4) **27.a3 Nb6!!** (now b3 has become weak!) **28.Kh2 Bd5 29.Kg2 Qc6 30.Nd2 a5! 31.Qc3** (Diagram 150a. In his trouble he decides after all to exchange Queens, but succumbs to the reflex weaknesses which have now arisen) **31...Bxf3+ 32.Nxf3** (if 32.Qxf3 Qc2) **32...Qxc3 33.Bxc3 a4!** (now the weakness of the White Queenside is evident) **34.bxa4 bxa4** and White lost, since the attempt to save himself by **35.Bb4** failed against **35...Bxb4 36.axb4 a3 37.Nd2 Nd5** whereby the approach of the White King via e2, d3, and c4 is prevented (the answer to Ke2 would always be ...Nc3+). What is remarkable in this fine ending, in addition to the transfer of the attack, is the masterly and varied use made of the d5 square.

On the manner of laying siege to an isolani I would make this additional remark, that nowadays it is no longer considered necessary to render an enemy isolani absolutely immobile. On the contrary, we like to give him the illusion of freedom, rather than shut him up in a cage. How this is done is shown in the following game. Lasker (whom we class under the moderns) -Tarrasch, Petrograd, 1914. **1.d4 d5 2.Nf3 c5 3.c4 e6 4.cxd5 exd5 5.g3 Nc6 6.Bg2 Nf6 7.0-0 Be7 8.dxc5 Bxc5 9.Nbd2** and now the isolani has the choice whether he will become weak on d5 or d4. Tarrasch chose the latter and there followed **9...d4 10.Nb3 Bb6 11.Qd3 Be6 12.Rd1 Bxb3 13.Qxb3 Qe7 14.Bd2 0-0 15.a4 Ne4 16.Be1 Rad8 17.a5!! Bc5 18.a6 bxa6** (if 18...b6, then 19.Qa4 threatening 20.b4) **19.Rac1**. Now all the pieces defending d4 are in the air. There followed **19...Rc8 20.Nh4 Bb6 21.Nf5 Qe5 22.Bxe4 Qxe4 23.Nd6** winning the exchange. Taking everything into consideration the isolani can be an effective weapon in the middlegame, but can also become very weak in the endgame.

♦ 7. *The isolated pawn couple.*

In the position on Diagram 151 Black can exchange at c3. If he then in the sequel succeeds in holding back White's c and d-pawns, and finally in blockading them absolutely, his otherwise rather doubtful strategy (...Nxc3) will have been justified, for to have the pawns tied down in their own camp and close to the frontier will be a great worry to White. The one trouble, namely the obligation to keep the c3 and d4 pawns protected, will be aggravated by the other, a cramped terrain. The pawns blockaded on c3 and d4, and only these, are what I call the isolated pawn couple. A good example is seen in game No. 11 (Thomas-Alekhine).

#151
The genesis of an isolated pawn couple, c3, d4 occurs after 1...Nxc3 2.bxc3

An essentially different picture is met when the beleaguered player succeeds in advancing his c-pawn. We then have White pawns on c4 and d4. These pawns we no longer call an "isolated pawn couple", but designate them instead as "hanging pawns".

It will not be difficult to decide where the preference lies between the isolated pawn couple, which as a rule has but slight mobility, and the two hanging pawns. It stands to reason that hanging pawns are much to be preferred, if only for the reason that they imply threats. Even if these should prove to be only apparent threats, a doubtful initiative is always better than a passivity which is dead beyond all manner of doubt, as we have discovered in the case of a blockaded isolated pawn couple in Game No. 11. We have then the following postulate for our guidance: The possessor of an isolated pawn couple (Diagram 151 after the moves ...Nxc3, bxc3) must do everything in his power to make c4 possible. He must not at any cost allow a blockade. He must regard the awkward formation c3, d4 as a transition stage to the mobile structure c4, d4, with its eternal threat of c5 or d5.

We now give an example of the case where Black, (who is saddled with an isolated pawn couple) struggles to make the desirable advance possible. Nimzowitsch-J. Giersing and S. Kinch, Copenhagen, 1924. **1.c4 e5 2.Nf3 Nc6 3.d4 exd4 4.Nxd4 Nf6 5.Nxc6 bxc6 6.g3 d5 7.Bg2 Bb4+ 8.Bd2 Bxd2+ 9.Nxd2 0-0 10.0-0 Rb8 11.Qc2** (White avoids 11.b3, as he wishes to keep this square available for piece maneuvers like Nb3 or Qa4) **11...Re8 12.e3 Be6 13.cxd5** (13.Nb3 dxc4 14.Nd4 was also to be considered), **13...cxd5.** (Diagram 151a). Black now has the isolated pawn couple in question. The pawn formation c7, d5 deserves the designation "isolated" even

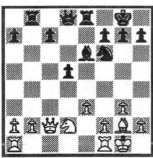

more than c6, d5. Black therefore quite rightly tries to make ...c5 possible. **14.Nb3 Qd6 15.Rfc1 Rec8 16.Qc5 Qxc5 17.Rxc5 Nd7 18.Ra5** (in order on the next move, by 19.Rc1 to establish an enduring blockade) **18...c5!! 19.Rxa7 c4 20.Nd4 Rxb2 21.Nxe6 fxe6 22.Rxd7 c3** (Black has purchased the mobility of his c-pawn at the cost of a minor piece! White cannot force a win). **23.Bh3 c2 24.Bxe6+ Kf8 25.Rf7+ Ke8 26.Bxc8 Rb1+ 27.Kg2 Rxa1** (if 27...c1=Q 28.Rxb1 Qxb1 29.Rf4) **28.Rc7 c1=Q 29.Rxc1 Rxc1** and the game was drawn on the 42nd move.

#151a

♦ *8. Hanging pawns. Their pedigree and what we can learn from it. The advance in a blocked position.*

The evolution, or the story of the genesis of hanging pawns, will be found illustrated in the trio of diagrams 152a, 152b, 152c. A glance at this shows that we are reminded to trace the descent of the hanging pawns from the isolani, and the "family tree" shows very clearly the generations: Isolani, the founder of the family. Isolated pawn couple. Hanging pawns.

This view, of which the soundness is demonstrable, will serve us well, for it will enable us to compare the hanging pawns with their anything but distinct motives, with their grandfather, the isolani whose motives are more plain.

#152a The Isolani

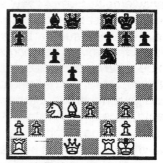

#152b The isolated pawn couple

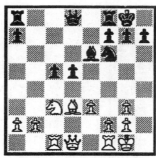

#152c The two hanging pawns

A short study of their family history should help us to a better understanding of one particularly "difficult" member of that family. From their grandfather the hanging pawns have inherited one essential trait, namely that curious mixture of static weakness and dynamic strength. But whereas in the case of an isolani both strength and weakness stand out clearly, with hanging pawns both are masked. In these highly problematical creatures two things only may be considered established. (i) that the two hanging pawns (see Diagram 152c) are "unprotected", meaning not defended by other pawns, and that the bombardment to which, being on open files, they are subjected, will be all the more harassing. (ii) that the possibility of attaining a comparatively secure position in which one of the pawns protects the other (d5, c4, or c5, d4), often presents itself.

The problem however is this: If this possibility, to attain relative security, is only to be bought at the cost of all initiative in the center, if the pawns in gaining this "security" can be blockaded, is it not more advisable to forego this offered security and let them remain "hanging"?

The answer to this is not easy. It depends entirely on the particular circumstances, namely on the manner and the details of the resulting blockade. To talk of the "security" in which such a blockaded complex can bask is greatly to stretch the meaning of the word. This I concede in advance, as blockaded pawns all too easily tend to become weaknesses. It would seem nevertheless, to be entirely fitting, in certain cases, to let the hanging pawns advance in a blocked position. These cases are as follows: (i) When the pawns in the enemy blockading ring are themselves attackable, as is the White b2 pawn in Diagram 152c. (ii) When the blockade would cost the enemy too much, either because the blockading apparatus is too great, or because the blockaders at his disposal prove to be for some reason unfitted for their task, whether for lack of elasticity or as having insufficient threat effect from their positions. As an antithesis to this we may point to Diagrams 153 and 154. Here the

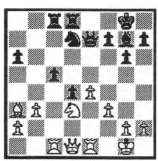

#153
E. Cohn-Duras
Carlsbad, 1911
The "security" achieved by the
hanging pawns was a very relative
one. The c5 pawn is weak even
though the d4 pawn is passed

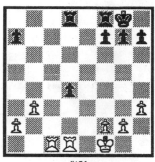

#154
The d4 pawn is the product of two
hanging pawns. Many moves ago
there occurred ...d4, exd4, ...cxd4.
This isolated d-pawn will now be
blockaded by Ke2-d3 and White will
have the advantage

"blockaded" security is shown to be deceptive. The advanced pawns become weak. Again the reason for this lies in the quality of the blockading forces: in Diagrams 153 and 154 the Nd3 and the Kd3 (after Ke2-d3) are respectively excellent blockaders, which sufficiently accounts for the miscarriage of the attempt to save the situation.

The truth seems, therefore, to lie in the following statement of the case: Just as our judgment on the isolani on d4 depended on the greater or lesser degree of initiative to which he could lay claim (of course the outpost station which he supports must have some importance), we also consider that we have the right to expect some measure of initiative in hanging pawns which have attained a "blockaded" security. Dead passivity has no prospects before it.

We will now give some examples:

In the position Rubinstein-Nimzowitsch, (returning to Diagram 152c), there followed **15.Qa4 Qb6** (Black holds tight) **16.Qa3 c4!** (steps into "blockaded" security, but here White's blockading ring is attackable (the b2 pawn). Black's advance was therefore justified). **17.Be2 a5 18.Rfd1 Qb4 19.Rd4 Rfd8 20.Rcd1 Rd7 21.Bf3 Rad8 22.Nb1** (a waiting measure would be better here, 22.R4d2, etc.) **22...Rb8 23.R1d2 Qxa3! 24.Nxa3 Kf8 25.e4** (leads in the end to the loss of a pawn, but White in any case stood badly. The equilibrium which still existed at move 21 has been disturbed. The b2 pawn has now become very weak, whereas the d5 pawn seems overprotected!) **25...dxe4 26.Rxd7 Nxd7 27.Bxe4 Nc5 28.Rd4** (or 28.Bc6! Rb4 29.Bd5 Na4 with advantage to Black) **28...Nxe4 29.Rxe4 Rxb2 30.Nxc4 Rb4 31.Nd6 Rxe4 32.Nxe4 Bxa2** and Black won. For the concluding moves the reader should return to Diagram 66.

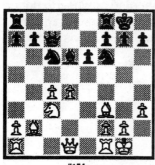
#154a

In master practice the move d5 (from the hanging pawn position c4, d4) occurs much more frequently. It leads quite prettily to the closing of the somewhat original circle, from isolani through the hanging pawns to isolani. The whole point now is whether the isolani which has newly come into existence can maintain itself or not. An example taken from the game Nimzowitsch-Tartakower, Copenhagen, 1923. **1.Nf3 d5 2.b3 c5 3.e3 Nc6 4.Bb2 Bg4 5.Be2 Qc7 6.d4 cxd4 7.exd4 e6 8.0-0 Bd6** (we now have a Queen's Gambit declined with colors reversed) **9.h3 Bxf3 10.Bxf3 Nf6 11.c4! dxc4 12.bxc4 0-0 13.Nc3** (Diagram 154a. The sequence Nd2-b3, Qe2, Rac1, and Rfe1 would here have been in the spirit of holding a tight policy, but I wanted to "realize" my stock-in-trade, by d5) **13...Rfd8 14.Nb5 Qe7 15.Qe2 Bb8 16.d5 exd5 17.Qxe7 Nxe7 18.Bxf6 gxf6 19.cxd5 Be5! 20.Rab1**, and the d-pawn not only managed to maintain itself, but also in the whole further course of the game formed a counterweight to Black's majority on the Queenside which was not to be underestimated. Tartakower did underestimate, and lost.

The game from which Diagram 155 was taken did not run so comfortable a course for the possessor of the hanging pawns. The game proceeded: **17.Qa3 Ne4 18.Rd3 Rfd8 19.Rfd1 Qe6 20.Nd2 Qb6 21.Nf1 Nf6 22.Ng3 Rac8 23.h3 h6 24.Ne2 Rd7 25.Nc3 Qe6 26.Qa5 d4!** (he is tired of the eternal threats and seeks to substitute for the "hanging position" the "blocked

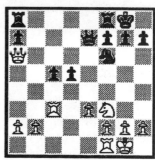
#155
Bernstein-Teichmann
Carlsbad, 1923
Some elegant pirouetting
by Black is seen

---

security" of which we have so often spoken, but it nearly cost him dearly) **27.exd4 cxd4 28.Nb5** (how is the newly arisen isolani to be saved?) **28...Qf5!** (now some dexterous parries follow) **29.Qa4! Rc1! 30.Rxc1 Qxd3 31.Rc8+ Kh7 32.Qc2 Qxc2 33.Rxc2 d3! 34.Rd2** (the isolani still seems to be in danger) **34...Ne4! 35.Rd1 Rb7** (the final liquidation!) **36.Nc3 Nxc3 37.bxc3 Rb2 38.Rxd3 Rxa2** and the players agreed to a draw.

The student should observe the way in which the d-pawn was indirectly protected. This stratagem furnishes the defending party with one chance more to emerge from the distress of his hanging pawn position to more settled circumstances.

The "hanging condition" must be regarded as a passing one and what we have to do is to find the proper moment for liquidating it. In general the defending party proceeds to this a move or two too soon, he does not hold tight long enough, perhaps because the consciousness of being "in the air" is not greatly to the taste of the human psyche. But if you have it in mind to realize your hanging pawns, do not do it unless you can sense behind the "blockaded security" which you crave, a glimmer of an initiative. Never let yourself be drawn into a dead blockaded position. It is much better to remain with options.

Other games illustrating the ideas of this chapter are Nos. 36 and 37.

CHAPTER 13

THE TWO BISHOPS

♦ *1. Introductory. Relative strength of Bishop and Knight.*

The two Bishops are a terrible weapon in the hands of a skillful fighter, yet I confess that for a moment I toyed with the blasphemous thought of omitting them from any detailed examination in my book. *My System*, I said to myself, only recognizes two things worthy of thorough investigation: the elements, and strategic devices. For instance, we regarded the isolani, which seemed to us in some way to have grown out of the problem of restraint, as a strategic device. Under what heading however were the proud Bishops to be placed?

This question which we have thrown out must not be dismissed as an idle or insignificant one, rather it appears to me to be one of decided theoretical interest. It would lead us too far to develop here the grounds on which my views on this are based, so I will content myself with giving the result. I have arrived at the conclusion that the advantage of the two Bishops can be called neither an element nor a stratagem. To me the two Bishops are, and can be, nothing else than a kind of weapon. The examination of the various kinds of weapons and the determination of their applicability to given cases lies totally outside the plan of this book. The reader, nevertheless, has the right to expect that I should enlighten him, as far as I can, on the dangers in which a pair of enemy Bishops may involve him.

The superiority of the Bishop over the Knight is strikingly shown in one of the two following diagrams. Each player has one or more passed pawns (Diagram 156) which are supported by their own King. The Bishop wins because he is outstanding at holding up the advance of passed pawns, or at slowing them down.

On the other hand the game in Diagram 157 shows up the principal weakness of the Bishop, namely that if his wish is to defend a terrain, he is usually helpless, for how shall a dark-squared Bishop protect light squares! Black's advance in Diagram 157 which puts the Bishop to shame would develop somewhat as follows: **1...Na5+ 2.Kc3 Ka4 3.Bf2 Nc6 4.Be3 Na7 5.Bf2 Nb5+ 6.Kd3 Kb3** and there eventually will follow a Knight check at b2 or b4 whereby the Black King will win the square c4.

We ask the reader to regard the cases in the positions on Diagrams 156 and 157 as the two poles between which all other cases occur. The advantage of the Bishop is that he can take long strides. The disadvantage lies in the weakness of the squares of the opposite color on which he operates.

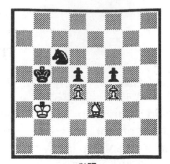

#156 Superiority of the long-striding Bishop over the short-winded Knight. Black's game could not be saved even if his Knight were at c3, d4, or f8

#157
White succumbs under the weakness of his light squares

In the position, White: Bg2, pawn c5. Black:Nb8, pawn c6 (with other pieces and pawns on the board), the advantage of the Bishop is as little demonstrable as its apparent inferiority in the position, White: Bb4, pawn c5. Black: Ne6, pawn c6. In both cases it is the strategic preponderance (the advantage of an active over a passive position of the pieces, which we analyzed in its place) which makes itself felt, not any possibly inherent superiority of the class of weapon in question.

We repeat, the principal weakness of the Bishop consists in its inability to attack or defend squares of opposite color, its main strength is in the fact that it is long-striding. Now it suddenly becomes plausible why two Bishops are held to be so strong. The reason is clear, their strength appears doubled, the weakness which we underlined is neutralized by the presence of the "other" Bishop. It is scarcely possible to set down on paper all the many and varied situations in which two Bishops may make themselves unpleasant. We will however, attempt to note the most important.

♦ *2. The Horrwitz Bishops.*

Two Bishops, when they rake two adjacent diagonals (for example Bb2, Bd3), and thus together bombard the enemy King position, are sometimes called the Horrwitz Bishops. Their effect is often devastating. One Bishop forces an enemy pawn move, which smooths the road for the second Bishop. For instance in Diagram 158 1.Qe4 forces the move ...g6 which loosens up Black's position upon which the Bf2 intervenes with decisive effect. Events took a similar course in the following game. **1.e4 e5 2.d4 exd4 3.c3 dxc3 4.Bc4 cxb2 5.Bxb2 Bb4+ 6.Nc3 Nf6 7.Nge2 Nxe4 8.0-0 Nxc3 9.Nxc3 Bxc3 10.Bxc3 0-0** (Black has castled and feels

#158 1.Qe4 forces Black to move the g-pawn, smoothing the road for 2.Bd4+

safe against **11.Qg4** [11...g6], or against **11.Qd4** [11...Qg5], but overlooks the combined play which is characteristic of the Horrwitz Bishops). **11.Qg4 g6** and only now **12.Qd4** and mate cannot be averted. The co-operation of the Bc4 lies obviously in the pinning of Black's f-pawn.

The Bishops in Diagram 159 I would call a variety of the Horrwitz Bishops, one indeed of the nobler sort. There is no talk of an attack on the King in this position. Yet the attack on a7 (I have included only the most important pieces), though not very intensive, is still unpleasant, and will in the end force the enemy to place his pawns on a7, b6, c5, at which time the road will have been smoothed for the other Bishop. White then follows with pawn moves to a4 and b3, and the squares a6, b5, and particularly c4 are made available for the White Bishop. Now Black's majority appears crippled.

#159 Two Bishops attack a pawn mass with the intention of winning stations for themselves

♦*3. The effective support afforded by the two Bishops to an advancing pawn mass. The hemming in of the enemy Knights.*

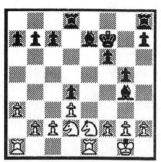

#160a
Tarrasch (Black) hems in the White Knights

A pawn mass, which need not by any means be a "majority," guided by a pair of Bishops can roll forward fairly far, and in the process lead to the imprisoning of the enemy Knights. The game Richter-Tarrasch may serve as an example. From Diagram 160a the game continued **19...c5 20.Ng3 h5 21.f3** (he does not show great skill in the defense. If the Knights are not to go under altogether, they must fight for stations for themselves. Indicated was 21.a4 followed by Nc4) **21...Bd7 22.Re2? b5! 23.Rae1 Bf8! 24.Nge4 Rg8** (in order to be able to play ...f5) **25.Nb3 Rc8 26.Ned2 Bd6 27.Ne4 Bf8 28.Ned2 f5 29.Re5 Bd6 30.R5e2** (30.Rd5? Rg6) **30...Ra8** (now the a-pawn is to advance) **31.Na5 Rab8 32.Nab3 h4 33.Kh1 Rg6 34.Kg1 Be6** (the barricading of the e-file effected by the Bd7 and Bd6 has been up to this move more of an "ideal" nature. With 34...Be6 this is changed into a "material" one, corresponding to the process we have before noted, where the "ideal" restraint of a passed pawn gave place to a mechanical stopping (blockade). So much on the strategic-theoretical meaning of the maneuver chosen. The practical significance of the move lies, however, as Dr. Tarrasch himself very rightly notes in the fact that fresh possibilities are opened up. (i) ...Ke7-d7 (ii) ...a6 ...Rc8, then ...Bb8-a7 followed finally by ...c4. I may add this remark that ...c4 must be regarded as without question the strategic plan indicated in this position. Why it is will appear in the note to White's 38th move. **35.Rf2 Ra8?** He is untrue to his main plan, ...c4, and again tries to make ...a5 possible. He succeeds, but only because his opponent neglects a subtle resource. Of course it is a fine thing to put into execution ...a4 and completely to drive back the enemy forces, but one should not go so far as to subordinate a plan indicated by the position to the idea of a broader decorative effect. But then the pseudo-classical school had an incredible weakness for such embroideries!) **36.Rfe2?** (a serious mistake. How could anyone allow ...a5 to be played without a fight!? In answer to 36.Na5 Dr. Tarrasch gives 36...Bc7 37.Nb7 Bf4 winning time for ...Rc8 and ...c4 by the threat of 38...Be3. He overlooks however, the hidden resource 38.Nxc5! Be3 39.c4 and Black cannot win, as the White Queenside is strong and the dark squares (c5 for the Knight), not less so. A plausible variation would be 39...bxc4 40.dxc4 Rc8 41.b4

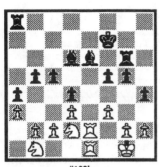

#160b
The hemming in accomplished

Rc7 42.Kf1 Bxf2 43.Kxf2 and White stands well). **36...a5 37.Nb1 a4 38.N3d2** (Diagram 160b. And now the breakthrough follows, and there is nothing logically surprising in this, for, as we know, Black has a decided "qualitative majority," as would show up even more obviously if we imagined a White pawn on e4 and a Black one on e5. Here the possibility of a breakthrough is still further enhanced by the miserable position of the White Knights, and by the large surface of friction [the four pawn front]) **38...c4 39.Nf1 Rc8 40.Kh1 c3 41.bxc3 dxc3 42.Ne3 b4** (Black's game plays itself. White resigned on the 47th move).

♦ *4. Fight against a pawn majority with simultaneous hemming in of the enemy Knights.*

The hemming in of the Knights with simultaneous fight against a pawn majority is a very different problem, the solving of which one would assume as requiring outstanding technical ability. But this is not so. Anyone who is moderately versed in the art of restraining and blockading pawn complexes, will soon find to his satisfaction that in the class of positions in question the hemming in of the Knights is more easily achieved than in the case just considered under part 3 of this chapter. We can say with some justice that the restraint of the pawn majority once in operation carries with it automatically the hemming in of the Knights. By this I mean the blockaded pawns may easily develop into obstructions to their own Knights. An example is found in the following game.

Harmonist-Tarrasch, 1889. **1.e4 e5 2.Nf3 Nc6 3.Bb5 Nf6 4.O-O Nxe4 5.d4 Nd6 6.Bxc6 dxc6 7.dxe5 Nf5 8.Qxd8+ Kxd8 9.Bg5+ Ke8 10.Nc3 h6 11.Bf4 Be6** (White's majority has only slight mobility) **12.Rad1 Rd8 13.Ne4 c5 14.Rxd8+ Kxd8 15.Rd1+ Kc8 16.h3 b6 17.Kf1 Be7 18.a3 Rd8 19.Rxd8+ Kxd8** (The exchange of

Rooks has increased the radius of action of the Black King) **20.c3 Bd5 21.Nfd2 Kd7 22.Ke2 g5 23.Bh2 Nh4 24.g3 Ng6 25.f4 Ke6 26.Ke3 c4 27.Nf3 gxf4+ 28.gxf4 c5** (Diagram 161). In the current position White's pieces are fairly well shut in. This gratifying state of affairs has followed almost automatically from Black's successfully executed blockade of the e6 and f5 pawns. This cannot surprise us, for have we not often experienced how the whole situation may be favorably affected, as if by a miracle, by a successful blockade? The game proceeded: **29.Ng3 Nh4 30.Nxh4 Bxh4 31.Ne4 Be7 32.Bg1 Bc6** (intending to move the King to d5 followed by

#161 Harmonist-Tarrasch , 1889
After 28...c5

#161a

...Bd7-f5 driving the Knight further back) **33.Bf2 Bd7 34.Bg3** (34.Nd6 offered the possibility of a draw, by playing for opposite colored Bishops) **34...Kd5 35.Nf2 h5 36.Kf3 Bf5** (Blockade!) **37.Ke3 b5 38.Kf3 a5** (Diagram 161a. White is "stalemated") **39.Ke3 b4 40.Kf3 Kc6 41.axb4** (White is lost) **41...cxb4 42.cxb4 axb4 43.Ne4 Kd5 44.Nd6 Bxd6 45.exd6 c3 46.bxc3 b3** and White resigned.

♦ *5. The two Bishops in the endgame.*

We regard as the ideal the transmutation of an advantage founded only in the class of weapon employed to one which is clearly and perceptibly strategic. For instance, that of the aggressive position of our pieces as opposed to the passive one of our opponent. Combined play with two Bishops, leading to such a transmutation as we have mentioned, comes out in the following example. See Diagram 162. Michel-Tartakower, 1925. White's position is well consolidated, the weakness of the dark squares c3 and d4 does not appear important. The game continued **40.Kg1 Kg7 41.Kf1 Bc6 42.Ng1 g5 43.Nf3 h5** (The two pawns advance, since they feel themselves to be a qualitative majority due to the exalted protection which they enjoy, supported as they are by the two

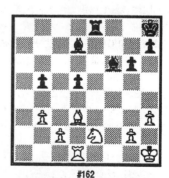

#162
Tartakower (Black) takes advantage one after another, of the various chances given to him by his Bishops

Bishops) **44.Be2 Re4! 45.Bd3 Rf4 46.Ke2 g4 47.hxg4 hxg4 48.Nh2 g3! 49.Nf3** (Black has quite correctly not pursued any further advantage to be obtained by hemming in the Knight. What he now has is more valuable. White's g2 pawn is marked for attack, and White's forces are from now on forced to keep perpetual watch over him. This strategic advantage very quickly brings a decision). **49...d4 50.Rf1 b4 51.Nd2 Rh4 52.Nf3 Rh8** (from here he threatens simultaneously the point h2 and the e-file) **53.Kd2** (for - with apologies to Goethe and his translator - where of good moves there's a failing, a botch steps promptly in as deputy!) **53...Rh2! 54.Nxh2 gxh2 55.Rh1 Be5 56.Bf1 Be4** (a charming situation!) **57.Kd1 Kf6 58.Kd2 Kg5 59.Kd1 Kg4** and White resigned..

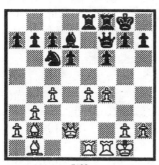

#163
Black's position appears defensible

We have now done enough for the glorification of the Bishops, and a few words may be added on situations in which they do not play as well. These are closed or half closed positions, (see for example games No. 15 and 38) while they are astonishingly weak against an unassailable, centrally posted Knight. Even in the position in Diagram 163, it seems to me that Black can maintain himself against the Horrwitz Bishops. In the next chapter we will pass to "overprotection".

An excellent example of play with two Bishops will be found in Game No. 41, Lasker-Burn, and also in No. 47, Gregory-Nimzowitsch.

CHAPTER 14

OVERPROTECTION

♦ *1. Why we should systematically overprotect our own strong points.*

A short chapter, which in particular may serve to illustrate the various forms under which "overprotection" may appear. We have already attempted to explain the spirit and inner significance of overprotection. We will therefore only repeat here that the contact established between the strong point and the "overprotector" can only be of advantage to both parties. To the strong point because the prophylactic induced by such a process affords it the greatest imaginable security against possible attack; to the overprotector, since the point serves him as a source of energy, from which he may continually draw fresh strength.

Overprotection clearly represents a maneuver, which from its very essence must have developed in close connection with positional play. Nevertheless even in the "Elements" we came across traces of overprotection; for example in the open file. White: Rd1, Nc3, pawn e4. Black: pawns c7, d6. The outpost Knight (after Nc3-d5) must, as was emphasized earlier, be protected not only by a pawn but also by a Rook. What can this compulsion signify other than the necessity of overprotecting the strategically important outpost!

Again, in the domain of the pawn chain overprotection is a stratagem which deserves every preference. Turn back to the game Nimzowitsch-Giese (Diagram 115), and notice in particular how the overprotection was not even intended for the base of the pawn chain, but rather for a more humble candidate for that position. We overprotected the e5 point since we had always to deal with an eventual and inevitable dxc5, when the e-pawn would be promoted to the base.

#163a

The wonderful vitality of the overprotector may here be demonstrated by two further examples. Nimzowitsch-Rubinstein, Carlsbad, 1911. **1.e4 e6 2.d4 d5 3.e5 c5 4.c3 Nc6 5.Nf3 Qb6 6.Bd3 cxd4 7.cxd4 Bd7 8.Be2 Nge7 9.b3 Nf5 10.Bb2** (At the moment d4 is barely protected, not more) **10...Bb4+ 11.Kf1 h5 12.g3 Rc8 13.Kg2 g6 14.h3 Be7** (intending to answer a possible g4 with ...Nh4+) **15.Qd2! a5 16.Rc1 Bf8 17.Qd1! Bh6 18.Rc3 O-O 19.g4 Nfe7 20.Na3** (Diagram 163a. Only now will it be clear why White delayed with the development of the Knight. An honorable post had been contemplated for him, namely as overprotector of the d4 pawn) **20...Nb4 21.Nc2** (there

---

now follows a surprising and effortless unraveling of the corps of White pieces on the Queenside) **21...Rxc3 22.Bxc3 Nxc2 23.Qxc2 Rc8 24.Qb2!** (whatever happens, the d4 pawn will stay overprotected) **24...Bb5 25.Bxb5 Qxb5 26.Bd2!** (the overprotector shows his teeth!)**26...Bf8 27.Rc1 hxg4 28.hxg4 Rc6 29.Qa3 Rxc1** (A pity!, for on 29...Nf5, White intended to offer a Queen sacrifice - 30.Rxc6 Bxa3 31.Rc8+ Kg7 32.gxf5 with a strong attack) **30.Qxc1** with the superior game.

#164
White develops his pieces
systematically to overprotect
the point d4

Nimzowitsch-Spielmann, Stockholm, 1920. **1.e4 e6 2.d4 d5 3.e5 c5 4.Nf3 Nc6 5.c3 Qb6 6.Be2 cxd4 7.cxd4 Nh6 8.Nc3 Nf5 9.Na4 Qa5+ 10.Bd2 Bb4 11.Bc3 Bd7** (preferable would have been 11...Bxc3+ 12.Nxc3 Qb4 [12...Qb6 13.Na4!] 13.Bb5 0-0 14.Bxc6 Qxb2 15.Na4 Qb4+ 16.Qd2. White would then have had the point c5, Black a backward pawn plus) **12.a3 Bxc3+ 13.Nxc3 h5 14.0-0 Rc8** (Diagram 164) **15.Qd2 Qd8** (threatening 16...g5) **16.h3** (in order to meet 16...g5 with the riposte 17.g4. e.g. 16...g5 17.g4 hxg4 18.hxg4 Nh4 19.Nxh4 Rxh4 20.Kg2 followed by 21.Rh1 with advantage to White) **16...Na5 17.Rad1 Qb6 18.Rfe1** (d4 and to a certain degree e5 are now systematically overprotected, and this strategy makes it possible later to be automatically master of the situation, whatever complications may arise) **18...Nc4 19.Bxc4 Rxc4 20.Ne2 Ba4 21.Rc1** (notice how available an overprotector is for service in all directions) **21...Bb3 22.Rxc4 Bxc4 23.Ng3 Ne7** and White with the better position won on the 61st move.

So much on the overprotection of the base. The overprotection of the following points is also of importance. (a) Overprotection of the central points. We have already on a previous opportunity emphasized the fact that the very common neglect of the central theatre of war is reprehensible. We are dealing here with a detail, or more accurately, with the examination of a quite definite, and, for the hypermodern style of play, typical situation. As is generally known, the hyper-modern knows admirably how to resist the temptation to occupy the center with pawns, at any rate not until a really favorable opportunity presents itself. If such an chance presents itself, he casts aside all shyness, and the pawns, supported by the fianchettoed Bishops, rush wildly forward, seize the center, and strive to crush the enemy. Against this threatened evil the overprotection of certain central points provides a thoroughly proven remedy, which cannot be too strongly recommended. Let us glance at the following opening of the game Reti-Yates, New York, 1924. **1.Nf3 d5 2.c4 e6 3.g3 Nf6 4.Bg2 Bd6 5.b3 0-0** (Why this hurry? To put the center in order was much more pressing. The moves ...c6, ...Nbd7 and ...e5 was the proper line of play) **6.0-0 Re8 7.Bb2 Nbd7 8.d3?** c6 **9.Nbd2 e5** (the position now reached is undoubtedly favorable to the second player. White should have played 8.d4) **10.cxd5 cxd5 11.Rc1 Nf8**

12.Rc2 Bd7 13.Qa1 Ng6 14.Rfc1. Diagram 165. White's Queen maneuver is significant. He intends to undermine the enemy center by d4 when opportunity offers and if Black replies ...e4, then Ne5. Black's duty therefore is to overprotect e5, to excess even. His best course was first 14...b5 aiming at White's Queenside which is compromised by the position of his Queen. If then 15.Nf1, there would follow 15...Qb8! (overprotection of e5) 16.Ne3 a5 and Black has the better game. For a game which took a most instructive course, and in which I employed the same Queen maneuver (...Qb8) see No. 38.

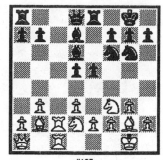

#165
Black to move. What point is worthy of his overprotection?

(b) The overprotection of the center as a measure of defense for our own Kingside.

The case which is about to be discussed in detail differs from that considered above under (a) in its general tendency, and is therefore treated here as an independent maneuver, not as a subdivision of that case. Earlier in the position of Diagram 124, a position was discussed which comes under the classification of the case now to be considered. Game No. 15 is also instructive in the same sense. In this game after Black's 13th move a position was reached which is shown in Diagram 166.

Black's move was **13...g4!**. To the reply 14.hxg4 hxg4 15.Qxg4, he had planned 15...Rxh2! followed by ...Bxe5+ and ...Bxb2. White, however, played **14.Re1**, and in doing something for his center he at the same time strengthens the power of resistance of his position against flank attacks as well. There followed **14...Kf8 15.Nc3!** (the prelude to a blockading maneuver) **15...Qe7 16.Bxf5 exf5 17.Qe3 Rh6 18.Ne2 c5 19.Nf4**, and White is better, for the two Bishops have little to say in view of the strength of the unassailable Knight, moreover, the collective mobility of Black is limited, for though the d5 and c5 pawns have a certain measure of mobility, the rest are blockaded.

#166
White parries every attempt at an attack on his King by overprotecting a central point. How does he do it?

Of quite special interest in the same sense is the position shown in Diagram 167 which is taken from game No. 39. Black is to play. That the Nd5 was the pride of Black's position is beyond all doubt. It was, however, not easy to devise a suitable plan. White was preparing one, though it is true it presented no great danger, namely Qd2 followed by Ne1-d3-c5. The train of thought which I followed in the game brought me on the track of a hidden maneuver which to this day I consider a good one. The separate links of this chain of ideas are as follows: (i) the Nd5 is strong, therefore (ii) the overprotectors, the Qd7 and Rd8 are also strong, but (iii) the Rd8

#167
Consultation game.
Three amateurs-Nimzowitsch

has a duty in connection with the King's position, which has a bearing on his strength in the center, therefore, surprisingly (iv) the R(h8) must come to d8! There followed **14...Kb8 15.Qd2 Rc8! 16.Ne1 Be7 17.Nd3 Rhd8**, and the deed is done! The Rook at d8 now feels that he can devote his whole attention to the center, since his colleague at c8 is looking out for the King. The further adventures of the Rd8 will be found in Game No. 39.

We could name many more "points" that are worthy of overprotection, but will limit ourselves to the few examples we have given here. Before passing on to the next strategic device, we must again stress the fact that only strategically valuable points should be overprotected, not a sickly pawn, or a Kingside which rests on a weak foundation. Overprotection must in no sense be regarded as an act of Christian meekness and lovingkindness! The pieces overprotect a point because they promise themselves strategic advantages to be gained from contact with it. We must therefore seek to establish connection with strong points. A weak pawn is only in a single exceptional case justified in claiming overprotection, and that is when he is engaged in looking after a potential giant of his species. For instance: White: pawns d4, e5. Black: pawns d5, e6. The d4 pawn as the base of White's pawn chain is nurse to the strategically important pawn on e5. Overprotection of the point d4 is therefore indicated.

♦ *2. How to get rid of weak pawns.*

We are not concerned here with the actual way by which we may get rid of weak pawns, but rather with the question of what pawns deserve to have this treatment meted out to them.

The situation is always the same: an otherwise sound pawn complex which, however, has to acknowledge a weakling in its body. We distinguish two cases:

(a) the weakness of the pawn is unmistakable.

(b) the weakness would only appear after a pawn advance, whether of our own or on the part of the enemy.

We shall give an example of each of these two cases. Diagram 167a.

(a) Nimzowitsch-Jacobson. **36.Rc5 Bd7** (if 36...Bd3+ 37.Kc1 Rd7 38.Rc8+ followed by 39.Rb8). **37.Rxd5.** White is now a pawn to the good. **37...Kf8 38.Kc2 b3+ 39.Kc3 Ke7** (White is in a position to bring his own flock of pawns, the e, f, and g-pawns, under one shelter, and to do this he has only to play e4. Everything will then be beautifully protected, and the shepherd, the Rd5, can with a clear conscience, turn his attention to other matters. Not quite!, for the stupid little sheep, the h-pawn, would scamper away from the shepherd - for at some time there would be threatened ...Ra1-h1 followed by the capture of this pawn) **40.h5 Be6 41.Rc5 Kd6 42.Rc6+ Kd7 43.hxg6 hxg6 44.Nxe6! fxe6** (44...Kxc6 45.Nd8+) **45.Rc5** to be followed by Rg5 and f4 with an easily won Rook and pawn ending. (The type of position reached after Black's 41st move has been considered earlier in Diagram 124).

#167a

(b) Tarrasch-Barthmann, played when Dr. Tarrasch was still a youth. See Diagram 168. Black played here **21...Rc6** and there followed **22.Rhc1 Rhc8 23.g4 g6 24.f5 gxf5 25.gxf5 Rg8?** (He shouldn't have allowed 26.f6+ at any price. Essential was 25...exf5 26.Nf4 Be6 27.Rg1, with a tough fight ahead) **26.f6+ Kf8 27.Rg1 Rxg1 28.Nxg1 Kg8** and Black's h-pawn is a glaring weakness.

This drawback could have been avoided had Black played 21...h5 with the idea of only allowing White to play his pawn to f6 on the stipulation that both the g and h-pawns should disappear in the exchange. The continuation might have been: 21...h5 22.h3 g6 (not 22...h4?, because of 23.Ng1 followed by Nf3) and Black, after a few moves, would have obtained a more favorable position than he did in this game.

Whereas case (a) does not make very great demands on the player, the right handling of the strategic weapon discussed under (b) is extremely difficult. It demands, above everything a pretty thorough knowledge of the various forms under which an advance of a compact pawn mass, may run its course, particularly on a wing. Many pages of this book have been devoted to this advance with all its consequences, and to deal with it we may therefore leave the kind reader to his own, as we hope, not less kind fate. Only let him keep well in view that the strategic necessity of getting rid of a troublesome pawn of his own may arise in the case of an advance of his pawns, just as much as in that of an

#168
Tarrasch-Barthmann

enemy advance. When the Black sheep of the family should be cast out, whether before the operation begins, or during it, can only be decided on the merits of each case.

For a very instructive game illustrating overprotection, see No. 39.

CHAPTER 15

MANEUVERING AGAINST WEAKNESSES

Maneuvering against an enemy weakness. The combined attack on both wings.

♦ *1. The logical components which go to make up a maneuvering action against a weakness.*

As an introduction to the following analysis I would like to try to present an idea for the operation which is to be considered. I picture the course of a maneuvering action somewhat as follows: An enemy weakness can be attacked in at least two ways. Each of these attempts at attack would be met by an adequate defense. In order that we might in the end conquer the enemy weakness in spite of this, we take advantage of the greater freedom of movement which belongs to our pieces, due to certain conditions of the terrain, so as to attack it in turn by different ways (maneuvering action), and thus oblige the enemy pieces to take up uncomfortable positions for its defense. Eventually an obstruction to the defense or something of the kind will intervene, and the "weakness" will prove untenable.

As we can see from this scheme, it would be quite a mistake to label this type of maneuvering as mere purposeless moving back and forth. On the contrary every move has set before it a clearly prescribed end with the conquest of a quite definite weakness in view. The ways which lead to this conquest are of a complicated nature.

♦ *2. The terrain. The conception of the pivot around which the maneuvering turns.*

The terrain over which any maneuvering action takes place must, if our plan is to succeed, be strongly built up. A characteristic of such action is that the different troop movements always cross a quite definite square (or line of demarcation). As an example see Diagram 169. Here it is the point d5 which the White pieces will wish to occupy, making it a base for further maneuvering. Accordingly the point d5 might be described as a fortified post in the lines of communication, and it is therefore right and proper to regard it as the pivot around which the whole maneuvering action turns. It is in virtue of this fortified post d5 that the whole operation is accomplished. Every piece, even the Rd1 strives to get there at some time or another. The law governing this maneuvering action moreover demands that d5 will be occupied by different pieces in turn, for this will always create new threats and thus help to embarrass the enemy. The relationship between the White pieces and the pivot

#169 White maneuvers against the d6 pawn using the point d5 as the pivot around which the operation runs

---

d5 exactly corresponds also to the "contact" between overprotectors and a strategically important point, which was discussed in the previous chapter. In this case the pieces strive to establish contact with d5. This speaks plainly for the strength of that point. Notice too, the device by which pieces exchange stations in, for example, the sequence of White moves Ne3-Qd5-Nc4. This operation serves well the purpose of the general plan of maneuvering action.

We now give some typical examples of this type of maneuvering.

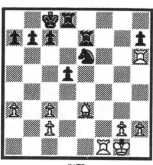

#170
Rubinstein-Selesnieff

(a) A pawn weakness which is to be brought under bombardment from the 7th rank. Rubinstein-Selesnieff, Diagram 170. There occurred **1...b6** (1...d4 deserved preference. For instance, 2.cxd4 Nxd4 3.Bg5 Ne2+ 4.Kf2! [otherwise 4...Rf7] 4...Rf8+ 5.Rf6 Rxf6+ 6.Bxf6 Re6). The game continued **2.Bf2 Rf8 3.Re1 Ref7 4.Rhxe6 Rxf2 5.Re8+ Kb7 6.Rxf8 Rxf8 7.Re7** (now some magnificent maneuvering begins against the h7 pawn) **7...Rh8 8.Kf2 Kc6 9.g4 Kd6 10.Rf7 a5 11.g5 a4 12.h4 b5 13.Kg3 c5** (Black now threatens to make a passed pawn by ...b4, so Rubinstein attacks the weakness, the h7 pawn, from the other side) **14.Rf6+!**
Kc7 15.Rh6 b4 16.cxb4 cxb4 17.axb4 Ra8 18.Rxh7+! (the "weakness" has fallen) **18...Kb6 19.Rf7 a3 20.Rf1 a2 21.Ra1 Kb5 22.g6 Kxb4 23.h5** Black resigns.

The following case is much more complicated.

#171
Dr. Kalaschnikow-Nimzowitsch, 1914

(b) Two pawn weaknesses (Diagram 171). Here c3 and h3 are both weak. The pivotal point, around which action against h3 turns (f4), seems to be threatened, but is rescued, and actually by timely attention paid to the weak c3 pawn on the other side of the board. We see here the two separated theatres of war logically connected one to the other. The game continuation follows: Dr. Kalaschnikow-Nimzowitsch. Black played **36...Ke7**. If White would only do nothing Black could get the advantage by a direct attack, by ...Kf7-g6 followed by ...f5. White would then have to defend with f3, and would thereby give his opponent the handle to
clutch which he has long wanted, namely (after of course moving the Nf4 out of the way) the posting of his Bishop at g3, when the threat to White's entire line of defense could not be parried. But White did not sit still. Instead he did his best to hinder his opponent in the execution of this plan, and played **37.Ng2!** With this he hopes to bring off a general exchange which would lead to a clear draw. The idea is 38.Bxf4

Nxf4 39.Nxf4 Bxf4 and there is nothing left. The pivotal point f4 could now not be held were it not for the maneuvering chance on the other side of the board. There followed: **37...Ra1+ 38.Rc1 Ra2! 39.Ne1!** (the relief expedition carried out by Black with his 37th and 38th moves has succeeded, for now with the Rook at a2 White's intended exchange would lead to his own disadvantage. For example 39.Bxf4 Bxf4! 40.Rd1 Bd2 41.Ne2 Nf4! and after the further moves 42.Ngxf4 gxf4 43.Kg2 Rc2 Black develops a remarkable appetite). **39...Kf7** Black has gained a tempo! Now the game starts anew. **40.Rc2 Ra3! 41.Ng2 Ra1+ 42.Rc1 Ra2! 43.Ne1 Kg6 44.Rc2 Ra3 45.f3** (this weakening move could not have been permanently avoided, otherwise ...f5 would follow, and if gxf5 ...Kxf5 followed by ...g4 creating a passed pawn) **45...f5.** It is accomplished! The end is peaceful. **46.Kf2 Kf6** (making room for the Knight) **47.Bc1 Ra1 48.Ke3 Ng6 49.Nd3 Bg3** (see note to Black's 36th move) **50.Ne2 Ngf4 51.Ng1 Nxd3 52.Kxd3 Bf4! 53.Ne2 Bxc1 54.Nxc1 Nf4+ 55.Ke3 Nxh3.** After a heroic defense the fortress falls (h3). There followed only **56.Ne2 f4+** and White gave up since ...Rf1 will win another pawn.

(c) The King as a "weakness". See Diagram 172. For the terrain there function here two possibilities of a driving action. As pivot we have a line of demarcation.

Nimzowitsch-Kalinsky, 1914. In this very piquant position there occurred first **1.Bb3** (the reply to 1.Bc2 f2 2.Rd1 would be 2...Ke6 and White cannot win.) **1...d4 2.Bd5 Rg4** (2...f2 3.Bxe4) **3.Rhh5 f2** and now White doubles his Rooks on the f-file with gain of tempo. **4.Rf6+ Ke7 5.Rhf5 Rg1+ 6.Ka2 d3.** We will use the position now reached as a touchstone of the correctness of our thesis. We explained in its place that a maneuvering action is only possible if certain conditions are fulfilled. These were: (a) the presence of a pivot, (b) a diversity of threats which might be directed against the weakness. The test turns out in

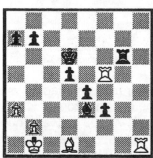

#172
Nimzowitsch-Kalinsky, 1914

our favor. Although this time the weakness is an ideal one, with no concrete pawn weakness, the circumstances (favoring a maneuvering action) are identical with those which we have laid down as typical. The variety of threats leaves nothing to be desired, for White plans by their means not only to force the King to the edge of the board, but determines also to arrange, when opportunity serves, a pretty Kinghunt, which drives him into the middle of the board. The requisite pivot is the f-file (line of demarcation which the King cannot pass). The game proceeded **7.Re6+ Kd7 8.Rf7+ Kd8 9.Ref6 d2** (the border mating position now reached cannot be taken advantage of, for on 10.Rh7, comes 10...f1=Q, and as 10.Rh6 is not possible, he maneuvers further) **10.Rf8+ Ke7 11.R6f7+ Kd6 12.Bb3 Bb6?** (perhaps 12...a6 would have been better as it gives the King an escape route to creep through) **13.Rf6+!!** Now the Black King has to face the choice. He may return to the edge of the board, where his position will now be untenable, or he must go out into the open, where fate in another form will overtake him. There followed **13...Ke5** (13...Ke7 14.R8f7+ Kd8 15.Rh6 and wins) **14.Re6+! Kd4 15.Rxf2! d1=Q 16.Bxd1 Rxd1 17.Re2!** winning the pawn and the game.

♦ *3. Combined play on both wings, with weaknesses which though for the moment are lacking are yet hidden.*

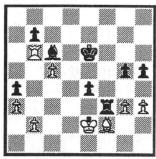

#173
v. Gottschall-Nimzowitsch
Hanover, 1926
Combined attack on both wings.
The White weaknesses are the
c-pawn, and as becomes
evident later, the h-pawn

Von Gottschall-Nimzowitsch, Hanover, 1926. (Diagram 173). A logical analysis of the position reveals the following data. White's pawn on c5 is, in view of the insecure position of the Bf2, to be regarded as a pawn weakness. On the other hand I cannot agree under any circumstances in branding the pawn mass g3, h3, as a "weakness," and this for the reason that here, on the Kingside, "terrain" is lacking. Black chose the following maneuver which at first sight looks most unintelligible. **39...Ke5 40.Rb4 Kd5**. The explanation of this combination which sacrifices a tempo lies in the following: With these moves a position is reached where White is in *Zugzwang*, for if the Rook goes back to b6 (and he as no other plausible move, for 41.Rd4+ fails against 41...Kxc5 42.Rxa4+? Rxf2+, etc., while 41.h4, as we will see, provides just that "terrain" which before was so sadly missed) **41.h4** (on 41.Rb6 h4 42.gxh4 gxh4 43.Bxh4 comes the intermezzo 43...Kxc5 threatening the Rook) **41...gxh4 42.gxh4 Rh3! 43.Rd4+ Ke6 44.Rd8 Bd5** and now Black began systematically to maneuver against the h4 pawn, with the square g4 as his pivot, and in fact by way of this point succeeded in breaking into his opponent's game.

The meaning of the strategy employed here appears out of the following scheme which is applicable to all analogous cases. We maneuvered first against the obvious weakness, the c5 pawn. By means of *Zugzwang* (with a slight mixture of threats) we succeeded in inducing our opponent to make a deployment (moving the pawn to h4). This, however, led to a weakness, which before h4 was played was merely latent, but afterwards became manifest and easily assailable. To recapitulate: Play on two wings is usually based on the following idea. We engage one wing, or the obvious weaknesses in it, and thus draw the other enemy wing out of its reserve, when new weaknesses will be created on that reserve wing, and so the signal is given for systematic maneuvering against two weaknesses, as in the game Dr. Kalaschnikow-Nimzowitsch which was given above.

This is the rule. As an interesting exception to the rule, I may call attention to the case where we may act as though the exposure of the weakness on the other wing had already taken place.

The following is an example of such an exposure. Von Holzhausen-Nimzowitsch, Hanover, 1926.

#174

(Diagram 174). Black here hastened to bring about the exposure and played **32...Rh6**. True, the real fight was on the Queenside (....b5), but I knew that after I had succeeded in opening up the game with ...b5 the advanced position of White's Kingside pawns could only serve my ends. There followed: **33.h3 Rg6 34.Re2 a6 35.Rf4 b5 36.b3 Rg5 37.g4 Rge5 38.Kc3 a5!** (the weakness h3 along with the chance of getting the e4 pawn unblocked made Black decisive in his demand for "terrain" with the pivot to go with it. It was for this that Black was fighting with his last moves) **39.Ref2 a4** (threatening 40...axb3 followed by ...bxc4 followed by an invasion by the Rooks via the now opened Queenside files) **40.bxa4 bxc4! 41.Rf8 R5e7 42.Rxe8 Rxe8 43.Nxc4 Nxc4 44.Kxc4 Ra8** (the desired terrain is now won; it consists of the a, b, and d-files. The pivot will be the point d4) **45.Rf7** (45.Kb3? Kd5!) **45...Rxa4+ 46.Kb3** (better was 46.Kc3) **46...Rb4+! 47.Kc3 Rb7 48.Rf5 Ra7 49.Kc4 Ra4+ 50.Kb3 Rd4** (the pivot!) **51.Re5 Kd6 52.Re8 Rd3+ 53.Kc4 Rxh3** (the proper use made of the "terrain" has not failed to yield fruit, as the "weakness" has fallen) **54.Rxe4 Ra3 55.Re2 Ra4+ 56.Kb5 Rxg4 57.a4 Rb4+** and Black won on the 71st move.

#175 Teichmann-Nimzowitsch
San Sebastian, 1911

In Diagram 175 an elegant mating threat is used merely as an instrument to carry out with gain of tempo a weakening attack on the enemy's Queenside. **31...Ne6** (threatening 32...Rxh2+ 33.Nxh2 Rxh2+ 34.Kxh2 Qf2+ 35.Kh3 Bf4! and wins) **32.Re2** (parries the threat, but now there follows a gain of tempo) **32...Nd4 33.Ree1** (if 33.Rf2 Be3!) **33...Qb7!** (now 34...Rc8 can be warded off only by a sacrifice) **34.Rxd4** (34.c3 bxc3 35.bxc3 Qb2+ and wins) **34...exd4** and Black won after a hard struggle. (See game No. 40)

We will now give two endgames which illustrate in miniature the combined attack on two wings. As the position in Diagram 176 shows, Black (Nimzowitsch) has first made a gesture as if he were going to attack the Queenside, but then has chosen

#176
Vestergaard-Nimzowitsch
From a simultaneous
display against 25 opponents

#177
Seifert-Nimzowitsch

the Kingside for his field of operation. White has taken up a tough defensive position. It was my move and after a little reflection I played **1...b5!!** Great astonishment among the spectators! On the Queenside Black surely has no troops for the attack. The game continued **2.cxb5 Rh2 3.Nxh2 Rxh2 4.Bf1 Bxb5!** Now we have daylight. The advance on the Queenside was conceived as a diversion against the Kingside. **5.Bxb5 Nh3+ 6.Kf1 Qxe3 7.Qe1 Qg1+ 8.Ke2 Qxg2+** and mate in two moves.

The next example also, Diagram 177, is characteristic of a surprising co-operation of two separate "diversions." It is taken from a game played in a tournament of the lighter order in Leipzig, 1926. The game proceeded **1...h4 2.Nxg3 hxg3 3.Rd2** and now there followed a thrust on the other wing. **3...a5.** My opponent parried with **4.b5** but after **4...Bxh3 5.gxh3 Qxh3+ 6.Kg1 d5!!** (the point), he resigned since the effect of the check at c5 is catastrophic. His right course would have been 4.Bf1 axb4 5.Rb2 c5 with a drawish position.

For further games illustrating this Chapter, see Nos. 40-45.

♦ *4. Maneuvering under difficult conditions, our own center lacking protection.*

In conclusion we will give a game inspired with the true spirit of this form of maneuvering. (Diagram 178). Black's cramped King position is here a glaring weakness, along with the weak d6 pawn. But his own weakness at e4 forces a certain reserve on White. The terrain bearing on the weak d6 pawn has little elasticity. This pawn can only be attacked by the Rook from d1 and from the diagonal. Somewhat more varied seem the possibilities of an advance on the Kingside, for Queen and Rook can at any time change places on the g and h-files. To make these not precisely impressive possibilities the basis of an effective operation demands the highest skill of a master. Lasker displayed it as follows in his game against Salwe. From the diagramed position the game continued **27...Qe8 28.Qf2!** (if 28.Nf4 the parry 28...Nh6 would be possible) **28...Rf8 29.Qd2** (by watching d6, she stops ...Nh6) **29...Qb8 30.Kh1 Rfe8 31.Rg4! Rg8** (if 31...Nh6 32.Nxf6 with advantage to White) **32.Rd1!** (because the pressure has been removed from e4) **32...Qb4** (with this the Black Queen eventually gets into wrong paths. 32...Qe8 was decidedly better, but it was difficult to foresee that the circle of influence of the Queen thus entering the enemy game would be so convincing). **33.Qf2 Qc3 34.Qh4** (now this old position taken up anew is stronger than ever) **34...Nh6 35.Rf4 Nf7 36.Kh2 Rge8 37.Qg3 Rg8 38.Rh4** (on 38.Rg4 Nh6 39.Rh4 the continuation could be 39...d5 40.exd5 cxd5 41.Rxd5 Bc6) **38...g5 39.fxg6**

#178
Dr. Lasker-Salwe, 1909

e.p. Rxg6 40.Qf2 f5 (to be rid of the weakness at f6) **41.Nf4 Rf6 42.Ne2 Qb2 43.Rd2 Qa1 44.Ng3 Kg8** (White threatened 45.exf5 Bxf5 46.Nxf5 Rxf5 47.Rxh7+) **45.exf5 Bxf5 46.Nd4! cxd4 47.Nxf5 Kf8 48.Qxd4 Qxd4 49.Nxd4 Ne5 50.Rh5 Ref7 51.c5 dxc5 52.Rxe5 cxd4 53.Rxd4 Rf2 54.Rd8+ Kg7 55.Ra5** and White won.

The way in which Dr. Lasker conducts this game is impressive. How he manages, despite the small variety of threats at his disposal, to dominate the whole board, while nearly eliminating his own weakness, is worthy of admiration. The student may learn from this game that the presence of a variety of objects of attack (enemy weaknesses), can compensate up to a certain point for a lack of variety in threat bearing lines of play.

With this magnificent example of master play we take leave of our readers.

PART 3

ILLUSTRATIVE GAMES

My System - 21st Century Edition

Game 1

Illustrating the consequences of pawn-snatching in the opening.

Nimzowitsch-Alapin
Carlsbad, 1911

1.e4 e6 2.d4 d5 3.Nc3 Nf6 4.exd5 Nxd5

Surrender of the center.

5.Nf3 c5

To "kill" the pawn (see chapter 1, on surrender of the center). "Restraint" might have been effected by ...Be7, ...0-0, ...b6, and Bb7.

6.Nxd5 Qxd5 7.Be3

It was to be able to make this move, which combines development and attack (the threat is 8.dxc5 winning a pawn), that White exchanged Knights.

7...cxd4

Disappearance of tempo spells a loss of time.

8.Nxd4 a6 9.Be2 Qxg2

Stealing a pawn. The consequences are disastrous.

10.Bf3 Qg6 11.Qd2 e5

The crisis. Black means to be rid of the unpleasant Knight so that he may catch up in development.

12.O-O-O! exd4 13.Bxd4

White's advantage in development is now too great.

13...Nc6 14.Bf6!

Travels by express. Any other Bishop move could have been answered by a developing move. Now there is no time for this; Black must take.

14...Qxf6 15.Rhe1+

Play in the d and e-files at the same time. The danger of a breakthrough is great.

15...Be7

If 15...Be6 16.Qd7 mate!

16.Bxc6+ Kf8

Or 16...bxc6 17.Qd8 mate.

17.Qd8+!! Bxd8 18.Re8 mate. 1-0.

Game 2

Teichmann-Nimzowitsch
Carlsbad 1911

1.e4 e5 2.Nf3 d6 3.d4 Nf6 4.Nc3 Nbd7

The Hanham variation. Development is more difficult, but it holds the center. To call the move "ugly" would be a question of aberration of taste. See game #40 between the same opponents.

5.Bc4 Be7 6.O-O O-O 7.Qe2 c6

Black at least establishes a sort of pawn majority in the center, though it is true that White for the time being, calls the shots.

8.a4

The closed character of the game allows pawn moves in the opening.

8...Qc7 9.Bb3 a6

In order to be able to eventually advance the c-pawn.

10.h3 exd4

Giving up the center must not here be regarded as illogical. Was happiness no happiness because it endured for just a short time? One cannot always be happy.

11.Nxd4 Re8

Restraint strategy, directed against the e-pawn.

12.Bf4 Bf8 13.f3 Nc5

The attentive student will here have expected Black to take possession of an advanced post at e5, but he wishes first to exchange. This is a commendable strategy in cramped positions.

14.Ba2 Ne6 15.Bxe6 Bxe6 16.Qd2 Rad8 17.Rfe1 Bc8 18.Rad1 Nd7

Now having harmoniously completed his development (though for harmony there was in truth not much room to spare in his cramped quarters), Black occupies the advanced post.

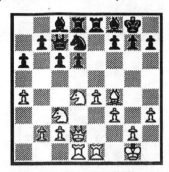

19.Nf5 Ne5

Controls the field with a large radius of attack. Any attempt to drive him away by f4 would weaken the e-pawn.

20.Nd4 f6

Observe the gradual paralyzing of the e-pawn.

21.Kh1 Qf7 22.Qf2 Qg6 23.b3 Nf7

Now ...f5 has been prepared. The student will perhaps ask what the Ne5 has accomplished. Quite enough, since White could undertake nothing.

24.Kh2 Re7 25.Nde2 (see next Diagram).

25...f5

Killing the paralyzed pawn.

26.Ng3 fxe4?

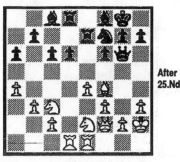

After 25.Nde2

Overhasty. 26...Rde8 should have been played. For example, 27. exf5 Bxf5 28.Nxf5 Qxf5 29.Bg3 Rxe1 30.Rxe1 Rxe1 31.Qxe1 Qxc2.

27.Ncxe4

After 27.fxe4? the e-pawn would have been very weak.

27...d5 28.Nc5 Rde8 29.Nd3 Rxe1

Black has equalized. 29...Nd6 would surrender the e5 square allowing 30.Be5.

30.Rxe1 Rxe1 31.Qxe1 Qe6 32.Qxe6 Bxe6 33.Be3

This good move puts Black's pawn majority under restraint. Black should now have contented himself with a draw; he wished to get more and lost the game as follows.

33...Bd6 34.f4 Kf8 35.Kg1 g6 36.Kf2 h5 37.Nc5 Bc8 38.a5 Nh6 39.b4 Kf7 40.c3 Ng8

40...Nf5 would have drawn.

41.Kf3 Nf6 42.Bd4 Bxc5 43.Bxc5 Be6 44.Bd4 Ne4 45.Ne2!

Not 45.Nxe4 dxe4+ 46.Kxe4 because of 46...Bd5+ and Bxg2.

45...Bf5

It's no use, Black is in effect a pawn down; his majority is paralyzed, White's is mobile.

46.g4 hxg4+ 47.hxg4 Nd2+

It would have been much better to keep the Bishop at home with 47...Bd7.

48.Kg3 Bc2 49.Ng1 Ke6 50.Kh4 Bd1 51.Nh3 Ne4

52.f5+

Ingeniously turns his majority to account.

52...gxf5

If 52...Kf7, then 53.fxg6+ Kxg6 54.Nf4+ would be unpleasant.

53.Nf4+ Kf7 54.g5! Bg4 55.g6+ Ke7 56.g7 Kf7 57.Ng6 1-0

Game 3

An excellent example of play in the open file. Black by this alone builds up a superior position and without the establishment of any outpost, he forces his way to the enemy's base.

Van Vliet - Znosko-Borovsky
Ostend, 1907

1.d4 d5 2.e3 c5 3.c3 e6 4.Bd3 Nc6 5.f4

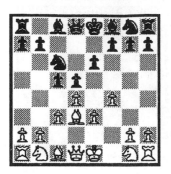

The Stonewall, a very close opening.

5...Nf6 6.Nd2 Qc7 7.Ngf3

Overlooks the threat involved in 6...Qc7. 7.Nh3 followed by 8.Qf3 would have been better.

7...cxd4! 8.cxd4

Positionally the right move here would usually be 8.exd4, giving White the e-file with an outpost station at e5, while the pawn at c3 closes the c-file, preventing its use by Black. Here, however it would lose a pawn. Nevertheless it was preferable to the text move, for 8.exd4 Qxf4 9.Nc4 Qc7 (9...Qg4 10.Ne3!) 10.Nce5 Bd6 11.Qe2, and White has a fairly protected outpost in the e-file, which Black cannot disturb even by 11...Bxe5 12.dxe5 Nd7 13.Bf4 f6?, for then comes 14.exf6 Qxf4 15.fxg7 Rg8 16.Qxe6+, and White wins. As long as the e-file with the outpost e5, or its full equivalent (a pawn at e5 for example), remains in White's possession, he

---

would stand excellently, despite being a pawn down.

8...Nb4 9.Bb1 Bd7 10.a3 Rc8

It is only by this subtle Rook move that the somewhat beginner-like Knight maneuver gets a meaning.

11.O-O Bb5 12.Re1 Nc2 13.Bxc2 Qxc2 14.Qxc2 Rxc2

Black has obtained the 7th Rank, the diagonal f1-a6 for his Bishop, and the e4 square for his Knight.

15.h3 Bd6 16.Nb1 Ne4

No outpost in our sense, as the open file behind is lacking, but yet a good substitute.

17.Nfd2 Bd3 18.Nxe4 Bxe4

18...dxe4 with the Bishop established at d3 would also have been good.

19.Nd2 Kd7 20.Nxe4 dxe4 21.Rb1 Rhc8 22.b4 R8c3 23.Kf1 Kc6 24.Bb2 Rb3 25.Re2 Rxe2 26.Kxe2 Kb5 27.Kd2 Ka4 28.Ke2 a5

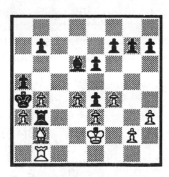

The decisive breakthrough. The position of Black's Rook, holding the

White e-pawn under continual threat, was also too strong to be withstood. The rest is easily understandable.

29.Kf2 axb4 30.axb4 Kxb4 31.Ke2 Kb5 32.Kd2 Ba3 33.Kc2 Rxb2+ 34.Rxb2+ Bxb2 35.Kxb2 Kc4 36.g4 Kd3 37.g5 Kxe3 and 0-1

Game 4

Lee-Nimzowitsch
Ostend, 1907

1.d4 Nf6 2.Nf3 d6 3.Nbd2 Nbd7 4.e4 e5 5.c3 Be7 6.Bc4 O-O 7.O-O exd4 8.cxd4 d5 9.Bd3 dxe4 10.Nxe4 Nxe4 11.Bxe4 Nf6 12.Bd3 Nd5 13.a3 Bf6

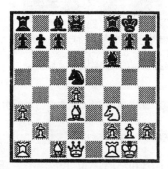

14.Qc2 h6 15.Bd2 Be6 16.Rae1 c6 17.Be3 Qb6 18.h3 Rad8 19.Rc1 Rd7

Quietly building up the position. The d-pawn cannot move, so why get excited?

20.Rfe1 Rfd8 21.Qe2 Qc7 22.Bb1 Ne7

His work done, (the Knight HAS been working), a change of air is good. The Knight is aiming for f5.

23.Ne5 Bxe5 24.dxe5 Qxe5 25.Bxa7 Qxe2 26.Rxe2 Rd1+

Black now invades the enemy position via the d-file.

27.Re1 Rxc1 28.Rxc1 Rd2

Now play on the 7th rank begins.

29.b4 Nd5 30.Be4 Nf6 31.Bc2 Nd5 32.Be4

32...Ra2

Allowing Bishops of opposite colors.

33.Bxd5 Bxd5 34.Rc3 f5!

All according to my system. Black seeks an object of attack on the 7th rank. Nothing can be done against the a-pawn, so the second player intends to lay bare White's h-pawn. This will be done by an advance on the Kingside.

35.Kh2 Kf7 36.Bc5 g5 37.Rd3 b5 38.Bd4 Be4 39.Rc3 Bd5 40.Bc5 Kg6 41.Rd3 h5 42.Bb6 f4 43.Bd4 Kf5 44.f3

White stood very badly. The threat was 44...g4, followed by ...g3+

44...g4 45.hxg4+ hxg4 46.Kg1 Re2

White's first rank is weak. ...g3 is threatened when the opportunity arises, and White has not a plethora of moves at his command.

47.fxg4+ Ke4! 48.Rd1 Bb3 49.Rf1 Kxd4 and 0-1 in a few moves.

In the two games which follow, the Knight as an outpost is the chief actor. In the first he is exchanged, but finds full compensation in the recapturing pawn. In the second his capacity to maneuver is exemplified.

Game 5

Dr. v. Haken-Giese
Riga, 1913

1.e4 e6 2.d4 d5 3.exd5 exd5 4.Nf3 Bd6 5.Bd3 Nf6 6.h3 O-O 7.O-O h6

In the exchange variation of the French defense with the KNs developed on f3 and f6 respectively, the pinning moves by the Bishops Bg5 and ...Bg4 furnish for both sides one of the leading motives. Here, however, this motif is

---

ruled out by the movement to h3 and h6 of the h-pawns. Except for a moment, we see and hear of, nothing but the e-file.

After 7...h6

8.Nc3 c6 9.Ne2 Re8 10.Ng3 Ne4

The outpost.

11.Nh5 Nd7 12.c3 Ndf6 13.Nh2 Qc7 14.Nxf6+ Nxf6 15.Nf3 Ne4 16.Bc2 Bf5

All pieces are directed towards the strategic point. This is also called emphasizing one's strength. Here we refer to the Knight on e4.

17.Nh4 Bh7 18.Be3 g5 19.Nf3 f5 20.Re1 Re7

The pressure in the file grows more acute move by move.

21.Nd2 f4 22.Nxe4 dxe4

The place of the outpost Knight is now worthily taken by a "half-passed" pawn.

23.Bd2 Rae8 24.c4 c5 25.Bc3 Bg6

In order to be able to play ...Kh7 and ...e3. A timely advance against the

pawn h3 is also threatened by ...h5 followed by ...g4.

26.Qg4 cxd4 27.Bxd4 Be5 28.Bxe5 Rxe5

29.Qd1

If 29.Rad1, then 29...e3 30.Bxg6 exf2+ 31.Kxf2 Qc5+ 32.Kf1 Qxc4+ 33.Kf2 Qc5+ 34.Kf1 Qb5+ 35.Kf2 Qxb2+ 36.Kf1 Qb5+ 37.Kf2 Qb6+ 38.Kf1 Qa6+ 39.Kf2 Qxa2+ 40.Kf1 Qa6+ 41.Kf2 Qb6+ 42.Kf1 followed by the double exchange on e1 and the capture of the Bg6. A fine example of the theme of winning a pawn with check.

29...Rd8 30.Qb1 Rd2 31.Bxe4 Qc5 32.Bd5+ Kg7 33.Qc1 Qxf2+ 34.Kh1 Rexd5 0-1.

The above game provides a transparent, therefore a good illustration to the outpost theme.

Game 6

A game from the early days of chess science.

Dr. Tarrasch-J. Berger
Breslau, 1889

After the opening moves:

1.e4 e5 2.Nf3 Nc6 3.Bb5 a6 4.Ba4 Nf6 5.Nc3 Bb4 6.Nd5 Be7 7.d3 d6, Tarrasch, with **8.Nb4 Bd7 9.Nxc6 Bxc6 10.Bxc6+ bxc6** gave Black a doubled pawn, whose weakness, however, must be considered for the present as problematic.

The game proceeded:

11.O-O O-O 12.Qe2 c5?

This move would today be considered bad. The weakness of the doubled pawn appears when Black advances, while an advance by White in the center would not reveal it. On the contrary, after d4, exd4 the pawn on c6 would attack White's outpost station on the Queen file! One can see how much easier thinking is made by the system.

Right was, therefore, 12...Re8 followed by...Bf8 awaiting events.

13.c3

To be able at any cost to play d4 as quickly as possible. We know today that the central attack is by no means the only one to bring happiness. The right course was Nd2-c4, followed after due preparation by b4 or f4, leaving the center passive.

13...Nd7 14.d4 exd4 15.cxd4 Bf6 16.Be3 cxd4 17.Bxd4 Re8 18.Qc2 Bxd4 19.Nxd4 Nc5

If this Knight is driven away, Black's c-pawn may become weak.

20.f3 Qf6 21.Rfd1 Reb8

White has the d-file with a point at d5. The e-file is of no value to Black, partly because of White's protected e-pawn, partly, however because his Rooks have been instructed to stop the move b4.

22.Rab1 a5 23.Kh1!

The idea of this subtle move is to use the center as a weapon of attack. The threat now after 23.Kh1! is 24.e5 Qxe5 25.Nc6 winning the exchange. This would have failed previously due to 25...Qe3+. Of positive value, however, there is little in this King move, for in any case Black would have to play ...Rb7 even if only to double Rooks. We see that Black operates in the b-file against the thrust b4.

23...Rb6

Not good, for White suddenly becomes strong on the d-file, as the outpost station at d5 will now be occupied with an attack on the Rb6. Better would have been 23...Rb7 (given by Steinitz) or some passive move like ...h6. For instance: 23...h6 24.e5 dxe5 25.Qxc5 exd4 26.Rxd4 a4 (the b-file is telling) 27.Rb4 Qd6, equalizing comfortably. Or 23...Rb7 24.Ne2 Rab8 25.Nc3 and now 25...a4 and the b-file makes itself felt.

24.Ne2 Ne6 25.Nc3 Rc6

It is intelligible that Berger should regard Nd5 as not conducive to his comfort, nevertheless, it would have been better to retreat in good order with 25...Qd8 26.Nd5 Rb7 followed by 27...Rab8.

26.Qa4 Rc5 27.Nd5 Qd8 28.Rbc1

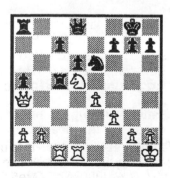

White's maneuver (Qa4, Rbc1) is as clear as daylight. White wishes to control the c-file, which is still in dispute, in order at the proper moment to play his trump card, Qc6.

28...Rxc1 29.Rxc1 c5

Puts c7 out of danger, but now the pawn on d6 has become a delicate child. Black, however, already stood unfavorably. He had in fact neglected the b-file.

30.Rd1 Nd4 31.Qc4

White wishes to exchange the Knight by the maneuver Nc3-e2 in order then to be able to attack the d-pawn to his heart's content. This attack must succeed, for the protecting pieces can easily get into uncomfortable positions (e.g. Black: Rd7, Qe7; White: Rd5, Qd3) in which the e-pawn will attack for the 3rd time and the Black d-pawn will be won. From our point of view it is of interest to notice how the White pieces have their eyes fixed on the point d5 (31.Qc4!). What happens is that if one is in possession of such a point as d5 is in this case, one embarks on protracted maneuvering with the point in question as base. That is to say one's own pieces come and go over the point d5. The poor Black d-pawn is attacked first in one way, now in another, and at last Black loses his wind, cannot keep pace with this tacking to and fro, which is intelligible enough since he not only has no base on which to pivot, but is in addition cramped for space (see Chapter 2 on maneuvering against enemy weakness). True, in this game it does not come to the sort of struggle we have sketched, for Black makes an error which takes the game out of the path of its logical development.

31...Rb8 32.b3 Rc8?

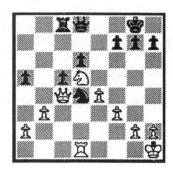

33.Rxd4 cxd4 34.Ne7+

and not 34.Qxc8? Qxc8 35.Ne7+, as the d-pawn would queen.

34...Qxe7 35.Qxc8+ Qf8 36.Qxf8+ Kxf8 and 1-0.

White won the pawn ending by means of the outside passed pawn. (See Diagram 58).

Game 7

Rabinowitsch-Nimzowitsch
Baden-Baden, 1925

1.d4 Nf6 2.c4 e6 3.Nf3 b6 4.Nc3 Bb7 5.Bg5 h6 6.Bh4 Be7 7.e3 d6 8.Bd3 Nbd7

Black has a solid but cramped game; such a game can as a rule only be slowly opened up.

9.0-0 0-0 10.Qe2 e5

Slower, therefore more true to type would be 10...Nh5.

11.dxe5 Bxf3!

Not 11...Nxe5 12.Nxe5 dxe5 13.Rfd1 with pressure on the d-file.

12.gxf3 Nxe5 13.Bxf6 Bxf6 14.Be4 Rb8

White with his d-file and Knight outpost at d5 will be able to force ...c6, that is already clear. True the Black d-pawn will not be difficult to defend, for it stands on a square of the same color of the Bishop, but what is going to happen on the g-file? This we shall soon see.

15.Rad1 Nd7! 16.Nd5 Nc5 17.Bb1 a5

No outpost, yet strong. The student should learn by careful practice how to establish Knights so that they cannot be driven away.

18.Kh1 g6

This would in any event be forced by Qc2.

19.Rg1 Bg7 20.Rg3 c6! 21.Nf4 Rb7!

The situation in the g-file may now be regarded as so far cleared up. It is evident that the threat consists in a sacrifice at g6 (the "revolutionary" type attack). A slow, undermining operation

---

by h4 and h5, on the other hand, would be difficult to carry through.

22.Qc2 Qf6 23.b3

He might have tried the "combination" 23.Nh5 Qxb2 24.Rxg6 fxg6 25.Qxg6, but the attack would hardly have succeeded.

23...Re8 24.Ne2

In order to bring the Knight to d4. White's dilemma consists in having two files, the d-file and the g-file. He cannot quite decide which one to use, and on this indecision his game goes to pieces.

Rd7 25.Rd2 Red8 26.Nf4 Kf8 27.Qd1 h5!!

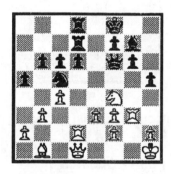

Not merely to make ...Bh6 possible, but also because the h-pawn has a great role to play.

28.Qg1 Bh6 29.Ne2 d5

Gets rid of the weakness at d6 and soon commands the d-file.

30.cxd5 Rxd5 31.Rxd5 Rxd5 32.f4

If 32.Nd4, then 32...Bf4 33.exf4 Qxd4 34.f5 h4! 35.Rg4 Qc3 and now the f3 pawn is difficult to defend.

32...Bg7

The decision to abandon the diagonal c1-h6, a difficult one to have to make is here comparatively easy to one who knows that there will be impediments (perhaps a Knight at d4) to be bombarded. I did not like 32...Rd2 at once because of the reply 33.Nd4 Bxf4 34.Rf3.

33.Qc1

I had expected here (at last!) the sacrifice at g6 and had prepared a real problem in reply. 33.Bxg6 h4! 34.Rg4 fxg6 35.Rxg6 Qf5! 36.Rxg7 Qe4+ 37.Qg2 (forced) 37...Rd1+ 38.Ng1, and now the point, 38...h3 39.Qxe4 Nxe4 threatening mate at f2.

33...Qd6

The exploitation of the d-file which now follows is all according to book (I mean my book), but is here embellished by a pretty feature.

34.Bc2 Ne4 35.Rg2 h4 36.Ng1

I was glad to be rid of the Knight and played...

36...Nc3

This Knight maneuver makes possible the invasion of the enemy's base (here his 1st and 2nd ranks).

37.a4

If 37.a3, then 37...Na2 winning the a-pawn.

37...Na2 38.Qf1 Nb4

Here I had the unpleasant feeling that I had let the Bishop escape, or at least allowed him elbow room .

39.Be4 Rd1

My first thought was: What a pity! Now the Queen will also find her way into the open, but then I saw the mating specter loom up, the same one which I had known well since the 33rd move.

40.Qc4 f5 41.Bf3 h3 42.Rg3 Nd3

43.Qc2 Rc1

Here I rejoiced over the Queen's involuntary return home.

44.Qe2 Rb1

and **0-1**, for the turning move 45...Rb2 will be in deadly effect.

The impression we get from this game is that the system supports combinative play most effectively.

And now a short game which is especially interesting since the outpost appears only as a threat, as a mere ghost, and yet its effect is enormous.

Game 8

Samisch-Nimzowitsch
Copenhagen, 1923

1.d4 Nf6 2.c4 e6 3.Nf3 b6 4.g3 Bb7 5.Bg2 Be7 6.Nc3 O-O 7.O-O d5 8.Ne5 c6

Safeguards the position.

9.cxd5 cxd5 10.Bf4 a6!

To protect the outpost station c4, by this move and ...b5.

11.Rc1 b5 12.Qb3 Nc6

The ghost! With noiseless steps he presses on to c4.

13.Nxc6

Samisch sacrifices two tempi (exchange of the tempo-eating Ne5 for the Nc6 which is almost undeveloped) merely to be rid of the ghost.

13...Bxc6 14.h3 Qd7 15.Kh2 Nh5

I could have supplied him with yet a second ghost by 15...Qb7, and

Nd7-b6-c4, but I wished to turn my attention to the Kingside.

16.Bd2 f5! 17.Qd1 b4! 18.Nb1 Bb5 19.Rg1 Bd6 20.e4

20...fxe4!

This sacrifice, which has a quite surprising effect, is based upon the following sober calculation: two pawns and the 7th rank, plus an enemy Queenside which cannot be untangled - all this for only one piece!

21.Qxh5 Rxf2 22.Qg5 Raf8 23.Kh1 R8f5 24.Qe3 Bd3 25.Rce1 h6!!

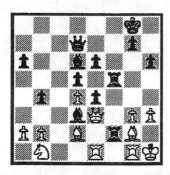

A brilliant move which announces the *Zugzwang*. White has not a move left. If 26.Kh2 or g4 then comes 26...R5f3. Black can now make waiting moves with

his King, and White must eventually throw himself upon the sword. **0-1**

Game 9

Nimzowitsch-Pritzel
Copenhagen, 1922

1.d4 g6 2.e4 Bg7 3.Nc3 d6 4.Be3 Nf6 5.Be2 O-O 6.Qd2

In order by Bh6 to exchange the Bg7.

6...e5 7.dxe5 dxe5 8.O-O-O

The plan chosen by White is seductive in the simplicity of the means to be employed. He intends after allowing the exchange of Queens, to get some advantage on the d-file.

8...Qxd2+ 9.Rxd2 c6

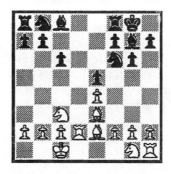

Moves which weaken such important points such as d6 should be avoided if in any way possible, and in fact a piece soon settles itself on this square. The important point to be observed by the student is that before Black's ...c6 the d-file was only under pressure, whereas after this move it is clearly weakened. It would have been better to forgo ...c6 and to instead have played 9...Nc6. For instance, the continuation might be 10.h3 (in order to be able to play 11.Nf3 without the fear of the reply 11...Ng4), 10...Nd4!? 11.Nf3! (but not 11.Bxd4 exd4 12.Rxd4 Ng4!), 11...Nxe2+ or 11...Nxf3 and White stands better after either recapture.

Nevertheless, 9...Nc6 was the correct move, but after 10.h3, Black must continue with 10...Be6. For example 10.h3 Be6 11.Nf3 h6 12.Rhd1 a6. In this position White has unquestionably full possession of the d-file. Since, however, neither an invasion of the 7th rank by Rd7 nor the establishment of an outpost by Nd5 lies within the realm of possibility, the value of the file would seem to be problematic. White's e-pawn is in need of protection and this circumstance has a considerable crippling effect.

Black has two courses open for consideration: (a) to play at once ...Rfd8, with the idea of the double exchange on d8 followed by Nxe5 and ...Nxe4 though this variation must be prepared for by ...Kh7 or ...g5 in order to safeguard the h-pawn against the Be3. (b) the slow maneuver ...Rfc8, followed by K-f8-e8, and finally the challenge of the Rooks by ...Rd8. The fact that this last line of play is possible is significant proof of the small amount of activity of White on the d-file.

10.a4

Apparently compromising, in reality, well thought out, for first b5, which would be an indirect and therefore unwelcome attack on the pawn at e4, must be prevented, and second, Black's Queenside is to be besieged. We feel ourselves justified in pursuing this ambitious plan since now that 9...c6 has been played our positional advantage in the center is unquestionable and should have a real effect even on the wings; a proposition which may be thus formulated: *a superior position in the center justifies a thrust on an extreme flank.*

10...Ng4 11.Bxg4 Bxg4 12.Nge2 Nd7

In unusual situations ordinary moves are, it would seem, seldom suitable. The proper system of development here was ...Na6, ...Rfe8, and ...Bf8. The weakness at d6 would then have been covered and the position would have been perfectly tenable.

13.Rhd1 Nb6 14.b3 Bf6 15.f3 Be6 16.a5 Nc8 17.Na4

It is now clear that the suggested development by 12...Na6 would have wasted less time than that in the text (Nd7-b6-c8). White now has a strong position on the Queenside and threatens to get a grip on the enemy with Nc5. We see that 10.a4! was valuable as an attacking move.

17...b6 (see next Diagram)

An excellent parry. If 18.axb6 axb6 19.Bxb6 (19.Nxb6 Nxb6 20.Bxb6 Bg5) naturally comes 19...Bg5.

18.Rd3 bxa5

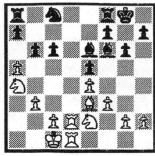

After 17...b6

Bad. The right move was 18...Rb8 and Black's position still had life in it.

19.Rc3 Ne7 20.Rc5 Rfb8 21.Nec3

The a-pawn won't run away.

21...a6 22.Rxa5 Kg7 23.Nb6 Ra7 24.Nca4

One Knight makes room for the other.

24...Rab7 25.Rxa6 Nc8 26.Nxc8 Rxc8 27.Nc5 Rbc7 28.Rd6

Now at last the point seized which Black weakened by his 9th move; but its occupation had always been in the air.

28...Rd8 29.Rxe6 1-0.

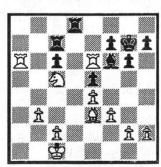

Final Position

In the notes to this game we have become acquainted with the resources at the disposal of the defender of a file. Since a knowledge of these is of the greatest practical value in the conduct of a game, we give another game which will be found instructive in the same sense.

Game 10

Nimzowitsch-Dr. Tarrasch
Breslau, 1925

1.Nf3 Nf6 2.c4 c5 3.Nc3 d5

Playable, but 3...e6 seems better. 3...e6 4.d4 cxd4 5.Nxd4 Bb4 or even 3...Nc6. For example 3...Nc6 4.d4 cxd4 5.Nxd4 g6, and now White could, it is true, by means of 6.e4, slowly try to tie up his opponent, but this attempt could be adequately parried by 6...Bg7 7.Be3 Ng4! (Breyer's move) 8.Qxg4 Nxd4 9.Qd1! Ne6! (suggested by Nimzowitsch). The position reached after 9...Ne6! is fairly rich in resources for Black. Development might continue with ...Qa5 ...0-0 followed by ...f5 ...b6 and ...Bb7. The student should examine for himself these lines of play.

4.cxd5 Nxd5 5.d4 cxd4

Best for Black would appear to be 5...Nxc3 6.bxc3 cxd4 7.cxd4 e6.

6.Qxd4 e6 7.e3 (see next Diagram)

A very cautious move, on which I decided because I recognized the more enterprising continuations 7.e4 and 7.Nxd5 exd5 8.e4, as leading to little for

---

After 7.e3

White. For instance 7.e4 Nxc3 8.Qxc3 (after 8.Qxd8+ and bxc3 he would have had a sick c-pawn on an open file to tend) 8...Nc6 9.a3 Qa5!; or 9.Bb5 Bd7 with equality. Or 7.Nxd5 exd5 8.e4 dxe4! 9.Qxd8+ Kxd8 10.Ng5 Bb4+ 11.Bd2 Bxd2+ 12.Kxd2 Ke7 with an equal game. The student who is interested in problems of development should test the following variation: 7.Nxd5 exd5 8.e4 Nc6 instead of 8...dxe4! as given by us. After 9.Qxd5 Qxd5 10.exd5 Nb4 there would follow 11.Bb5+ Black would have difficulty in finding a good continuation.

7...Nc6 8.Bb5 Bd7 9.Bxc6 Bxc6 10.Ne5 Nxc3 11.Nxc6 Qxd4 12.Nxd4 Nd5 13.Bd2

The position here shown is for all its harmless appearance full of poison.

White threatens to take possession of the c-file, moreover he has at his disposal a convenient square for his King (e2). Black on the other hand enjoys this last advantage in only a restricted fashion See note to move 17. In such positions the defense must be very carefully played.

13...Bc5

In order to drive the Knight away from the center, but as the Knight moves to b3 in order to promote c5 into an outpost station, 13...Bc5 proves to be pleasant for White. Best appears to be 13...Be7 intending ...Bf6. For example 13...Be7 14.e4 Nb6 15.Rc1 0-0 16.Ke2 and now White is full of pride in his developed King. His Black majesty however, can in this case give up all thought of development since the Be7 is a crafty minister, who likes to keep the reins of government in his own hands. For instance: 16...Bf6! 17.Be3 Rfc8 18.b3 Bxd4 19.Bxd4 and now 19...Nd7, or else 19...Rxc1 20.Rxc1 Rc8 21.Rxc8+ Nxc8 22.Kd3 and though it is true that the White King is now able to make his influence felt, it is questionable whether Black will not overtake his opponent. 22...f6 23.Kc4 Kf7 24.Kb5 a6+! (else the Bishop sacrifice) 25.Kc5 Ke7 followed by ...Kd7 with a draw. It follows that 13...Be7 was the correct defense.

14.Nb3 Bb4

Either 14...Bb6 or 14...Be7 would have been decidedly better. 14...Bb6 would have safeguarded c7 against invasion, and this in the defense is an imperative duty. After 14...Bb6 15.e4 Ne7 White's advantage would have been infinitesimal.

15.Rc1 Rd8 16.Bxb4 Nxb4 17.Ke2

Black has cleared a square for himself, but at what a cost of valuable time (...Bc5-b4).

17...Ke7 18.Rc4 Na6

An unpleasant retreat. If 18...Nc6, then not 19.Nc5 because of 19...Na5 and 20...b6, but rather a doubling of Rooks, and Black's position would not be favorable.

19.Rhc1 Rd7

Black's position still makes an impression which inspires confidence in it, and this at a moment when it carries the seeds of death in itself. The next two moves of White reduce Black's d-file to passivity.

20.f4! Rhd8 21.Nd4 f6

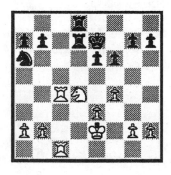

22.a4!

Even the full advance of a pawn can imply a waiting policy. White does not fear ...e5 in the least for after 22...e5 23.fxe5 fxe5, Black's e-pawn would be weak. The more energetic 22.b4 was also to be considered, but would have been less advantageous because of the reply 22...b5. Now, however this move

(b4) threatens to confine Black within still narrower limits.

22...e5

In a cramped position the attempt to strike out is explicable on psychological grounds, even if it is not always equally justified if viewed dispassionately. So too, here. It is true that in any case Black stands badly.

23.fxe5 fxe5 24.Nf3 Ke6 25.b4 b6 26.R1c2!

One of those unpretentious moves which are more disagreeable to a cramped opponent who is threatened on all sides than the worst direct attack. The move is a defending and a waiting move, and moreover involves a threat, though this from the nature of things is but a small one, and is in fact of but secondary importance. The slight threat is 27.Ng5+ and Ne4 followed by b5, driving the Black Knight back to b8.

26...h6 27.h4! Rd6 28.h5

As a result of 26.R1c2! entirely new attacking possibilities have arisen. Black's pawn on g7 has become backward. The maneuver Rg4 would, however, not only help to expose the weakness of the g-pawn, but, what is more important, put the Black King in an extremely disagreeable situation. All this fell like ripe fruit into White's lap simply and solely as the logical result of the waiting move 26.R1c2!. The finest moves are after all, waiting moves!

28...Rd5 29.Rg4 R5d7 30.Rc6+ Rd6

If 30...Kf5?, then 31.Rcg6 followed by mate. If 30...Kd5 31.Rcg6 e4!, there

---

would follow 32.Nd2 Nxb4 33.Nxe4 with advantage to White.

31.Rg6+

The possession of the points c6 and g6 insures the complete investment of the enemy King. Observe how the c-file has been used as a jumping off place to get into the g-file.

31...Ke7

On 31...Kd5 there would have followed a pretty little catastrophe. 32.Rcxd6+ Rxd6 33.e4+ Kc6 34.b5+ and the Knight, who had felt so thoroughly safe at a6, to his intense surprise meets his doom!

32.Rxg7+ Kf8 33.Rxd6 Rxd6 34.Rxa7 Nxb4 35.Nxe5 Re6

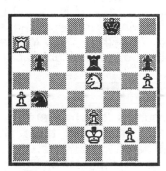

White wins. To make effective use of a superiority in material is one of the most important things which a student has to learn. He cannot practice himself enough in it. White has now won two pawns. A glance at the position shows (1) that White commands the 7th rank; (2) that White's e-pawn is isolated and his g-pawn is backward. The policy, therefore, is, taking full advantage of the 7th rank, to unite our isolated or badly placed detachments. To this end the

Knight will be brought, with gain of tempo, to f5.

36.Ng6+ Kg8! 37.Ne7+ Kf8 38.Nf5 Nd5 39.g4

The Knight at f5 has the effect planned for him, he protects the e-pawn, attacks the h-pawn, and makes Kf3 possible.

39...Nf4+ 40.Kf3 Nd3

In order, if 41.Rh7, to protect the h-pawn by 41...Ne5+ and 42...Nf7.

41.Ra8+! Kf7 42.Rh8 Nc5 43.Rh7+

One always returns to his first love!

43...Kg8

For if 43...Kf8, White gets a mating attack or the advance of his g-pawn cannot be stopped.

44.Rxh6 Rxh6 45.Nxh6+ Kf8 46.Nf5 Nxa4 47.h6 Kg8 48.g5 Kh7 49.Kg4 Nc5 50.Kh5

According to the motto, the line will advance!

50...Ne6 51.g6+ Kg8 52.h7+ Kh8 53.Kh6 1-0

Game 11

Sir George Thomas-Dr. Alekhine
Baden-Baden, 1925

1.e4 Nf6 2.d3 c5 3.f4 Nc6 4.Nf3 g6
5.Be2 Bg7 6.Nbd2 d5 7.O-O O-O
8.Kh1 b6 9.exd5 Qxd5 10.Qe1 Bb7
11.Nc4

The position of this Knight is all White
has as poor compensation for the lack
of harmony in his position (the Be2 is
clearly limited in scope). Black stands
much better. White on his 5th move or
even sooner should have played c4.

11...Nd4

Outpost on the d-file.

**12.Ne3 Qe6 13.Bd1 Nd5 14.Nxd4 cxd4
15.Nxd5 Qxd5 16.Bf3 Qd7 17.Bxb7
Qxb7**

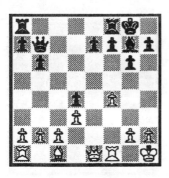

White has eased his position by the
exchanges, but the open c-file forces the
next disorganizing move.

**18.c4 dxc3 e.p. 19.bxc3 Rac8 20.Bb2
Rfd8 21.Rf3 Bf6 22.d4**

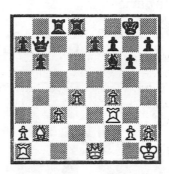

We have now arrived at a well-known
position in the QP opening but with
colors reversed. Compare the opening
to the following game, Nimzowitsch vs.
Professor Kudrjawzew and Dr. Landau
(in consultation) Dorpat, 1910 1.d4 d5
2.Nf3 Nf6 3.c4 e6 4.Nc3 c5 5.cxd5 exd5
6.Bg5 cxd4 7.Nxd4 Be7 8.e3 O-O 9.Be2
Nc6 10.Nxc6 bxc6 .

**Nimzowitsch vs. Kudrjawzew and
Landau , Dorpat 1910**

And now we have the same pawn
configuration (with colors reversed) as
in the game Thomas-Alekhine. The
game went on: 11.O-O Be6 12.Rc1 Rb8
13.Qc2 Bd7 14.Rfd1. The well-known
theme of isolated pawns now comes up
for discussion. 14...Ne8 15.Bxe7 Qxe7
16.Na4 Nf6 17.Nc5 Rb6 18.Rd4! Rfb8
19.b3 Be8 20.Bd3 h6 21.Qc3 Bd7
22.Ra4 with a marked advantage in

---

position. We now revert to the Thomas-Alekhine game -

22...Qd5 23.Qe3 Qb5 24.Qd2 Rd5 25.h3 e6 26.Re1 Qa4 27.Ra1 b5 28.Qd1 Rc4

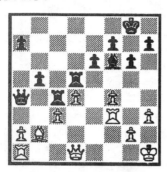

The "restricted advance", or else the c-file used as a jumping off place for the a-file. Observe the similarity of the maneuver in this game and the consultation game quoted above.

29.Qb3 Rd6 30.Kh2 Ra6

The d-file is also used as a jumping off place!

31.Rff1 Be7 32.Kh1 Rcc6

Very fine! The regrouping ...Qc4, ...Ra4, and...Rca6 is planned.

33.Rfe1 Bh4 34.Rf1

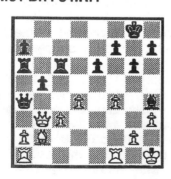

White dare not weaken his own base by 34.Re5? Qxb3 35.axb3 Rxa1 36.Bxa1 Ra6 37.Bb2 Ra2 and wins.

34...Qc4! 35.Qxc4 Rxc4

The exchange is grist to Black's mill, for now White's a-pawn has become very weak. The student should notice that the exchange is the direct, almost automatic result of the quiet seizing of strategically important points. The beginner seeks to bring about an exchange in other ways; he pursues the piece, which tempts him, with offers to exchange only to have them refused. The master occupies the strong points and the exchange which seems desirable to him falls like ripe fruit into his lap.

36.a3 Be7 37.Rfb1 Bd6 38.g3 Kf8 39.Kg2 Ke7

Bringing the King to the center.

40.Kf2 Kd7 41.Ke2 Kc6 42.Ra2 Rca4 43.Rba1 Kd5

Centralization is now complete.

44.Kd3 R6a5 45.Bc1 a6 46.Bb2 h5

A new attack and yet the logical consequence of the play on the

Queenside, for the White Rooks are chained to the a-pawn, and even if we assumed the Black Rooks to suffer from a like immobility, which is not the case since they can be brought into play via c4 against the White c-pawn, there remains to Black an indisputable advantage in the more enterprising position of his King. That this advantage should weigh in the balance at all, we have once more only to thank the fact that as a consequence of Black's diversion the White Rooks have lost their wind. If they were mobile, White's advantage derived from his King position would be illusory. Thus the attack on the extreme flank has not immaterially increased the importance of the mobility of Black's King. The strategic contact between the two seemingly separated theatres of war is now made clear. And now on the Kingside Black's ...h5 is intended to provoke h4, in order that, with White's g3 exposed, ...e5 may exercise its full effect. A very instructive case which is recommended for study.

47.h4 f6 48.Bc1

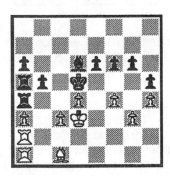

48...e5

The breakthrough which sets the seal on White's downfall.

49.fxe5 fxe5 50.Bb2 exd4 51.cxd4 b4!

As obvious as this move is, it must yet delight every connoisseur, that the sole purpose of the breakthrough was to get the disturbing White c-pawn out of the way.

52.axb4 Rxa2 53.bxa5 Rxb2 0-1.

The restricted advance was in this game carried out with great virtuosity.

Game 12

P.S. Leonhardt-Nimzowitsch
San Sebastian, 1912

1.e4 e5 2.Nf3 d6 3.d4 Nf6 4.Nc3 exd4

Surrender of the center. Black will seek to keep White's e-pawn under restraint. See game #2.

5.Nxd4 Be7 6.Be2 O-O 7.O-O Nc6 8.Nxc6 bxc6

This exchange creates advantages for both sides. Black gets a more compact pawn formation in the center, safeguards for instance, d5 against its possible occupation as an advanced post by a White Knight, but his a-pawn is isolated, moreover, as in the game continuation, c5 may become a weak point.

9.b3 d5

Very playable here would also have been ...Re8 and ...Bf8, directed at the restraint of the White e-pawn.

10.e5 Ne8 11.f4 f5

Otherwise 12.f5 with a strong attack.

12.Be3 g6!

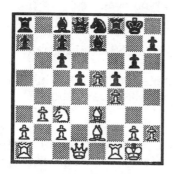

13.Na4! Ng7 14.Qd2 Qd7

In order to follow with ...Rd8 as soon as possible.

15.Qa5

Combines continued pressure on c5 (see note to move 8) with play against the weak, isolated Black a-pawn.

15...Ne6 16.Rad1 Rd8 17.Nc5?

A positional mistake. White should seek to keep the Knight as a potential blockader, or at any rate only exchange him for a Knight. The situation is this: the two Knights are here the chief actors (because they are most effective in blockade) and whoever gives up his proud horseman for a Bishop gets in this case the worst of the bargain. 17.Bc5 was the correct move.

17...Bxc5 18.Bxc5 Bb7 19.Rf3 Kf7 20.Rh3 Kg7 21.Rf1 Re8 22.Rhf3 Rad8

The a-pawn is poisoned. 23.Qxa7? Ra8 24.Qxb7 Reb8. There is little that White can undertake.

23.Rd1 a6 24.b4 Kh8 25.Qa3 Rg8 26.Qc3 Rg7 27.Kh1 Rdg8

Black plans ...g5, and in this the blockading Knight at e6 would render priceless service. A comparison between the two blockading pieces, the Black Knight at e6, and the White Bishop at c5, is here all in favor of the Knight. The Bishop does his work as a blockader pure and simple enough, but his effective range of action is very limited.

28.Be3 c5!

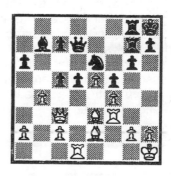

The advance which we have so often discussed! The Bishop's diagonal is opened by the pawn sacrifice. It may be objected that the c-pawn is here neither a passed pawn or even a candidate, yet logically he must be filled with that ambition to expand, for otherwise White would not have kept him under blockade for so long. Now he takes vengeance for the restraint he has had to suffer.

29.Rg3

Best, as given by Schlechter would have been 29.bxc5 d4 30.Rxd4 Nxd4 31.Bxd4 Bxf3 32.Bxf3 with two Bishops and two pawns in exchange for two Rooks.

29...d4 30.Qa3 g5 31.Bc4 gxf4

31...Bd5 would have been good, if only to preserve the Knight.

32.Bxe6

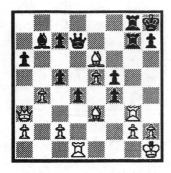

32...Bxg2+!

Now the Bishop runs amok! The death of the Knight makes him utterly reckless.

33.Kg1

But behold he still lives! Indeed after 33.Kxg2 (33.Rxg2? Qc6) 33...Qc6+ 34.Kf1 fxg3 35.Bxg8 gxh2 he would be bloodily avenged.

33...Qxe6

He who would regard 32...Bxg2+! as a bolt from a clear sky, shows that he has not fully grasped the logic which lay in this sudden irruption of the Bishop, which had been kept under restraint for such ages.

34.Bxf4 Bb7 35.bxc5 Qd5

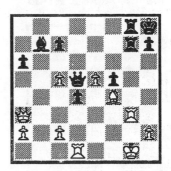

36.c6 Bxc6 37.Kf2 Rxg3 38.hxg3 Qg2+ 39.Ke1 Bf3 40.Qxa6 Qg1+ 0-1.

Game 13

An instructive example of the method of dealing with the supports of a blockader. In the endgame they are usually driven away, in the middlegame, on the other hand, they are kept busy.

Nimzowitsch-von Gottschall
Breslau, 1925

1.Nf3 e6 2.d4 d5 3.e3 Nf6 4.b3 Nbd7

He should have played 4...c5 and ...Nc6.

5.Bd3 c6 6.O-O Bd6 7.Bb2 Qc7

In order to play ...e5 opening up the game. To prevent this, White counterattacks.

8.c4 b6 (see next Diagram)

If 8...e5, the continuation would be 9.c5 Be7 (9...e4 10.cxd6 Qxd6 11.Ba3) 10.dxe5 Ng4 11.b4 Ndxe5 12.Nxe5

Nxe5 13.f4 Nxd3 14.Qxd3 and White commands the diagonal a1-h8.

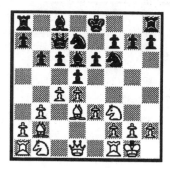

9.Nc3 Bb7 10.Rc1 Rc8 11.cxd5 exd5 12.e4

Opening up all the lines.

12...dxe4 13.Nxe4 Nxe4 14.Bxe4 O-O 15.d5 c5

The two Bishops now have a clear line of fire to the enemy Kingside. Impressed by this Black underestimates the fact that the d-pawn is now passed, in fact he overlooks it altogether. And indeed what possible role could this most carefully blockaded passed pawn play? In fact a reserve blockader is already stationed at d7! But things turn out quite otherwise.

16.Re1 Qd8 17.Bb1

The attack leads to the instructive result that the blockading pieces, the Bd6 and Nd7 are either cut off or killed.

17...Re8 18.Qd3

18.Rxe8+ first would have been more precise.

18...Nf8

And here too, 19...Rxe1+ would have been better.

19.Rxe8 Qxe8 20.Nh4! f6 21.Nf5 Rd8

Black is about to try to show the weakness of White's d-pawn, when he is awakened from his dream by the flash of a sacrifice.

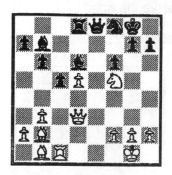

22.Bxf6 Bxh2+!

In order not to lose a pawn Black had to submit to this indirect exchange of his Bishop. If 22...gxf6 23.Nxd6 Rxd6 24.Qg3+ followed by 25.Qxd6.

23.Kxh2 gxf6

What a change! The Bishop on d6 has disappeared and the reserve blockader, the Nd7, will soon be landed at g6 leaving the White d-pawn free!

24.Qg3+ Ng6 25.f4

To allow the Rook to go to e1. The d-pawn is indirectly protected.

25...Kh8

Not the capture of the White d-pawn by the Rook or Bishop because of Re1 followed by Ne7+.

26.Re1

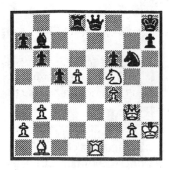

26...Qf8!

If 26...Qg8, the passed pawn would have come into his own in a most interesting way. 27.Ne7 Nxe7 28.Rxe7 (7th rank) 28...Qxg3+ 29.Kxg3 Rg8+ 30.Kf2 Rg7. Apparently the 7th rank is now neutralized, but the passed pawn has something to say about that. 31.d6 Rxe7 32.dxe7 Bc6 33.Be4 Be8 34.f5! Kg7 35.Bd5 and e7 is unassailable. 35...Kh6 36.Kf3 Kg5 37.Ke4, and Black cannot stop the threat of Bb7 followed by Kd5 and Bc6. The blockading Bishop must die.

27.d6! Rd7

Why not 27...Bc8? Would not this have led to the winning of the passed pawn? The answer is no, for the continuation would have been 28.Ne7 (By playing the pawn to d6 White has provided the Knight an outpost at e7) 28...Qh6+ (Best) 29.Kg1 Nxf4, and now 30.Nxc8 Rxc8 31.d7 wins.

28.Qc3

Threatening 29.Re8! Qxe8 30.Qxf6+ Kg8 31.Nh6 mate. Accordingly the 8th rank must be safeguarded by the retreat

28...Rd8, but in this case the 7th rank will be left without protection and White will win by playing the Rook to e7. Note that the winning moves Re7 or Ne7 (as in the last note) must be regarded as a direct consequence of the advance of the d-pawn.

28...Rxd6

A desperate gasp. If 28...Rf7, then 29.d7 Rxd7 30.Re8! would have been decisive.

29.Nxd6 Qxd6 30.Bxg6 hxg6 31.Re8+ Kg7 32.Qg3

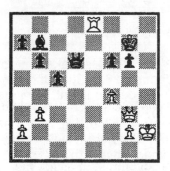

and White went on to win as follows:

32...Bc6 33.Re3 Bd7 34.f5 Qxg3+ 35.Kxg3 Bxf5 36.Re7+ Kh6 37.Rxa7 Bb1 38.Ra6 b5 39.a4 bxa4 40.bxa4 Kg5 41.Rb6 Be4 42.a5 f5 43.a6 c4 44.a7 c3 45.Rb3 f4+ 46.Kf2 c2 47.Rc3 1-0

Game 14

Nimzowitsch-C.Behting
Riga, 1919

1.e4 e5 2.Nf3 f5

According to C. Behting's view, which I am inclined to share, this move is quite playable. At any rate I do not know a refutation to it.

3.Nxe5 Qf6 4.d4 d6 5.Nc4 fxe4

6.Ne3!
Against this move speak (1) tradition, which demands 6.Nc3; (2) the principle of economic development, moving each piece only once in the opening; (3) the apparently small threat effect of the blockader. And yet 6.Ne3, taken with the following move is in every respect a master move. Even if all the rest of the world would play here 6.Nc3, I yet hold my move 6.Ne3 to be more correct, and this for reasons based on the "system."

6...c6 7.Bc4!!

The point. In order to be able to castle Black must now play 7...d5, but this move will hold out another field for the Knight after Bb3 and c4.

7...d5 8.Bb3 Be6

or 8...b5 9.a4 b4 10.c4,etc.

9.c4 Qf7 10.Qe2 Nf6 11.O-O

Not 11.Nc3 because of 11...Bb4. White wants to bring the maximum pressure to bear on d5. If we look at the blockading Ne3 more closely, do we find that it meets the requirements asked of a blockader? Yes, for (1) he establishes a strong blockade, hindering the approach of enemy pieces to g4(2) exercises threats from where he is stationed; (3) is very elastic, as we shall see later. In short, the Ne3 is an ideal blockader.

11...Bb4! 12.Bd2 Bxd2 13.Nxd2 O-O 14.f4

Threatening f5, winning the d-pawn.

14...dxc4 15.Ndxc4 Qe7 16.f5 Bd5

Black seeks to maintain the point d5.

17.Nxd5 cxd5 18.Ne3

Hardly has the Ne3 disappeared than a new one stands in his place. Against such "elasticity" not even Death can prevail.

18...Qd7 19.Nxd5!

The threat effect of the blockader from his post culminates in this decisive sacrifice.

19...Nxd5 20.Qxe4 Rd8 21.f6!

The point of the combination and at the same time a further illustration of the pawn's lust to expand, as the f-pawn was a "candidate".

21...gxf6

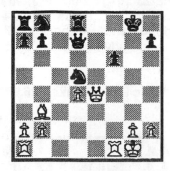

If 21...Nc6 22.f7+ Kh8 23.Bxd5 Qxd5? 24.f8=Q+, followed by 25.Qxd5. If 22...Kf8, then 23.Bxd5 Qxd5 24.Qxh7 and wins.

22.Rf5 Kh8 23.Rxd5 Re8

If 23...Qe8 24.Bc2! wins a whole Rook.

24.Rxd7 Rxe4 25.Rd8+ Kg7 26.Rg8+ Kh6 27.Rf1 1-0

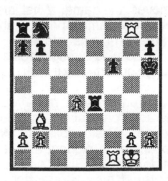

And now the companion picture to the above game.

Game 15

Nimzowitsch-von Freymann
Wilna, 1912

1.e4 e6 2.d4 d5 3.e5 c5 4.Nf3 cxd4

4...Qb6 seems to be better.

5.Nxd4 Nc6 6.Nxc6 bxc6 7.Bd3 Qc7 8.Bf4 g5

Not quite sound but leading to interesting play.

9.Bg3 Bg7 10.Qe2 Ne7 11.O-O h5 12.h3 Nf5 13.Bh2

If 13.Bxf5 exf5 14.e6 f4 15.exf7+ Kxf7 and Black is better.

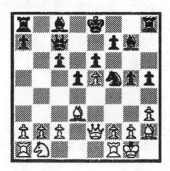

13...g4

The pretty point of the attack started by 8...g5.

14.Re1

The answer to 14.hxg4 hxg4 15.Qxg4 would be 15...Rxh2 16.Kxh2 Bxe5+ followed by ...Bxb2.

14...Kf8 15.Nc3

This Knight proposes to make his way to f4 after the Black Knight on f5 is exchanged off.

15...Qe7 16.Bxf5 exf5 17.Qe3 Rh6 18.Ne2 c5 19.Nf4!

This Knight is to be regarded as primarily the blockader of f5 and its adherent mass of pawns; but in addition he acts as an "anti-blockader" for his pawn at e5.

19...d4 20.Qd3 Qd7 21.Qc4 Qc6

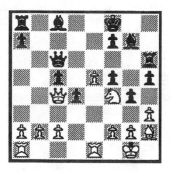

22.hxg4!

The necessary prelude to Nd3. If at once 22.Nd3 there would have followed 22...gxh3 23.Qxc5+ Qxc5 24.Nxc5 Rg6 25.g3 and White stands badly.

22...Ba6

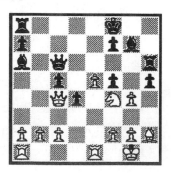

23.Qd5!! Qxd5

More interesting would have been 23...hxg4; the result would have been a triumphant march of the e-pawn. For instance 23...hxg4 24.e6 with attack on the Queen 24...Qxd5 25.e7+ Ke8 26.Nxd5 followed by check at c7. The "unexpected advance of the unstopped pawn."

24.Nxd5 Bc4 25.Nf6 hxg4 26.Bf4 Rg6 27.Nd7+

1-0 in 47.

Winning the c-pawn and after twenty more moves, the game. What interests us in the above game is primarily the role which the Nf4 has played. As a blockader he was strongly posted and excellently supported by the Bh2. Again, he had a crippling effect on Black's Bg7 and Rh6. Further, his "threat effect" was considerable, particularly on the points d5 and e6. (The mobility of White's e-pawn affords a piquant antithesis to the immobility of Black's f5 pawn). Lastly, the Knight's elasticity was striking, for he could composedly go on his travels, leaving the Bishop to take his place.

The three following games show the connection between the "pin" and the center.

Game 16

Nimzowitsch-P.S. Leonhardt
San Sebastian, 1911

1.e4 e5 2.Nf3 Nc6 3.Nc3 Nf6 4.Bb5 Bb4 5.O-O O-O 6.Bxc6 dxc6 7.d3

White now has a solid position, since the enemy d-file "bites on granite" (the protected d-pawn). This solidity, however, also finds expression in the fact that White's e-pawn can never be troubled by an advance of the Black d-pawn. In other words the center cannot be opened.

7...Bg4

The pin.

8.h3 Bh5 9.Bg5

9.g4 would have been premature because of 9...Nxg4 10.hxg4 Bxg4 followed by ...f5.

9...Qd6 10.Bxf6 Qxf6 11.g4

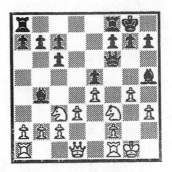

The "question" is here indicated, since the Bishop will be driven into a desert, which, because of the impossibility of ...d5, can never be transformed into a "flowering garden". Observe how the White h and g pawns slowly develop into storm troops.

11...Bg6 12.Kg2 Rad8 13.Qe2 Bxc3

Otherwise Nd1-e3-f5 would have followed.

14.bxc3 c5 15.Nd2

White now intends to bring his Knight to f5 via c4 and e3. He also proposes to prevent the embarrassing move ...c4 for as long as possible without having to play c4, as this move would leave an outpost at d4 unguarded.

15...Qe7 16.Nc4 b6 17.Ne3 f6

In order to free the Bishop. This move however, invites g5 when the opportune moment comes.

18.Rg1 Qd7 19.Kh2 Kh8 20.Rg3 Qb5 21.Qe1 Qa4 22.Qc1 Rd7 23.h4 Bf7 24.c4

Black has succeeded in provoking c4. In the meantime, however, White has

---

beautifully arranged the Kingside to suit his purposes.

24...Be6 25.Qb2 a5 26.Rag1 Qc6

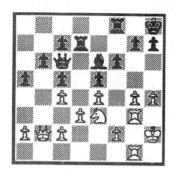

27.R1g2!!

White quietly makes his last preparations for a worthy reception of the enemy Queen at d4, for which she is striving. Observe how White has succeeded in combining the defense of the center with his plans for an attack on the Kingside.

27...Qd6 28.Qc1 Qd4?

29.Nd5!

Winning the Queen, or as in the game, sufficient material for victory. This "trap" was everywhere applauded. That it was subordinate to those strategic ends I had set myself in this game was taken into consideration by nobody. The aim of my strategy was to prevent a breakthrough or any maneuvering in the center and to make possible the ultimate advance g5 with the attack. There followed:

29...Rxd5 30.c3 Qxd3 31.exd5

31.cxd5 was more accurate,

31...Qxc4 32.dxe6 Qxe6 33.Qc2 c4 34.Qf5 Qxf5 35.gxf5 and 1-0.

The student may see from the laborious and tedious defense which White adopted see moves 21, 22, 25, 28 that he fully recognized the fact that the disposition of his Kingside pawns on h3 and g4 demanded a closed center. This game elucidates the problem of the "question" in an instructive manner.

Game 17

Nimzowitsch-Dr. Fluss
Correspondence, 1913

1.e4 e5 2.Nf3 Nc6 3.Nc3 Nf6 4.Bc4 Bc5 5.d3 d6 6.Bg5 h6 7.Bh4 (see next diagram).

7.Be3 was of course also playable.

7...g5

Here 7...Be6 was probably better (see discussion of Diagram 88).

After 7.Bh4

8.Bg3 Bg4 9.h4 Nh5 10.hxg5

White here ought to have given more attention to the problem of the center. For instance 10.Nd5 Nd4 11.c3 and White is better.

10...Nd4

And here Black by 10...Nxg3 11.fxg3 Nd4, could have utilized the center which White has neglected. As we have already said (in our discussion of Diagram 88), 12.Nd5 would not be sufficient, since Black has the Queen sacrifice at his disposal. (12...Bxf3 13.gxf3 Qxg5 14.g4 c6 15.Rh5 cxd5!), nor would the sacrificial combination 12.Bxf7+ Kxf7 13.Nxe5+ dxe5 14.Qxg4 be enough, for after 14...Qxg5 15.Qd7+ Kg6, Black is safe. The move 10.hxg5 instead of the central thrust 10.Nd5, which we indicated,would seem to be a decisive mistake, of which Black could have taken advantage by 10...Nxg3 followed by 11...Nd4.

11.Bxe5!

A disconcerting evasion. White gives up the Bishop, but leaves Black with a Knight in the air, and a King in much the same state.

11...Bxf3

If 11...dxe5 immediately, then 12.Bxf7+ Kxf7 13.Nxe5+ Kg8 14.Qxg4 and wins.

12.gxf3 dxe5 13.Rxh5 Rg8

On the surface White's position is by no means enviable, for the Nd4 exerts pressure and the g-pawn seems doomed.

14.f4

The saving move.

14...exf4 15.Qg4

The point. White isn't afraid of Black's attack ...Nxc2+, which is only a flash in the pan.

15...Nxc2+ 16.Kd2 Nxa1

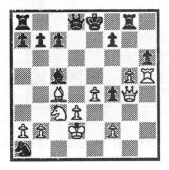

17.Bxf7+! 1-0.

For if 17...Kxf7 18.Qf5+ Ke8 19.Qe6+ Kf8 20.g6 and wins. On 19...Qe7 20.Qxg8+ Qf8 21.Qh7 Qe7 22.g6 Qxh7 23.gxh7 Bd4 24.Nb5!. Or 22...Bd4 23.Nb5 Qb4+ 24.Kd1 and wins.

Game 18

This game introduces a whole assortment of pins, poisonous and harmless ones following in quick succession.

Rubinstein-Nimzowitsch
Marienbad, 1925

1.d4 Nf6 2.Nf3 b6 3.g3 c5 4.Bg2 Bb7 5.dxc5 bxc5 6.c4

The line of play chosen by White is certainly not to be blamed. He holds the d-file with the outpost station at d5, whereas Black's majority in the center (the c, d, and e pawns against the White c and e pawns) gives evidence of but slight mobility.

6.... g6 7.b3 Bg7 8.Bb2 O-O 9.O-O

Each side castles now with a clear conscience, for not even the most hypermodern pair of masters can produce more than four fianchettoed Bishops!

9...Nc6

A normal move which has a deeper meaning. The Knight is better placed at

c6 than at b6 (Nd7-b6), for White is clearly planning the configuration Nc3, Qc2, followed by e4. Black therefore relies on the counter configuration ...Nc6, ...d6, ...a5, followed by ...Nd4 and when the opportunity presents itself, ...a4, thus sheltering his d-pawn behind the Nd4.

10.Nc3 a5 11.Qd2 d6 12.Ne1

The start of a tiring journey: Ne1-c2-e3-d5. More natural would have been 12.Nd5. For instance, 12...Nxd5 13.Bxg7 Kxg7 14.cxd5.

12...Qd7 13.Nc2 Nb4! 14.Ne3 Bxg2 15.Kxg2

Taking with the Knight would mean straying off the road to the goal of the journey, d5.

15...Qb7+ 16.f3

If 16.Kg1 Ne4 17.Nxe4 Qxe4 and the pawn at a5 becomes an actual menace.

16...Bh6

A pin of the harmless order, since obviously this last move creates a serious weakening of the Black Kingside.

17.Ncd1

Now the threat is 18.Bxf6 exf6 19.Qxd6.

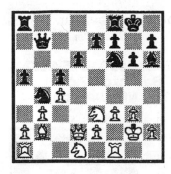

17...a4

See note to move 9.

18.bxa4 Rfe8!!

This purely defensive move against the previously mentioned threat of Bxf6 is surprising, since after the energetic thrust at move 17, which had been so eagerly looked forward to for so long, anything but a defensive move was to be expected. This amalgamation of attack and defense stamps the combination as a truly original one.

19.Bxf6 exf6 20.Kf2

Now White plans to break the pin by f4, after which he would be in a position to take possession of the d5 point once and for all.

20...f5!!

Revealing Black's plan. He threatens 21...f4 22.gxf4 Bxf4 with an enduring pin on the one hand, and 21...Bg7 followed by ...Bd4 with an equally chronic pin on the other. White is defenseless.

21.Qxd6 Bg7! 22.Rb1 Bd4

Threatening 23...Nd3+

23.Kg2

The poor Knights! At the 17th move they had to break their journey, and now they actually both have to die before reaching their journey's end. In reply to 23.Rb3, Black, with 23...Re6 24.Qf4 Qe7 (threatening 25...Nc2) 25.Kg2 Rae8 would have pushed forward the siege in the most energetic way.

23...Bxe3 24.Nxe3 Rxe3 25.Qxc5

Now it is White's turn to pin.

25...Rxe2+ 26.Rf2 Rxf2+ 27.Qxf2

Forced, for 27.Kxf2 Nd3+ and 28...Nxc5 protecting b7 would lose at once.

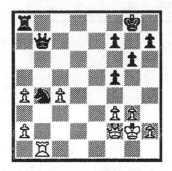

27...Rxa4!

The "immediate unpinning" by 27...Qe7 is avoided, as White can get no profit out of the pin.

28.a3

If 28.Qb2, then 28...Qc8! This is the only feasible retreat for the piece behind the pinned one.   28...Qc7 would be bad because of 29.Re1, just as 28...Qc6 would be because of 29.Rd1. Obviously 28...Rxa2? would be a gross error because of 29.Qxa2.

28...Rxa3 29.Qe2 Ra8

Now he goes back home, tired but happy.

30.c5 Qa6

Unpinning.

31.Qxa6 Nxa6 32.Ra1

A last pin.

32...Nc7

And a last unpinning.

33.Rxa8+ Nxa8

And White resigned on the 38th move.
0-1

There follow six games illustrating the Pawn-Chain.

Game 19

Louis Paulsen-Dr. Tarrasch
Played in 1888

1.e4 e6 2.d4 d5 3.e5 c5 4.c3 Nc6 5.Nf3 Qb6 6.Bd3 cxd4 7.cxd4 Bd7 8.Be2 Nge7 9.b3 Nf5 10.Bb2 Bb4+

11.Kf1

Forced, for otherwise the d-pawn falls.

11...Be7

In order to keep up the pressure on the d-pawn (12.g4 Nh4), but Black should have played to take direct advantage of White's spoiled Kingside with 11...0-0!

12.g3 a5?

In order to exploit the new "weakness" at b3. The only pity is that this point is no weakness; he should have gone for the weakened White King's position.

13.a4 Rc8 14.Bb5

The square b5 now becomes a good pivot for White's pieces.

14...Nb4 15.Bxd7+?

Quite wrong. With 15.Nc3 (see next game) White could have overcome all difficulties. For instance, 15.Nc3 Bxb5+ 16.Nxb5 Nc2 17.Rc1 Nce3+ 18.fxe3 Nxe3+ 19.Ke2 Nxd1 20.Rxc8+ Kd7 21.Rxh8 Nxb2 22.Rc1 and wins.

15...Kxd7

16.Nc3 Nc6 17.Nb5 Na7 18.Nxa7?

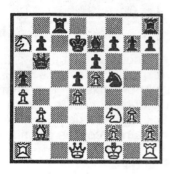

Never in this life should White have relinquished his Nb5. Instead 18.Qd3 Nxb5 19.axb5 would have sufficed. We can see what harm Black's a-pawn has done him.

18...Qxa7 19.Qd3 Qa6! 20.Qxa6

Now we shall see how a weakened "base" becomes a weakness in the endgame.

20... bxa6 21.Kg2 Rc2 22.Bc1 Rb8 23.Rb1 Rc3 24.Bd2 Rcxb3 25.Rxb3 Rxb3 26.Bxa5

Now White is happily rid of his weakness at b3 on an open file!, but the pawns on a4 and d4 are hard to defend.

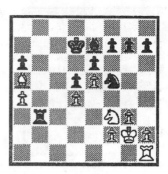

26...Rb2

Not 26...Ra3 because of 27.Rc1, but now the answer to 27.Rc1 would be 27...Ne3+ followed by ...Nc4.

27.Bd2 Bb4 28.Bf4 h6

There is no harm in this; Black's position can stand this little weakness. The pawn on h6 is now a possible objective.

29.g4 Ne7 30.Ra1 Nc6 31.Bc1 Rc2 32.Ba3 Rc4

32...Bxa3 would have been simpler.

33.Bb2 Bc3 34.Bxc3 Rxc3 35.Rb1 Kc7 36.g5 Rc4

Finally!

37.gxh6 gxh6 38.a5 Ra4 39.Kg3

A last desperate attempt to continue the attack begun by 36.g5.

39...Rxa5 (see next diagram)

and Black won as follows:

40.Kg4 Ra3 41.Rd1 Rb3 42.h4 Ne7 43.Ne1 Nf5 44.Nd3 a5 45.Nc5 Rc3

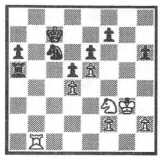

After 39...Rxa5

**46.Rb1 Nxd4 47.Na6+ Kd8 48.Rb8+
Rc8 49.Rb7 Ke8 50.Nc7+ Kf8 51.Nb5
Nxb5 52.Rxb5 Ra8 0-1.**

We recommend to the student to study
this well-played ending by Dr. Tarrasch.

Game 20

Nimzowitsch-Dr. Tarrasch
San Sebastian, 1912

**1.e4 e6 2.d4 d5 3.e5 c5 4.c3 Nc6 5.Nf3
Qb6 6.Bd3 cxd4 7.cxd4 Bd7 8.Be2
Nge7 9.b3 Nf5 10.Bb2 Bb4+ 11.Kf1
Be7 12.g3 a5 13.a4 Rc8 14.Bb5 Nb4
15.Nc3!**

15...Na6

For 15...Bxb5+ 16.Nxb5 Nc2, see the
note to move 15 in game 19.

**16.Kg2 Nc7 17.Be2 Bb4 18.Na2 Na6
19.Bd3 Ne7 20.Rc1 Nc6 21.Nxb4
Naxb4 22.Bb1**

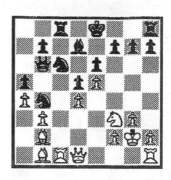

White has now overcome the difficulties
of development, the base d4 is now
thoroughly protected. The game can
now take another course. White opens
an attack against the Black Kingside
which is cramped by the pawn at e5.

22...h6 23.g4

To make castling appear unhealthy. The
maneuver Rc3-e3 was perhaps even
better here.

**23...Ne7 24.Rxc8+ Bxc8 25.Ne1 Rf8
26.Nd3 f6 27.Nxb4 Qxb4 28.exf6 Rxf6**

29.Bc1

The courage required to deliberately let oneself be kept under pressure for hours, simply for the sake of a remote chance of attack, now has its reward. White gets a direct attack. Note the dark-squared Bishop which has been roused to activity.

29...Nc6 30.g5 hxg5 31.Bxg5 Rf8 32.Be3

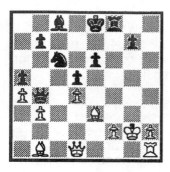

32...Qe7 33.Qg4 Qf6 34.Rg1 Rh8 35.Kh1 Rh4 36.Qg3 Rxd4

Despair! Both 37.Qxg7 and 37.Bg5 were threatened.

37.Bxd4 Nxd4 38.Qxg7 Qf3+ 39.Qg2 Qxg2+ 40.Rxg2 Nxb3 41.h4   1-0.

Final Position

Amos Burn remarks on this game:

"An excellent game on the part of Herr Nimzowitsch, well illustrating his strategic skill. Dr. Tarrasch, himself one of the greatest masters of strategy, is completely outplayed." Flattering as this praise is, I must, nevertheless, remark that it is probably not so very difficult to maneuver well if one has a complete system to fall back on. A pawn on e5, as I even then knew, seriously cramps Black's Kingside, and if White succeeds in holding d4 without any counterbalancing disadvantage elsewhere, a moment must sometime come when fortune will smile on him, in the form, that is, of an attack with his pieces on the Black King's cramped position, or else a vigorous onslaught on the chain by f4-f5 followed by fxe6. Today all of this seems plausible. At the time this game was played it seemed nothing short of revolutionary.

Game 21

The following game illustrates my idea of the two theatres of war in a particularly striking manner.

Professor Becker-Nimzowitsch
Breslau, 1925

1.e4 e6 2.d4 d5 3.Nc3 Nc6

The "odds-giving" style to use Dr. Lasker's expression. Lasker meant by this that one chooses a variation which one considers inferior, with the idea of setting the opponent a difficult problem to solve. Lasker played by preference - and with inimitable virtuosity - this style. It is this that might make people believe that the heel of Achilles lay for Lasker in his treatment of the openings. Such a judgment rests, however, on an entire misconception.

The move 3...Nc6 was introduced by Alapin. The Black c-pawn is obstructed, and in the event of White's playing a pawn to e5, there is a very dark side to Alapin's innovation.

4.Nf3 Bb4 5.e5 Bxc3+ 6.bxc3 Na5 7.a4

Not very intelligible. Better was 7.Nd2 Ne7 8.Qg4. Black would then have had laboriously to defend himself by 8...Nf5 9.Bd3 Rg8 10.Qh3 h6.

7...Ne7 8.Bd3 b6

Preparing to attack the White base d4 by ...c5.

9.Nd2 c5 10.Qg4

How is Black to defend his g-pawn?

10...c4

The answer is not at all, for all direct defenses would here be compromising.

11.Be2

If 11.Qxg7? Rg8 followed by cxd3.

11...Nf5

The g-pawn is protected, but the pressure on d4 has been removed and now White gets a free hand for play on the Kingside.

12.Nf3 h6

In order to be able to maintain the Nf5 at his good post. The threat was 13.Bg5 Q moves 14.Nh4. Lasker rightly preferred the elastic defense 12...Nc6, and if 13.Bg5, then 13...f6. Another interesting possibility is 12...Nc6 13.a5!? Nxa5 14.Bg5 f6 15.exf6 gxf6 16.Bh4 and now 16...Nxh4 would fail to 17.Qg7!. On the other hand 16...Qe7 would seem to consolidate the position sufficiently.

13.Qh3 Kd7

My King likes going for walks.

14.g4 Ne7 15.Nd2

With the threat of 16.Qf3 followed by 17.Qxf7 or 17.Nxc4!

15...Qe8

The Queen takes possession of the throne, which the King has vacated! She has her eye on the a-pawn for which she seems to have a fancy.

16.f4

The scene shifts! The old theatre of war vanishes in a flash and new plans of attack appear. White intends to attack the base of the chain by f5.

16...Kc7

The King proceeds on his walk.

17.Ba3 Bd7 18.Qf3 h5

White's Kingside provides him with a terrible instrument of attack. To blunt this was the object of Black's last move. 18...Bc6, (to counter the threat 19.Nxc4) would not have sufficed. 18...Bc6 19.f5 followed by f6 and the wedge would have been unendurable.

19.Nxc4!

If 19.gxh5 then comes 19...Nf5, and the Kingside, which had been all ready to march to the attack, is crippled. White should try 19.h3. then 19...hxg4 20.hxg4 Rxh1+ 21.Qxh1.

19...Nxc4 20.Bxc4 hxg4

Naturally not 20...dxc4?? 21.Bd6+ followed by 22.Qxa8+.

21.Qg2 Nf5 22.Bd3 Bxa4!!

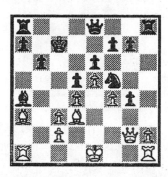

Lunch under dangerous conditions!

23.Bxf5 exf5 24.Qxd5

24.c4 would also have been difficult to parry. The defense would be found in 24...Qc6 25.Qxd5 (and not 25.cxd5 because of 25...Qc3+) 25...Qxd5! 26.cxd5 Bb5!!, for then the establishment of the Bishop at d5 via c4 could not have been prevented.

24...Bc6

Black's position is threatened on all sides, but the situation is not hopeless.

25.Qd6+ Kc8

Having regard for the planned combination. An alternative was 25...Kb7 26.d5 Bb5.

26.d5 Rh6 27.e6 (see next Diagram) **27...Bxd5!**

This was afterwards pronounced the "only move". Black had, however, another one, namely 27...Rxe6+. If now

After 27.e6

28.dxe6 Bxh1 29.0-0-0 Bf3! (and not 29...Be4? because of 30.e7 followed by 31.Qe5 and the White Queen now has new squares for decisive operations) 30.exf7 Qxf7 31.Qd8+ Kb7 32.Rd7+ Ka6 and the Black King is safe.

28.Qxd5 Qxe6+ 29.Qxe6+ Rxe6+

White now has a piece for two pawns, but his own pawns are weak.

30.Kd2 Kb7 31.Rae1 Rh8 32.Rxe6! fxe6 33.Re1! Rxh2+ 34.Kd3 g3

Anything but a passive Rook (34...Rh6?).

35.Rg1

After 35.Rxe6 would come 35...g5! 36.fxg5 g2 and the White pawn on g5 would be an obstruction.

35...Rh3

Much better than 35...g2, for it is soon clear that Black must have a route to c2.

36.Kd4 Kc6 37.Rg2 a5 38.c4 Rh2! 39.Rxg3 Rxc2 40.Rxg7 Re2 41.Bc1 Re4+ 42.Kd3 b5 43.cxb5+ Kxb5 44.Be3 Kc6 45.Rf7 a4 46.Rf8 a3 47.Ra8 e5 48.Ra6+ Kb5 49.Rb6+

Professor Becker is absolutely bent on winning, and so it comes about that in the end he loses.

The game continued:

49...Ka5 50.Rf6 a2 51.Bd2+ Kb5 52.Bc3 Rd4+

After six hours of hard fighting to get such a problem check is hardly pleasurable!

53.Ke2

Correct was 53.Kc2 Rc4 54.Kb2 Rxc3 55.Rxf5.

53...Rxf4 54.Rf8 Kc4 55.Ba1 Re4+ 56.Kd2 f4

White is lost.

57.Rc8+ Kd5 58.Rd8+ Ke6 59.Re8+ Kf5 60.Rg8 f3 0-1.

The following game shows how an advance on the wrong wing should be punished.

Game 22

Opocensky-Nimzowitsch
Marienbad, 1925

1.d4 Nf6 2.c4 e6 3.Nc3 Bb4 4.Qc2 b6 5.e4 Bb7

The expansive power of White's center pawns is less than might at first sight appear.

6.Bd3 Nc6 7.Nf3 Be7!

By this unexpected retreat, which threatens 8...Nb4, Black manages to muzzle White's mass of pawns in the center, while still keeping his valuable dark-squared Bishop.

8.a3 d6 9.O-O e5 10.d5

The muzzling.

10...Nb8 11.b4 Nbd7

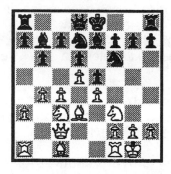

12.Bb2

The pawn formation called for White to play, after proper preparation, the move c5. For of the two theatres of war resulting from 10.d5, only one is available, namely an attack on the Black pawn base at d6. The other theoretically possible plan, an advance with pieces against the wing cramped by the d5 pawn, must be regarded as nipped in the bud by the presence of an obstruction at c4. The only plan of action feasible here (c5) could, however, have been prepared by 12.h3 followed by 12.Be3. For instance, 12.h3 h6! (the best chance) 13.Be3 g5 14.Nh2. Black will try to attack White's Kingside, but White's attack on the Queenside (Na4 followed by c5) is quickly put into motion, while his castled position is defendable. 12.h3 to be followed by 13.Be3 was therefore the correct continuation.

12...O-O 13.Ne2

White's pieces desert the Queenside in order to demonstrate on the other wing. By this movement, however, the effect of his own center is weakened. For with the Knight still at c3, ...c6 could be answered by dxc6, while this Knight at the same time casts a threatening eye on the d5 square as an outpost station. If, however, the Nc3 has gone on a journey, the thrust ...c6 gains in effect. True for the moment this thrust is not a threat, for on the Queenside Black is weaker. In the end, however, this will change. The way in which the theatre disdained by White is made a base of operations by his opponent makes the game of fundamental interest to the student.

13...Nh5 14.Qd2

The answer to 14.g4 would have been 14...Nf6. Black wants to be attacked on the Kingside as he regards that theatre as unavailable. (See note to move 12).

14...g6 15.g4 Ng7 16.Ng3 c6!

What sense can there be in this move? If in the end ...cxd5 is played, then the answer cxd5 would attain nothing other than the exposure of his own base at d6. Black in this case would have worked for his opponent, for with the Black pawn still at c7 the strategic advance indicated for White, c5-cxd6, would lead to exactly the same pawn configuration, the one which is the object of White's efforts!

This calculation contains, however, two logical errors. First White in advancing c5 will certainly not content himself with cxd6; this is only a threat. The insertion of a wedge, in other words the shifting of the attack by c6, would be a much sharper threat. Second, White by Bb2, and Ne2-g3 has been untrue to his Queenside. The just punishment will lie in Black's becoming strong there!

17.Qh6 Rc8 18.Rac1

18...a6!!

A very difficult move. The answer to 18...cxd5 could be 19.exd5 and Black could get two powerful pawns by 19...f5 20.gxf5 gxf5. After 21.Kh1 and 22.Rg1, however, Black would stand badly. The mobility of his e and f-pawns would prove to be illusory, whereas White's

Kingside attack would be very real. Black intends to play ...cxd5 at a moment when the recapture exd5 is not feasible.

19.Rfd1 Rc7 20.h4? cxd5 21.cxd5

Since 20.h4? has still further weakened White's position (the square g4), 20...cxd5 seems correct. The answer to 21.exd5 would have been 21...Nf6 as in the game. In addition, the threat of a breakthrough by ...b5 would be in the air.

21...Rxc1 22.Rxc1 Nf6 23.Nh2 Kh8

The White Queen goes in danger of her life. For instance if now 24.f4?? Ng8. If 23.Ng5, then 23...Qd7 24.f3 Rc8, and the Bishop threatens to attack her from f8.

24.Qe3 Nd7 25.Nf3 Nf6 26.Nh2 Ng8 27.g5 f6 28.Nf3 fxg5 29.hxg5 Bc8 30.Rc6

A very clever resource, which is extraordinarily difficult to parry. Observe too, that in the current position it looks as though White had operated exclusively of the Queenside by c4-c5-cxd6, and Black, on the other hand had sought salvation by a counterattack directed against the base of the White pawn chain, e4.

30...Bd7 31.Bxa6

31.Rxb6? would have been answered by 32...Rxf3. The sacrifice of the exchange is very promising.

31...Bxc6 32.dxc6 Qc7 33.b5

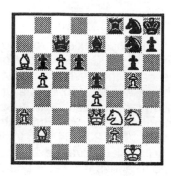

33...h6!

This pawn sacrifice yields Black freedom to maneuver. Without this move sacrifices at e5 or d6 would have been possible for White. Take for example the following variation. 33...Ne6 34.a4 Bd8 35.Ba3 Qf7 36.Bxd6! Qxf3 37.Bxe5+ Ng7 38.Qxf3 Rxf3 39.c7.

34.gxh6 Ne6 35.a4 Bd8 36.Ba3 Qf7

For now if 37.Bxd6 Qxf3 38.Bxe5+ would be answered by 38...Kh7.

37.Nxe5 dxe5 38.Bxf8 Qxf8 39.a5 (see next Diagram)

39...Nxh6

Black has also his 33rd move to thank for the possibility of this Knight's intervention.

After 39.a5

40.axb6 Ng4 41.c7 Nxe3 42.c8=Q Qf3 43.fxe3 Qxg3+ 0-1.

Black will take the e-pawn with check followed by the capture of the b6 pawn.

Game 23

Rubinstein-Duras
Carlsbad, 1911

1.c4 e5 2.Nc3 Nf6 3.g3 Bb4 4.Bg2 O-O 5.Nf3 Re8 6.O-O Nc6

The exchange 6...Bxc3 was to be considered.

7.Nd5 Bf8 8.d3 h6 9.b3 d6 10.Bb2 Nxd5 11.cxd5 Ne7 12.e4 c5

In the long run, something must be done for the c-pawn.

13.dxc6 e.p. Nxc6 14.d4 Bg4 15.d5 Ne7

We now have our pawn chain, and the Black base, the pawn on d6, already seems exposed from the side, just as if the typical attack had been made on it by c4-c5-cxd6 with Black recapturing cxd6.

16.Qd3 Qd7 17.Nd2

The Knight is already being sent forward to attack the exposed base.

17...Bh3 18.a4

To safeguard the Knight's position at c4.

18...Bxg2 19.Kxg2 Reb8 20.Nc4 b5 21.axb5 Qxb5 22.Ra3

In this and similar positions the question arises, which pawn is weaker, the White b-pawn or the Black a-pawn? In the present case this problem could be solved by logical deduction. Since the square d6 is weaker than d5, a like

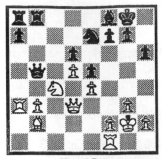

After 22.Ra3

relationship must exist throughout the remainder of the Queenside. Were this not the case then White's 18.a4 must have been wrong, and that is unlikely. Was he in fact not justified in supporting the Knight move to c4? But that would be absurd. No, 20.Nc4 was indicated, similarly 18.a4. Therefore 20...b5 must have led to a less favorable position for Black. The course of the game proves the correctness of this judgment.

22...Ng6

22...Nc8 would perhaps have been better.

23.Rfa1 a6 24.Bc1 Rb7 25.Be3 f6 26.f3

If Black could manage to play ...f5, his position would not be so bad. But this is out of the question and he is besieged.

26...Ne7 27.Qf1

Threatening 28.Nxd6

27...Nc8 28.Nd2 Qb4 29.Qc4 Qxc4 30.Nxc4 Rab8 31.Nd2 Rc7 32.Rxa6

The masterly and varied uses made of the points d2 and c4 will be noted.

32...Rc2 33.R6a2 Rxa2 34.Rxa2

The rest of the game, which consists of bringing the King to the center followed by an advance in close order of the King, Bishop, and Knight is easily understood.

There followed:

34...Be7 35.Kf2 Kf7 36.Ke2 Ke8 37.Kd3 Kd7 38.Kc3 Bd8 39.Nc4

c3 is our shelter.

39...Bc7 40.g4 Bd8 41.Ra6 Bc7 42.h4 Bd8 43.h5 Bc7 44.b4 Rb7 45.Ra8 Kd8 46.Kb3 Rb8 47.Rxb8 Bxb8 48.b5 Ne7 49.b6 f5

There is nothing left to hope for.

50.gxf5 Ng8 51.Bf2 Nf6 52.Bh4 1-0

In the following game the transference of the attack from one point to another is carried out in classical style.

Game 24

Maroczy-Suchting
Barmen, 1905

1.d4 d5 2.c4 e6 3.Nc3 Nf6 4.Bg5 Nbd7 5.e3 Be7 6.Nf3 O-O 7.Qc2 c6 8.a3 Nh5

Better would have been 8...Re8 or 8...h6.

9.h4 f5

9...f6 would be answered by 10.Bd3.

10.Be2 Ndf6 11.Ne5! Bd7 12.Qd1 Be8 13.c5

Weaving the chain.

13...Qc7 14.b4 a5 15.g3!

Nobody knows better than Maroczy how to prevent freeing moves (here ...f4).

15...axb4 16.axb4 Rxa1 17.Qxa1 Ne4 18.g4! Nxc3 19.Qxc3 Nf6

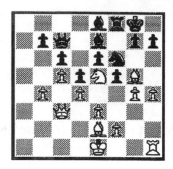

20.Bf4!

Threatens 21.Ng6 and thereby gains time for 21.g5

20...Qc8 21.g5 Nd7 22.Nd3!

The exchange would make it more difficult to break through.

22...Bf7 23.Kd2 Bd8 24.Ra1

Only now does play begin in the real theatre. The idea is naturally to attack the base c6 by b4-b5.

24...Bc7 25.Ra7 Re8 26.Bxc7 Qxc7 27.f4

Stops all attempts to break through by ...e5.

27...Rb8 28.b5

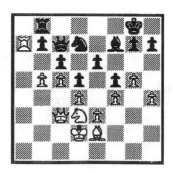

At last!

28...Qc8

Or 28...cxb5 29.Nb4.

29.b6

With this White transfers the attack to the new base, the pawn on b7. Play against the base c6 could have been pursued by 29.Nb4 followed by Qa3-a4, but attacking b7 is even stronger, and above all, safer. Suchting is now helpless.

29...Be8 30.Nc1 Nf8 31.Nb3 e5!

The only way of saving the b-pawn, otherwise comes Na5, Nxb7, and if ...Rxb7, Ba6.

32.dxe5 Ne6 33.Bd3! g6 34.h5 Bf7 35.Na5 Nd8 36.e6!

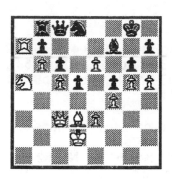

Our sacrificing advance of the unblockaded passed pawn. The pieces to the rear now come to life.

36...Qxe6 37.h6 d4 38.Qxd4 Qa2+

And White won as follows:

**39.Ke1 Ne6 40.Qe5 Re8 41.Nxb7 Qb3
42.Be2 Qb1+ 43.Kf2 Qh1 44.Nd6
Qh4+ 45.Kg2 Nxf4+ 46.Qxf4 Bd5+
47.Bf3 Bxf3+ 48.Kxf3 1-0**

Game 25

*This game illustrates the idea of collective mobility,
and touches also on the problem of prophylactic.*

Nimzowitsch-Dr. Michel
Semmering, 1926

1.Nf3 d5 2.b3 Nf6 3.Bb2 c5 4.e3 e6

A new idea. Black avoids developing
the Knight at c6, since it might be pinned
by Bb5.

5.Ne5 Nbd7 6.Bb5 a6?

6...Bd6 here was much better than the
text move, first with regard to his
development, and second because
White threatens to make strong use of
the diagonal a1-h8, particularly to
support his outpost at e5. A prophylactic

measure was urgently needed. For
instance 6...Bd6! 7.Nxd7 Bxd7 8.Bxd7+
Qxd7 9.Bxf6 gxf6 and the doubled pawn
has both its dark and bright sides.
Further we consider 6...Be7 also better
than the text move.

7.Bxd7+ Nxd7 8.Nxd7 Bxd7 9.O-O f6

An admission of weakness on the long
diagonal. There came under
consideration also 9...Bd6 10.Qg4 Qc7
followed by ...0-0-0.

10.c4 dxc4

The threat was 11.cxd5 exd5 12.Qh5+
followed by Qxd5.

11.bxc4 Bd6 12.Qh5+ g6 13.Qh6 Bf8

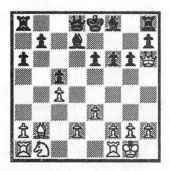

14.Qh3!!

The best place for the Queen and one
difficult to find. 14...e5 would now only
surrender the point d5 to White. For
instance, 14...e5 15.Qg3 (with the threat
of 15.Bxe5) 15...Bg7 16.e4 followed by
17.d3 and Nc3-d5 with advantage to
White.

14...Be7 15.Nc3 O-O 16.a4!

White plans to place his pawns on e4 and f4, which would leave his d-pawn backward. As he thus sacrifices the effective power of his d-pawn, he first paralyzes the three Black Queenside pawns.

16...Bd6 17.f4 Qe7 18.e4 Bc6 19.g4

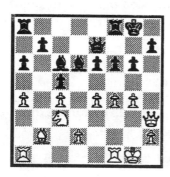

A "pawn roller" which can hardly be rendered innocuous.

19...f5

If Black does nothing, White has the choice between a direct attack on the one hand and play against the c-pawn on the other. On 19...Rae8, for example, the latter could be carried out by 20.Qe3 followed by a5 and Ba3, and finally driving away the defending Bishop with e5. After the text move a mating attack wins the game in short order.

20.gxf5 exf5

On 20...gxf5 21.Kf2

21.e5

The following variation may be dedicated to those who love combinative complications. On 21.Nd5 (instead of 21.e5) Qxe4 22.Rae1 Qxc4 23.Ne7+ Bxe7 24.Rxe7 Rf7 25.Rxf7 Qxf7 26.Qc3 Kf8! and Black appears to have a sufficient defense.

21...Bc7 22.Nd5 Bxd5 23.cxd5 Qd7 24.e6! 1-0.

For if 24...Qxd5, 25.Qh6 forces mate or the loss of a Rook. If 24...Qe7 the fatal Queen goes to c3 and there is no good answer.

The following game shows how easily the early surrender of the center can lead to disaster. Nevertheless, this procedure seems to us to be in itself quite practicable, provided we bring to bear on the problem all the tenacity which we possess, and do not allow ourselves to be forced down a dead end road.

If we do this our prospects for the future are good. See game 28 as another example.

Game 26

Dr. Tarrasch-J. Mieses
Berlin 1916

1.e4 e6 2.d4 d5 3.Nc3 dxe4

Gives up the center, but opens the d-file and the long diagonal a8-h1 for pressure on White's center.

4.Nxe4 Nd7 5.Nf3 Ngf6 6.Bd3 Nxe4

Better would be 6...b6, but the text move is playable.

7.Bxe4 Nf6 8.Bd3

If 8.Bg5 Be7 9.Bxf6, then best for Black would be 9...gxf6.

8...b6 9.Bg5 Bb7 10.O-O Be7 11.Qe2 O-O 12.Rad1 h6?

The tenacity of purpose so necessary to tournament play fails him here. Why not 12...Qd5? If then 13.c4 Qa5 14.d5, then 14...Rae8! with strong counterthreats. For instance, 15.dxe6? Bxf3 followed by 16...Qxg5. Why the mere contact with the square d5 must bring a blessing is evident. This point in the first place is the outpost station on the d-file, and in the second the same thing on the diagonal a8-h1, and finally, the square d5 is a blockading point. The enormous strategical importance to Black of the point d5 makes it clear that any, even the most passing contact with it must work wonders.

13.Bf4 Qd5

Now this move is unfavorable, as the c-pawn is hanging. Black's position is not enviable.

14.c4 Qa5 15.Bxc7 Bxf3

15...Rac8 was to be considered here, and after 16.Be5 Rfd8, the advance of White's pawn majority is very much hindered.

16.gxf3! Qxa2?

Black will not resign himself to the loss of pawn and loses his Queen in an attempt to maintain material equality. With 16...Rfc8 17.Be5 Nd7! (with a view to the threatened 18.Kh1 followed by Rg1), he could have put up a resistance. For if now 18.Be4, 18...Nxe5 19.Bxa8 Ng6 and Black threatens 20...Nf4 with a later ...Bd6 and ...Qh5.

17.Ra1 Qb3 18.Bc2 Qb4 19.Ra4 1-0.

The Queen is prettily trapped.

Game 27

In a situation very similar to that in the preceding game Tartakower succeeds in making the point d5, which Mieses so badly neglected, the basis of an undertaking which he carries out with great virtuosity.

Grunfeld-Dr. Tartakower
Semmering, 1926

1.d4 d5 2.c4 dxc4 3.Nf3 Bg4 4.Ne5 Bh5 5.Nxc4

The best answer to 5.Nc3 would be 5...Nd7, and the proud Ne5 would be forced to declare his intentions.

5...e6 6.Qb3

Threatening both 7.Qxb7 and 7.Qb5+.

6...Nc6 7.e3

7...Rb8!

He does not hesitate to employ the Rook for the protection of a pawn.

8.Nc3 Nf6 9.Be2 Bxe2 10.Nxe2 Bb4+ 11.Nc3 O-O

Both sides have now completed their

development, and the game is about equal. White's center, which is otherwise well protected, betrays a striking measure of immobility. *"My System"* however, teaches that every immobile complex tends to become a weakness. The truth of the proposition will here be shortly manifested.

12.O-O

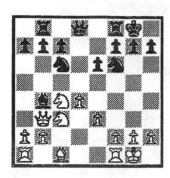

12...Nd5!

The Knight feels at home here, as 13.e4 is not possible because of 13...Nxd4.

13.Nxd5

If 13.Ne4, the result would be the mobilization of Black's Queenside by 13...b5 14.Ne5 Nxe5 15.dxe5 c5 16.a3 c4. On 14.Ncd2 e5 and White's game is disorganized.

13...Qxd5! 14.Qc2 e5

White's center is already being demolished.

15.Nxe5 Nxe5 16.dxe5 Qxe5 17.Bd2 Bxd2 18.Qxd2 Rfd8 19.Qc2 Rd5!

He makes use of the point d5 in excellent fashion.

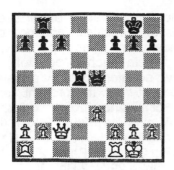

20.Rad1 Rbd8 21.Rxd5 Rxd5 22.Rd1 g6 23.Rxd5 Qxd5 24.a3 c5

Black has a decided advantage for the endgame. He has a pawn majority on the Queenside, possession of the d-file, and last but not least the central position of his Queen. The advantage is still, however, only small.

25.h3 b5 26.f4 c4

Centralization proceeds! White's pawn majority is much less easily realizable than Black's (if for instance 26.f3, Black plays 26...f5 with control of e4).

27.Qc3 Qe4! 28.Kf2 a5

The entire ending is played by Tartakower with wonderful precision and true artistic elegance. (*Tartakower was considered by Nimzowitsch to be third among all masters of his time, in the artistry of endgame play-Ed.*).

29.g4 h6 30.h4 Qh1!

Only now, and this tardiness is to his credit, does he give up the central position in favor of a diversion.

31.Kg3 Qg1+ 32.Kf3 Qh2! 33.g5 h5 34.Ke4 Qxh4 35.Qxa5 Qh1+ 36.Ke5 Qc6!

In order on 37.Qe1 to put in operation the following maneuver. 37...Qc5+ 38.Ke4 Qf5+ followed by ...Qc2 and wins.

37.Qa7 h4 38.f5 gxf5 39.Kxf5 Qf3+ 40.Ke5 h3 41.Kd4 Qg4+ 0-1.

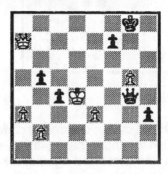

The following game illustrates the plan of action "center file's attack on a flank.".

Game 28

Kline-Capablanca
New York, 1913

1.d4 Nf6 2.Nf3 d6 3.c3 Nbd7 4.Bf4 c6 5.Qc2 Qc7 6.e4 e5 7.Bg3 Be7

White has the attacking position in the center. This is unquestionably an advantage. The weakness of e4, however, (we shall quickly see why e4 is weak) will soon force White to surrender this advantage.

8.Bd3 O-O 9.Nbd2 Re8! 10.O-O Nh5

In order to exchange the Bishop.

11.Nc4 Bf6 12.Ne3 Nf8

13.dxe5

Since the Bishop is needed at d3 for the protection of the e-pawn, the d-pawn can only be protected against a Knight at e6 by exchanging himself. The student should consider carefully the motif used, aimed at forcing the opponent to declare himself (whether for 13.dxe5 [as in this case], or 13.d5).

13...dxe5 14.Bh4 Qe7 15.Bxf6 Qxf6 16.Ne1 Nf4?

With this and the next move a diversion is put in place which may be said to be counter to the spirit of the opening. The right line of play consisted in ...Be6 and the doubling of Rooks on the d-file. By this means advantage could have been taken of the uncomfortable position of White's Bd3. Black's simplest course would have been to play ...Be6 on the 14th move.

17.g3 Nh3+ 18.Kh1 h5 19.N3g2 g5 20.f3 Ng6 21.Ne3! h4

The entry of the Knight at f5 would, according to my analysis, have decided the game in White's favor. The retreat of the Black Knight at h3 is cut off. The

attempt at a rescue undertaken by means of a reckless advance of the Kingside pawns gives opportunity, often occurring in such a position, for a decisive counterstroke, by an invasion in the center (in the present case by Nf5). For instance 22.Nf5 hxg3 23.hxg3 Bxf5 24.exf5 Ne7 25.Kg2 Kg7 (is the pawn sacrifice 25...g4 26.fxg4 Ng5 any better?); 26.Kxh3⁻ Rh8+ 27.Kg2 Qh6 28.Kf2 Qh2+ 29.Ng2 Rh3 30.Ke1 Rxg3 31.Ne3. Moreover, the move 26.Rh1 is also playable, which I showed to be a win for White in analysis I published in the *Rigaer Rundschau*.

22.g4?? Nhf4

Now the Knight rejoices in his rediscovered freedom, and Black, after this doubtful excursion, which could have ended fatally for him, takes up the right line, play on the d-file, and pursues it with complete mastery to victory. What remains needs but few remarks. The continuation was:

23.Rf2 Nxd3 24.Nxd3 Be6 25.Rd1 Red8 26.b3 Nf4 27.Ng2 Nxd3 28.Rxd3 Rxd3 29.Qxd3 Rd8

The move 29...Bxg4 may have been better.

30.Qe2 h3 31.Ne3 a5 32.Rf1 a4 33.c4 Rd4 34.Nc2 Rd7 35.Ne3 Qd8 36.Rd1 Rxd1+ 37.Nxd1 Qd4

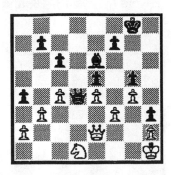

Centralizing and taking the d-file.

38.Nf2 b5 39.cxb5 axb3 40.axb3 Bxb3

Threatening 41...Qa1+.

41.Nxh3 Bd1 42.Qf1 cxb5 43.Kg2 b4 44.Qb5 b3 45.Qe8+ Kg7 46.Qe7 b2 47.Nxg5 Bb3 0-1.

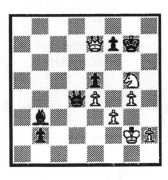

The next game illustrates the following plan of action - Play in a file against the enemy center: First restrain, then blockade, and finally destroy!

Game 29

Rubinstein-Levenfish
Carlsbad, 1911

1.e4 e6 2.d4 d5 3.Nc3 Nf6 4.Bg5 Be7 5.e5 Nfd7 6.Bxe7 Qxe7 7.Qd2 O-O 8.f4 c5 9.Nf3 f6

It would be more in the spirit of a correct attack on a pawn chain to first play 9...cxd4 10.Nxd4 and only then ...f6. But after 10...f6 11.exf6 Qxf6 the position is after all similar to the game.

10.exf6 Qxf6 11.g3 Nc6 12.O-O-O a6 13.Bg2 Nb6

The diagonal attacking range (from g2 to d5) is a necessary element in White's plan of operations. The Bishop on g2 holds up the freeing thrust e5 better than any other possible disposition could.

14.Rhe1 Nc4 15.Qf2 b5 16.dxc5!

Bravo! The flank attack ...Nxb2 has no terror for him, since a flank attack by itself can never ruin a strongly centralized game. White's game is centralized, for he holds the center files and pressure on them is already making itself felt. Further he has the prospect of

---

occupying the central points d4 and e5. Observe now how Black's wing attack is thrown back by action in the center.

16...Nxb2 17.Kxb2 b4 18.Nd4! bxc3+ 19.Ka1

A Rook will soon gobble up the Black c-pawn.

19...Nxd4

If 19...Bd7, then 20.Nxe6 Bxe6 21.Rxe6 followed by 22.Bxd5

20.Qxd4 Rb8 21.Re3 g5

Now Black has a go on the other wing.

22.Rxc3 gxf4 23.gxf4 Bd7 24.c6 Qxd4 25.Rxd4 Be8 26.Bh3 Rf6 27.c7

It would have pleased me even more if the decision had been brought about in a Bishop ending instead of through the somewhat "tacked on" action of the passed c-pawn. For instance, from such a position as follows: White Ke5, Bh3, pawns a2, c3, f4, h2; Black: Ke7, Bf7, pawns a6, d5, e6, h7. White plays 1.f5 exf5 2.Bxf5 and White will win the d-pawn and with it the game. We should then have the general idea more markedly brought out, namely first to keep the e-pawn and d-pawn under

restraint, then to blockade them, and only in the end to destroy them. But as played, the game was instructive enough! (Note moves 13, 16, and 18).

27...Rc8

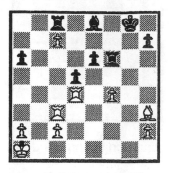

28.Rxd5 Rxc7 29.Bxe6+ 1-0.

The following game is instructive for the way in which Black turns his majority in the center to account despite disturbing countermeasures.

Game 30

Bugoljubow-Nimzowitsch
London, 1927

1.c4 e6 2.Nc3 Nf6 3.e4 c5

Since 4.e5 did not seem dangerous.

4.g3

There was also to be considered 4.Nf3 Nc6 5.d4 cxd4 6.Nxd4 Bb4 7.Qd3 (Bugoljubow's suggestion).

4...d5 5.e5 d4 6.exf6 dxc3 7.dxc3

An interesting idea. White, so to speak, sacrifices a pawn, in that he makes his

---

pawn majority on the Queenside of no value. He hopes, by occupying certain central points, to be able to bring counterpressure to bear. See next note.

7...Qxf6 8.Nf3 h6 9.Bg2 Bd7! 10.Nd2

White's command of the diagonal h1-a8 coupled with control of e4 is no small embarrassment to Black. If now 10...Qe5+?, then 11.Ne4 followed by Bf4 .

10...Bc6 11.Ne4 Qg6 12.Qe2 Be7

Not 12...f5 because of the reply 13.Bf3 followed by 14.Nd2 and e5 remains weak.

13.O-O O-O

14.h4

An ingenious move, which, however, brings about a disturbance of the equilibrium which up to now existed. Better was 14.f4! Nd7 15.Bd2 Kh8! 16.Rae1 Nf6 17.Bc1. After the text move the balance weighs in Black's favor.

14...f5 15.Nd2 Bxg2

Not 15...Bxh4 because of 16.Nf3!

16.Kxg2 Nc6 17.Nf3 f4

Otherwise 18.Bf4 and the balance is readjusted.

18.Re1 Rf6 19.Qe4

The game is already lost for White, for the occupation of the point e4, which seems to consolidate the position proves to be deceptive. In fact, g3 is sick unto death.

19...fxg3 20.fxg3 Bd6 21.g4 Qxe4 22.Rxe4 Raf8 23.Re3 Rf4 24.g5

24.Rxe6 Rxg4+ 25.Kf2 Ne5 would lead to a massacre.

24...Rg4+ 25.Kh1

Or 25.Kf2 Ne5 26.Ke2 Rg2+ 27.Kf1 Rg3 winning a piece.

25...hxg5 26.hxg5 Kf7

27.Ng1

If 27.g6+, best would be 27...Kf6 (not 27...Ke7 because of 28.Nh2 Rh8 29.Re2 Rgh4?? 30.Bg5+).

27...Rh8+ 28.Nh3 Ke7 29.b3 Bf4 30.Rf3 Ne5 0-1.

Game 31

A game in which seven White pawns show greater collective mobility than eight Black ones. A case of mind's dynamic effect over matter.

Nimzowitsch-Anton Olson
Played in 1924

1.f4 c5 2.e4 Nc6 3.d3 g6 4.c4 Bg7 5.Nc3 b6 6.Nf3 Bb7 7.g4

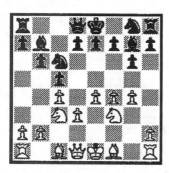

The collective mobility of White's Kingside pawns already makes itself quickly felt.

7...e6 8.Bg2 Nge7 9.Nb5!

In order to provoke ...a6, after which the lack of protection from which the b-pawn will suffer from is to form the basis of a sharp combination.

9...d6 10.O-O a6 11.Na3 O-O 12.Qe2 Qd7 13.Be3 Nb4

Otherwise White would play 14.Rad1 followed by d4 with advantage.

14.Nc2! Bxb2 15.Rab1 Bc3 16.Nxb4 Bxb4

or 16...cxb4 17.Bxb6 See note to White's 9th move.

17.Bc1!

White has succeeded in wresting the long diagonal from his opponent.

17...f6 18.Bb2 e5 19.g5

The connection between "sacrifice" and "blockade" would have been more definite had the continuation been 19.f5 g5 20.h4 with an enduring attack, while Black's pawn plus would have but an illusory value.

19...Nc6

or 19...fxg5 20.Nxg5 threatening 21.Bh3.

20.gxf6 Qg4 21.fxe5 dxe5 22.Qe3 Qh5

To hold the e-pawn.

23.Ng5 Bc8 24.f7+ Kg7 25.Qf4 Kh6

Forced.

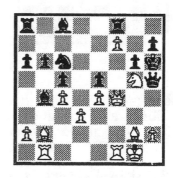

26.Ne6+! exf4 27.Bg7 mate. 1-0

In the following game we have an example of a "mysterious" Rook move, also a striking example of the difference between a true and a false freeing move. As this game also illustrates very clearly our conception of prophylactic strategy, it is inserted here.

Game 32

Blackburne-Nimzowitsch
Petrograd, 1914

1.e3 d6 2.f4 e5 3.fxe5 dxe5 4.Nc3 Bd6

The best move, for the early development of the Knights advocated by Lasker would not get at the root of the matter here. This root lies rather in the pawn configuration and in the prevention of any freeing pawn moves.

5.e4 Be6

Preventing 6.Bc4.

6.Nf3 f6

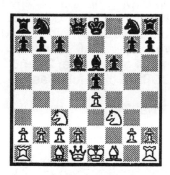

Black plays (as will become evident on his 8th move) to prevent the advance to d4, which would in a certain sense have a freeing effect, as it would make White's majority in the center felt. Black, as he plays it, succeeds in completely crippling the enemy majority in the center. The reader may ask, why does Black give White the opportunity of playing d4 on his 7th move?

7.d3

White forgoes the advance, and rightly, for 7.d4 would here be the typical false liberating move, which merely creates new weaknesses. For instance, 7.d4 Nd7! 8.d5 (otherwise ultimately ...exd4 with play against the isolated White e-pawn), 8...Bf7 followed by the occupation of the square c5 by a Knight or Bishop.

7...Ne7 8.Be3 c5!

With the aid of the resources he has on the d-file, Black now succeeds in forcing his opponent to the defense. See Black's 9th and 10th moves.

9.Qd2 Nbc6 10.Be2 Nd4 11.O-O O-O 12.Nd1 Nec6 13.c3

The reward which Black's systematic scheme of operations has earned for him. d3 is now a weakness.

13...Nxe2+ 14.Qxe2 Re8!

The "mysterious" Rook move, which in the event of White playing d4, threatens to make things uncomfortable for him on the e-file. In addition to this, it makes room for the Bd6 at f8.

15.Nh4 Bf8 16.Nf5 Kh8!

White has made pertinent use of the open f-file, his one advantage. Black's move, for all its unpretentiousness, has its significance in positional play. Black insures the eventual possibility of

---

playing ...g6 and ...f5 without being disturbed by a Knight check at h6.

17.g4 Qd7!

Renders possible a parry to the ever threatening advance g5. For example 18.g5 g6 19.Ng3 f5! with an excellent game (see previous note).

18.Nf2 a5

White's a-pawn is constantly threatened, and if now 19.b3, 19...a4 is possible. It is evident that White's Queenside is sympathetically affected by the weakness of his center.

19.a3 b5

19...Bb3 would have been a strong move here, although by it Black would have to forgo this parry he had planned to b4. Nevertheless, 19...Bb3 could have composedly have been played (one should not be a slave to one's parries!), 19...Bb3 20.g5 fxg5 21.Bxg5 c4! (Lasker's suggestion) 22.dxc4 Qe6 23.Ne3 Qg6 24.Qg4 Bc5! and wins. Or 23.Qf3! Bxc4 24.Rfd1 and Black has a slight advantage.

20.Rad1 Rab8

Some tempi could have been saved by playing 20...b4 at once.

21.Rd2 b4 22.axb4 axb4!

if 22...cxb4, then 23.d4!

23.c4

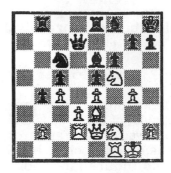

Black ought now to play his trumps.

23...Ra8?

Black had brought about a strategically won position, only he should not have delayed playing his trumps any longer. These consisted of ...Nd4, which would have led to Bxd4 by White, and ...g6 followed by ...Bh6 dominating the diagonal. For example, 23...g6 24.Ng3 Nd4! 25.Bxd4 cxd4 followed by ...Bh6.

24.Qf3 Ra2?

There was still time for ...Nd4.

25.g5

Thanks to a tactical shot (White's 26th move) this thrust which was thought to have been prevented, is now possible after all.

25...g6 26.Ng4!

This move robs Black of the fruits of his deep plan of campaign. There followed:

26...gxf5 27.Nxf6 Nd4 28.Qf2

28.Qh5 would have won more quickly.

28...Qc6 29.Nxe8 Qxe8 30.Bxd4 exd4 31.exf5

White won easily. **1-0.**

What we have to learn from this game is the ability to distinguish between true and false freeing moves. The manner in which Black was able to hold in check the thrusts d4 and later (until the moment of aberration) g5 is worthy of special notice.

The following game illustrates the effect of preventive measures and the idea of collective mobility.

Game 33

Nimzowitsch-Rubinstein
Dresden, 1926

1.c4 c5 2.Nf3 Nf6 3.Nc3 d5 4.cxd5 Nxd5 5.e4

A novelty, which at the price of a backward d-pawn, aims at securing other advantages.

5...Nb4

Preferable was 5...Nxc3 6.bxc3 g6.

6.Bc4! e6

It was not possible here to take immediate advantage of White's weakness at d3. For example, 6...Nd3+ 7.Ke2! Nf4+ 8.Kf1 with the threat of 9.d4. Or 6...Nd3+ 7.Ke2 Nxc1+ 8.Rxc1 Nc6 8.Bb5 Bd7 10.Bxc6 with the better ending.

7.O-O N8c6

Better here was 7...a6, though it is true that even then White with 8.a3 N4c6 9.d3 followed by 10.Be3 would have an excellent game.

8.d3 Nd4

9.a3 was threatened.

9.Nxd4 cxd4 10.Ne2

White now stands very well. Any weakness at d3 is covered up, the collective mobility of White's Kingside (f4!) is considerable, and most important, the apparently blocked Bc4 plays a preventive role (directed against a possible ...e5) from the background, all of which goes far in leading to a White advantage.

10...a6

Directed against the threat of 11.Bb5+ Bd7 12.Nxd4.

11.Ng3 Bd6 12.f4

12.Qg4 would have been very strong here. 12.Qg4 0-0 13.Bg5! Be7 14.Bh6 Bf6 15.Bxg7 Bxg7 16.Nh5; or else 13...e5 14.Qh4 with the sacrifice at g7 to follow (Nh5, Nxg7). The best answer to 12.Qg4 would have been 12...Qf6. For example, 12.Qg4 Qf6 13.f4, but even in this case White's superiority in position would have been very great. After the less incisive text move Black can equalize.

12...O-O 13.Qf3

A direct mating attack is no longer feasible. For example: 13.e5 Bc7! 14.Qg4 Kh8 15.Nh5 Rg8 16.Rf3 f5! 17.exf6e.p. gxf6 18.Qh4 Rg6 19.Rh3 Qe7 and Black threatens to consolidate his position by ...Bd7 and ...Rag8.

13...Kh8 14.Bd2 f5 15.Rae1 Nc6

Rubinstein has defended himself skillfully, but White has a trump in hand, the e-file.

16.Re2 Qc7

Not good. In cramped positions one should never give away the possibility of a future move. But here ...Qc7 gives away the possibility of playing ...Qf6 after exf5 ...exf5. The right move was therefore 16...Bd7, and if then 17.exf5 (best) 17...exf5 18.Rfe1, 18...Qf6 and Black stands much better at any rate than he does in the game.

17.exf5 exf5

18.Nh1

The Knight starts on a long journey with g5 as his goal, in order to support with all the means at his disposal the King Bishop which now wakes up and throws off his preventive role for one of direct activity. In the meantime White's e-file, thrown, so to speak, on its own resources, makes a desperate but successful struggle for existence. This vitality of the e-file gives point to the Knight's maneuver.

18...Bd7 19.Nf2 Rae8 20.Rfe1 Rxe2 21.Rxe2 Nd8

We see now that 21...Re8 would be met by 22.Qd5.

22.Nh3 Bc6

And here 22...Re8 would lead to a combination full of pleasantries. 22...Re8 23.Qh5! Rxe2 24.Ng5 h6 25.Qg6 hxg5 26.Qh5 mate.

23.Qh5 g6 24.Qh4 Kg7 25.Qf2

Black's castled position was still too

strongly defended, so White intends to first force a regrouping of the enemy forces.

25...Bc5

Or 25...Qb6 26.b4 followed by Bc3!

26.b4 Bb6 27.Qh4

The switchback theme, such as usually only occurs in problems. 27.Qe1 would also have been good. 27.Qe1 Be4 28.Nf2 winning a pawn by Nxe4, etc.

27...Re8

The answer to 27...Rf6 would have been 28.Ng5 h6 29.Nh7 winning at once.

28.Re5! Nf7

If 28...h6 there would follow 29.g4 with a very strong attack. After the text move White forces an elegant win.

29.Bxf7 Qxf7

If 29...Rxe5 30.fxe5 Qxf7 31.Ng5 Qg8 32.e6 Bd5 33.Qf4 with an easy win.

30.Ng5 Qg8 31.Rxe8 Bxe8 32.Qe1!

32...Bc6

If 32...Kf8, White wins by 33.Qe5 Bd8 (best) 34.Ne6+ Ke7 35.Qc5+ Kd7 36.Nf8+! Observe how White on his 35th move forgoes the discovered check and how the Black King has gotten tangled up with his own pieces.

33.Qe7+ Kh8

On 33...Kh6, obviously comes 34.Ne6.

34.b5

Tightening the noose! If 34...axb5 35.Ne6 h5! 36.Qf6+ Kh7 37.Ng5+ Kh6 38.Bb4 leads to mate.

34...Qg7

Desperation.

35.Qxg7+ Kxg7 36.bxc6

And White won. **1-0.**

Game 34

Illustrates the restraint of a double complex in an extraordinarily striking manner.

Nimzowitsch-Marquis S. Rosselli del Turco
Baden-Baden, 1925

1.Nf3 d5 2.b3 c5 3.e3 Nc6 4.Bb2 Bg4 5.h3 Bxf3 6.Qxf3 e5 7.Bb5 Qd6 8.e4

We have here a position in which White does not immediately double the Black pawns by 8.Bxc6+ bxc6, but brings this about by a roundabout way. After 8.Bxc6+? bxc6, we would never be able

---

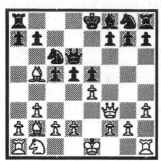

After 8.e4

to force our obstinate opponent to accommodate us by playing ...d4. Black would (after 8.Bxc6 bxc6 9.e4) simply play 9...Nf6.

8...d4 9.Na3

Threatening 10.Nc4 Qc7 11.Bxc6+ bxc6 and the weakness of the doubled pawns is now evident.

9...f6 10.Nc4 Qd7 11.Qh5+

The maneuver of the Queen is intended to help prevent Black's castling on the Queenside, not on the Kingside as one might think.

11...g6 12.Qf3 Qc7

Not 12...0-0-0 because of 13.Na5 and the covering move ...Nge7 is ruled out as the f-pawn would hang.

13.Qg4!

Now she rejoices in the observation post she has won for herself. This Queen maneuver has quite a hypermodern air to it.

13...Kf7

The threat was 14.Qe6+ Kd8 (14...Be7 15.Na5) 15.Bxc6 and the unpleasant doubled pawn is a fact.

14.f4 h5 15.Qf3 exf4

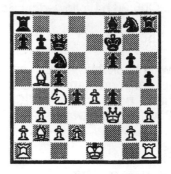

16.Bxc6

At the right moment, for the Queen dare not recapture. If 16...Qxc6 17.Qxf4 Re8 18.0-0!! Qxe4 (18...Rxe4 19.Ne5+!) 19.Qc7+!! and wins (19...Qe7 20.Nd6+ followed by ...Nxe8).

16...bxc6

At last White has attained his end, at the cost it is true of a pawn, but this plays a subordinate role in this case.

17.0-0 g5

Black's position can be broken up. White must prevent the maneuver Ng8-e7-g6-e5. To break up Black's game three pawn moves are necessary. (1) c3 (2) e5 and (3) h4. If White contented himself with only two of these, his work would be only half done. In the game all three are brought about.

18.c3 Rd8

Now this Rook is happily chained to the d4 pawn.

19.Rae1! Ne7 20.e5 Nf5

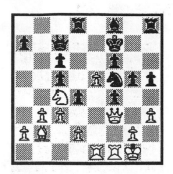

21.cxd4! Nxd4

If 21...cxd4 22.exf6 Kxf6 23.Qe4 and 23...Ng3 fails because of 24.Bxd4+.

22.Qe4 Be7

The reply to 22...f5 would have been 23.Qb1, an attacking move in the best modern spirit! For example, 22...f5 23.Qb1 Ke6 (protecting the f-pawn) 24.Qd3! and Nd6! with a decisive attack.

23.h4

Now the undermined Black position tumbles like a house of cards.

23...Qd7 24.exf6 Bxf6 25.hxg5 1-0.

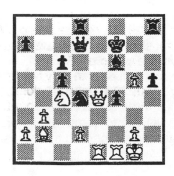

For after 25...Bg7 26.Ne5+ Bxe5 27.Qxe5, Black's King in his helplessness is a pathetic figure.

Game 35

Illustrates a position held under complete restraint, and may serve as a pendant to my game (No.8) against Samisch.

Johner-Nimzowitsch
Dresden, 1926

1.d4 Nf6 2.c4 e6 3.Nc3 Bb4 4.e3 O-O

Black intends to bring into existence the double complex only under conditions favorable to himself. (see game 34).

5.Bd3 c5 6.Nf3 Nc6 7.O-O Bxc3 8.bxc3 d6

The prognosis for the pawn complex c3, c4 is slightly favorable for Black. Yet after 9.e4 e5 10.d5 Na5 Black would not have been able to bring about the barricade which he achieves cheaply in the game, as his c-pawn would have been much better placed at c7 in this case.

9.Nd2!

A fine idea. In reply to 9...e5 10.d5 Na5, the intention is to bring the Na5 to reason by 11.Nb3.

9...b6 10.Nb3?

There was time enough later for this. 10.f4 should have first been played. If then 10...e5, there would follow 11.fxe5 dxe5 12.d5 Na5 13.Nb3 Nb7 14.e4 Ne8, and the weak point c4, which now can be attacked from d6, will be protected by Qe2, while White for his part can use the f-file together with a4-a5 as a base of operations. The game would then stand about even.

10...e5 11.f4

For the reply to 11.d5 would now be 11...e4! Thus 11.d5 e4! 12.Be2 Ne5!; or 12.dxc6 exd3 with advantage to Black.

11...e4

11...Qe7 was also possible. If 12.fxe5 dxe5 13.d5, then 13...Nd8 14.e4 Ne8 and Black by ...Nd6 and ...f6 gets a strong defensive position.

12.Be2 Qd7

Black sees in White's Kingside pawns (f, g, and h-pawns) a qualitative majority. The text move involves a complicated system of restraint. A simpler one could have been brought about by 12...Ne8. For example 13.g4 (or 13.f5 Qg5), 13...f5 14.dxc5! (observe the "dead" Bishop at c1 and consider further how ineffectively posted the White pieces are for an attack to be launched on the g-file). 14...dxc5 15.Qd5+ Qxd5

16.cxd5 Ne7 17.Rd1 Nd6 and Black has the better game.

13.h3 Ne7 14.Qe1

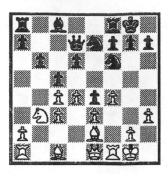

14...h5! 15.Bd2

15.Qh4 will not do because of 15...Nf5 16.Qg5 Nh7 17.Qxh5 Ng3.

15...Qf5!

The Queen is bound for h7! Here she will be excellently placed, for then the crippling of White's Kingside by ...h4 will at once be threatened. It must be conceded that the restraint maneuver ...Qd7-f5-h7 represents a remarkable conception.

16.Kh2 Qh7! 17.a4 Nf5

Threatening 18...Ng4+ 19.hxg4 hxg4+ 20.Kg1 g3!

18.g3 a5!

In this position the backwardness of the b-pawn is easy to put up with.

19.Rg1 Nh6 20.Bf1 Bd7 21.Bc1 Rac8

Black wishes to force d5 in order to operate undisturbed on the Kingside.

22.d5

Otherwise ...Be6 would follow and d5 would be forced anyway.

22...Kh8 23.Nd2 Rg8

And now comes the attack. Was ...Qd7-f5-h7 actually an attacking maneuver? Yes and no. No, since its whole idea was to restrain White's Kingside pawns. Yes, since every restraining action is the logical prelude to an attack, and since every immobile complex tends to be a weakness and therefore must sooner or later become an object of attack.

24.Bg2 g5 25.Nf1 Rg7 26.Ra2 Nf5 27.Bh1

White has very skillfully brought up all of his defensive forces.

27...Rcg8 28.Qd1 gxf4

Opens the g-file for himself, but the e-file for his opponent. This move therefore, demanded deep deliberation.

29.exf4 Bc8 30.Qb3 Ba6 31.Re2

White seizes his chance. Black's e-pawn now needs to be defended. If he had limited himself to purely defensive measures, as perhaps 31.Bd2, a pretty combination would have resulted. 31.Bd2 Rg6! 32.Be1 Ng4+ 33.hxg4 hxg4+ 34.Kg2 Bxc4! 35.Qxc4 and now follows the quiet move 35...e3 and ...Qh3 mate can only be parried by Nxe3 which, however would cost White his Queen.

31...Nh4 32.Re3

32...Bc8 33.Qc2 Bxh3 34.Bxe4!

34.Kxh3 Qf5+ 35.Kh2 would have led to mate in three.

34...Bf5

Best, for ...h4 can no longer be withstood. After the fall of White's h-pawn the defense is hopeless.

35.Bxf5 Nxf5 36.Re2 h4 37.Rgg2 hxg3+ 38.Kg1 Qh3 39.Ne3 Nh4 40.Kf1 Re8! 0-1.

A precise finish, for now there is threatened 41...Nxg2 42.Rxg2 Qh1+ 43.Ke2 Qxg2+! and against this threat White is defenseless. If 41.Ke1 Nf3+ Kd1 (or f1) ...Qh1+ leads to mate. One of the best blockading games that I have ever played.

Game 36

This game illustrates the isolated d-pawn.

Nimzowitsch-Taubenhaus
Petrograd, 1913

**1.d4 d5 2.Nf3 Nf6 3.c4 e6 4.e3 c5
5.Bd3 Nc6 6.O-O dxc4 7.Bxc4 cxd4
8.exd4 Be7 9.Nc3 O-O 10.Be3**

10.d5 would be bad because of 10...Na5
11.b3 Bb4. On 10.Bg5, Black plays
10...b6.

10...b6

10...a6 followed by ...b5 would
unnecessarily weaken c5.

**11.Qe2 Bb7 12.Rfd1 Nb4 13.Ne5 Rc8
14.Rac1 Nbd5 15.Nb5**

A strategically noteworthy conception.
White says to himself: in the center I am
strong, therefore a strategic diversion is
justified; moreover, I have no particular
wish after 15.Ba6 or Bd3 to be saddled
with hanging pawns. The right move
was, nevertheless, 15.Ba6. There
would follow 15...Nxc3 16.bxc3 Qc7
17.Bxb7 Qxb7 18.c4 with a4 and a5 to
eventually follow.

15...a6 16.Na7! Ra8

If 16...Rc7 17.Bxa6.

17.Nac6 Qd6 18.Nxe7+ Qxe7 19.Bd3!

19...Nxe3

There was no occasion for this. There
were other lines of play to be
considered. (1) 19...a5 and ...Rfc8, or
(2) 19...Rfd8 followed by ...Nd7-f8.

20.fxe3 b5

Creates a weakness of the point c5. After
20...a5 followed by 21...Rfc8, Black is ok.

21.Rc5

By controlling this outpost station, Black
gets play on the c-file.

21...Rfc8 22.Rdc1 g6 23.a3

What now follows could serve as a text book example for play in an open file. The slowness with which White step by step gains in terrain is also of significance from the point of view of positional play.

23...Ne8 24.b4 Nd6

On 24...Qg5 25.Nxf7!

25.Qf2 f5

In order to relieve the f-pawn and make ...Qg5 possible.

26.Qf4 Ne8

Black can undertake nothing.

27.Be2 Nd6 28.Bf3

Breaks down the opposition on the c-file.

28...Rxc5 29.dxc5 Ne8

If 29...Ne4, then 30.c6! g5 31.cxb7 Rf8 32.Rc8 and wins.

30.Rd1 Nf6

31.c6

The c-pawn, the fruit of the operations on the c-file, now brings a decision.

31...Bc8 32.c7 Ra7 33.Rd8+ Kg7 34.Rxc8 Rxc7 35.Nxg6 1-0.

Game 37

This game is dedicated to hanging pawns, and is characteristic of these though only in a quite special sense. It shows the frightful dangers to which hanging pawns are exposed at birth. Infant mortality is very high among them, and appreciably exceeds the mortality of grown up hanging pawns, who if worst comes to worst can seek refuge in "blockaded security."

Rubinstein - Znosko-Borovsky
Petrograd, 1909

1.d4 d5 2.c4 e6 3.Nc3 Nf6 4.Bg5 Be7 5.e3 Nbd7 6.Nf3 O-O 7.Qc2

7...b6

7...c5 is possible here. For instance, 8.cxd5 Nxd5 9.Bxe7 Qxe7 10.Nxd5 exd5 11.dxc5 Nxc5 and the isolani doesn't look so bad.

8.cxd5 exd5 9.Bd3 Bb7 10.O-O-O Ne4 11.h4 f5 12.Kb1 c5

The correctness of this move stands or falls by that of the pawn sacrifice recommended in the next note. Sound and good is, instead of 12...c5, 12...Rc8 as given by Dr. Lasker. For instance, 13.Qb3 Nxc3+ followed by ...c5. Not quite so good, yet by no means bad would seem to be 12...h6 13.Bf4 Bd6 14.Bxd6 cxd6.

13.dxc5 bxc5

13...Rc8 was possible here. If then 14.cxb6 Nxb6 Black would have attacking chances. The answer to 14.Nd4 might be 14...Ndxc5. The outcome of the game would have been doubtful in either case, whereas now there is no doubt whatever. It may be observed that if 13...Ndxc5, the 14.Nxd5 Bxd5 15.Bc4! wins.

14.Nxe4 fxe4 15.Bxe4 dxe4 16.Qb3+ Kh8 17.Qxb7 exf3 18.Rxd7 Qe8 19.Rxe7 Qg6+ 20.Ka1 Rab8 21.Qe4

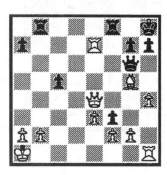

Lasker praised this move, but 21.Qd5 seems to do as well. After 21.Qd5 fxg2

22.Qxg2 Qc2, comes 23.Bf6! True, many roads lead to Rome.

21.... Qxe4 22.Rxe4 fxg2 23.Rg1 Rxf2 24.Rf4 Rc2

If 24...Rbxb2 25.Rf8+ wins outright.

25.b3 h6 26.Be7 Re8 27.Kb1 Re2 28.Bxc5 Rd8 29.Bd4 Rc8 30.Rg4 1-0.

Game 38

This game takes an instructive course. It was played in a simultaneous exhibition in Leipzig in 1926. White was played by Schurig and K. Laue together up to the 12th move and from that point on played alone by Schurig.

Allies-Nimzowitsch

1.Nf3 e6 2.g3 d5 3.Bg2 c6 4.b3 Bd6 5.Bb2 Nf6 6.d3 Nbd7 7.Nbd2 Qc7

7...e5 was also possible. With the text move an original maneuver begins. Black plans an attack on the Queenside, but before launching it he wishes to safeguard his center against the possible threat of e4-e5. Accordingly, he first sees to the overprotection of e5. Further, from where the Black Queen stands she has at her disposal a reserve square in b8 to which she can withdraw if the need arises, perhaps on the opening of the c-file.

8.O-O a5 9.c4 b5

The question whether a flank attack is admissible or not can only be solved by

---

reference to the actual position in the center. If this is secure a flank attack cannot be totally amiss. This is true here. What matters is that the King has not yet castled. As it is he is unassailable.

10.cxb5 cxb5 11.Rc1 Qb8

The withdrawing room.

12.Qc2

12.e4 seems more to the point.

12...O-O 13.e4 Bb7 14.Nd4 Rc8 15.Qb1 Rxc1 16.Rxc1 b4 17.Nc6

A bit premature in my opinion.

17...Bxc6 18.Rxc6 a4

Every free moment is used to the strengthening of the position on the Queenside.

19.d4

This move must be credited to Black's strategy in overprotecting e5. The valuable diagonal a1-h8 is now obstructed, but by no other means could the thrust e5 have been effected. Those engaged in this overprotection have

once more stood the test excellently. They have had to put up with no inconveniences, but have made themselves felt in all directions.

One variation should be mentioned, namely 19.f4, in order to keep the d-pawn at d3. The continuation might have been 19...Bc5+!, and White has after all to submit to playing 20.d4, and after 20...Bf8 21.e5 we will have arrived at the position in the text.

19...Bf8 20.e5 Ne8

The White Bishops have small possibilities of action.

21.f4 Qb5

21...a3 at once would have been more precise.

22.Qc2 a3 23.Bc1

It was essential to interpolate 23.Bf1 here.

23...Bc5

This interesting combination should begin with 23...Nc5! Instead of 23...Bc5. The difference will soon be manifest.

24.Rxc5 Nxc5 25.dxc5?

The interpolation here of 25.Bf1 (which would not have been possible if Black had played 23...Nc5) would have yielded him an extra tempo for the endgame.

25...Rc8

We can see by his face that White's a-pawn is marked for death.

26.Nb1 Qxc5+ 27.Qxc5 Rxc5 28.Bxa3

Or 28.Bd2 Rc2 29.Bf1 Rxa2 30.Bxb4 Rg2+! and wins (On 31.B or Kxg2, comes 32...a2). If White had one tempo more (see note to move 25), this combination would have been impossible.

28...bxa3 29.Nxa3 Ra5 30.Nc2 Rxa2 31.Nd4 Rb2 32.f5 Nc7 33.fxe6 Nxe6 34.Nc6 d4 0-1.

Game 39

Illustrates overprotection and also the problem of the isolated d-pawn.

Three Swedish Amateurs-Nimzowitsch
Played in 1921

1.e4 Nc6 2.d4 d5 3.e5 f6 4.Bb5

4.f4 would have been better.

4...Bf5 5.Nf3 Qd7 6.c4 Bxb1!

With this exchange, which is anything but obvious. Black plans to win the square d4 for his Knight.

7.Rxb1 O-O-O

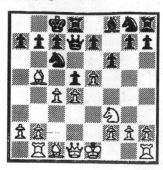

8.cxd5

If 8.c5 then 8...g5. A fight would then take place for possession of the point e5. For example, 8.c5 g5 9.Qe2 (to threaten e6 shutting Black in), 9...Qe6 10.a3 Nh6, followed by ...Nf7 or else ...Nb8. In either case Black would not stand badly.

8...Qxd5 9.Bxc6 Qxc6 10.O-O e6 11.Be3 Ne7 12.Qe2 Nd5

We may with a clear conscience regard White's d-pawn as isolated. His weakness (for the endgame!) is evident. Black has in the square d5 a very strong point. As regards any compensating advantage for what we have called his isolated d-pawn, White has the outpost station c5 which will serve some purpose. On the other hand e5 is of no use to him as a station for his Knight. The game is about equal.

13.Rfc1 Qd7

It is very questionable whether 13.exf6 would not have been better for White than the Rook move. True his opponent would have had the g-file and a centrally posted Bishop at d6, but the e-file must not be despised, at any rate as a counterweight. A rather curious overprotection is now built up in moves 13-18 and has been previously discussed in Diagram 167.

14.Rc4 Kb8 15.Qd2 Rc8 16.Ne1 Be7 17.Nd3 Rhd8 18.Qc2 f5

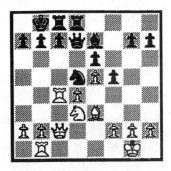

Having consolidated his position, Black passes to the attack, which is not easy to conduct, since for one thing objectives are lacking and for another White has attacking chances of his own.

19.Rc1

Without question 19.b4 should have been played here, with the intention of playing 20.Nc5 Bxc5 21.bxc5. The question now arises, is Black's position strong enough to bear weakening? Two moves in particular come under consideration in answer to 19.b4, namely 19...b6, and 19...b5. If 19...b6, then 20.Nc5! can be played, but after 20...Bxc5 21.bxc5 c6, Black would stand very well. He must, however, emphatically not accept the Knight as the following combination proves. 19.b4! b6 20.Nc5 bxc5 21.bxc5+ Ka8? (the return sacrifice 21...Nb6 was essential). 22.c6 Qe8 23.Ra4 (threatening 24.Rxa7+), 23...Nb6

24.d5!! Rxd5 25.Rxa7+ Kxa7 26.Qa4+ Kb8 27.Bxb6 cxb6 28.Rxb6+ Kc7 29.Rb7+ Kd8 30.c7+! Rxc7 31.Rb8+ Rc8 32.Rxc8+ Kxc8 33.Qxe8+ and White wins. A true Morphy combination.

We may quietly note the fact that his overprotected central position is so strong that Black can here without a qualm leave himself unprotected and yet remain master of the situation as he was before, for he is in a position laughingly to evade any enemy combination, be it ever so diabolical.

We have still to show what would happen if Black played 19...b5 in reply to 19.b4. In this case, too, Black would not fare badly. 20.Rc6 Kb7 21.Nc5+ Bxc5 22.Rxc5 Nb6 followed by ...c6, and Black is strong on the light squares.

19...g5 20.Nc5 Bxc5 21.Rxc5 Rg8 22.Qe2 h5! 23.Bd2

23.Qxh5? g4 and ...Rh8.

23...h4 24.a4 g4 25.a5 a6! 26.b4 c6

White has spent his last fury.

27.Rb1 Qf7 28.Rb3 f4 29.Qe4

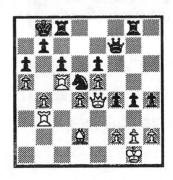

29...f3!

White would not be able to hold out after 30.gxf3 gxf3+ 31.Kf1 Rcf8. (stronger than 31...Rg1+).

30.Rc1 fxg2 31.Kxg2 Rcf8

Note with what surprising ease the Black Rooks are brought into action, a further proof, in my opinion, of the enormous vitality of overprotecting pieces.

32.Rf1 g3! 33.hxg3 hxg3 34.f4

After 34.Rxg3 Rxg3+ the King would be exposed.

34...Ne7 35.Be1 Nf5 36.Rh1 Rg4 37.Bxg3 Qg6 38.Qe1 Nxg3

Decisive, though so simple and even insipid. It wins the pawns which are so conveniently exposed on the 4th rank.

39.Rxg3 Rfxf4 40.Rhh3 Rxd4 41.Qf2 Rxg3+ 42.Rxg3 Qe4+ 43.Kh2 Qxe5 44.Kg2 Qd5+ 1-0.

One of my favorite games.

Game 40

The Hanham defense. Illustrates combined play on both wings. The fearlessness with which Black is able up to a certain point to ignore his own weakness at d6 is noticeable.

Teichmann-Nimzowitsch
San Sebastian, 1911

1.e4 e5 2.Nf3 d6 3.d4 Nf6 4.Nc3 Nbd7 5.Bc4 Be7 6.O-O O-O 7.Qe2 c6 8.Bg5

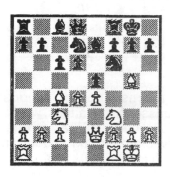

8.a4 would have been preferable.

8...h6 9.Bh4 Nh5 10.Bg3 Nxg3

10...Bf6 was also to be considered.

11.hxg3 b5 12.Bd3 a6!

Black's pawn mass is now of such a constitution (I mean inner structure), that they must inspire respect. Notice the two-fold possibility of deployment by ...c5 or, on occasion ...d5.

13.a4

He tries to nip the latent strength of Black's pawns in the bud.

13... Bb7 14.Rad1 Qc7 15.axb5 axb5 16.g4 Rfe8 17.d5 b4 18.dxc6 Bxc6 19.Nb1 Nc5 20.Nbd2 Qc8

White's attempt to pick a quarrel, must be regarded as having failed, for d6 is easily defendable, while the two Bishops in conjunction with the a-file and the threatening diagonal c8-h3, exercise significant influence.

21.Bc4

A witty defense of the g-pawn. (21...Qxg4?? 22.Bf7+).

21...g6 22.g3 Kg7 23.Nh2 Bg5!

The weakness of d6 is here of only slight importance.

24.f3

24.f4? exf4 25.gxf4 Bf6 winning a pawn.

24...Qc7

Threatening 25...Na4, and if 25.Rb1, then 25...Bxd2 followed by 26...Bxe4 and the Bc4 hangs.

25.Rfe1 Rh8 26.Ndf1 h5

The following moves lead to the occupation of the important files and diagonals.

27.gxh5 Rxh5 28.Bd5 Rah8 29.Bxc6 Qxc6 30.Qc4 Qb6 31.Kg2

A weakness has now slowly crystallized; namely that of White's base. With the Black Knight placed at d4 the invasion of White's 2nd rank would be decisive.

31...Ne6

He has his eye now on d4 but at the same time threatens the Kingside by 32...Rxh2+ 33.Nxh2 Rxh2+ 34.Kxh2 Qf2+ 35.Kh3 Bf4! and wins. (36.Rg1 Ng5+ 37.Kg4 Qxf3+; or 37.Kh4 Qh2+)

32.Re2

Were it not for the threat mentioned in the last note, White might find an adequate defense by 32.Qd5 Nd4 33.f4.

32...Nd4

This move now takes place with the win of a tempo.

33.Ree1

or 33.Rf2? Be3!

33...Qb7

34...Rc8 cannot be parried. A good example of how one can devote one's attention to several weaknesses at the same time.

34.Rxd4

After 34.c3 bxc3 35.bxc3 Qb2+, the weakness of White's 2nd rank would be shown.

34...exd4 35.Ng4

or 35.Qxd4+ Bf6 36.Qxd6 Rd8

35...Qb6

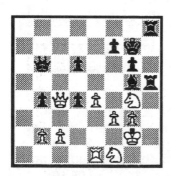

36.f4 Be7 37.Rd1 f5 38.Nf2 fxe4 39.Qxd4+ Qxd4 40.Rxd4 d5 41.g4 Bc5

42.Rd1 Rh4 43.Rxd5 Bxf2 44.Kxf2 Rxg4

Black, in order to maintain his advantage had always to try to combine attack on the Kingside with play in the center. See his 40th and 41st moves.

45.Ke3 Rc8

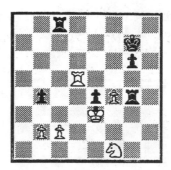

And now White's Queenside is brought in, too.

46.Kxe4 Rc4+ 47.Kd3 Rcxf4

Now things go easier.

48.Ne3 Rg3 49.Re5 Kf6 50.Re8 Kf7 51.Re5 Rf6 52.c4 b3 53.Ke4 Re6 54.Rxe6 Kxe6 55.Nd5 g5 0-1.

Game 41

A most complicated game in the strategic sense. Lasker maneuvers on one wing and breaks through on the other. The why and the wherefore of this procedure will be found in the notes.

Dr. Lasker-Amos Burn
Petrograd, 1909

1.e4 e5 2.Nf3 Nc6 3.Bb5 a6 4.Ba4 Nf6 5.O-O Be7 6.Re1 b5 7.Bb3 d6 8.c3 Na5 9.Bc2 c5 10.d4 Qc7 11.Nbd2 Nc6 12.Nf1

12...O-O

Black should have tried to force White to declare his intentions in the center by 12...cxd4 13.cxd4 Bg4.

13.Ne3 Bg4 14.Nxg4

The reply to 14.Nd5 would have been 14...Qa7 15.Nxe7+ Nxe7! With the text move Lasker plays for the advantage of the two Bishops.

14...Nxg4 15.h3 Nf6 16.Be3 Nd7 17.Qe2 Bf6 18.Rad1 Ne7 19.Bb1 Nb6 20.a3 Ng6 21.g3 Rfe8

Black has consistently kept his goal in sight - to prepare for ...d5. Lasker is now forced to play d5 blocking his own Bishop. The game enters a new stage.

22.d5 Nd7 23.Kg2 Qd8

Instead of this he should have played ...c4 followed by ...Nc5. The Knight would have been well posted, and more important would have a preventive effect, as White was preparing to play f4.

24.h4 Be7 25.h5 Ngf8 26.Rh1 h6 27.Rdg1 Nh7

The point g5 seems well fortified.

28.Kf1 Kh8 29.Rh2 Rg8 30.Ne1

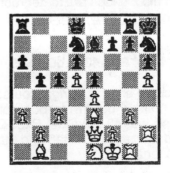

If 30.Nh4, Black would simply exchange (30...Bxh4 31.Rxh4) and the game would then take on a somewhat rigid aspect. Lasker, wisely avoids this move and seeks to preserve whatever latent dynamic force is in the position, even though little remains.

30...Rb8 31.Nc2 a5 32.Bd2 Bf6 33.f3 Nb6 34.Rf2

White intends to play the Knight to e3 and wishes to hold the move f4 in readiness should Black play ...Bg5 (Lasker).

34...Nc8 35.Kg2 Qd7 36.Kh1 Ne7 37.Rh2 Rb7 38.Rf1 Re8 39.Ne3 Ng8 40.f4 Bd8 41.Qf3

Lasker has succeeded in carrying out f4 under circumstances favorable to himself. Black's pieces must keep on the watch against the threat of an invasion by Nf5 and are less well posted in the case of an attack on the Queenside. We may say that Lasker has laid the Kingside under siege in order to bring the enemy pieces out of contact with their own Queenside and will now roll up the Queenside and thus score a double advantage. Definite weaknesses are to be created, and in addition his Bishops are to get room for maneuvering. Play might go c4 ...b4 Bc2 followed by Qd1 and Ba4.

41...c4 42.a4 Bb6 43.axb5 Qxb5

The decisive error. The right course, as Lasker pointed out in the book of the Congress, was 43...Bxe3 44.Bxe3 Qxb5 followed by ...a4 and ...Ra8 and Black's game is tenable.

44.Nf5 Qd7 45.Qg4 f6

The Knight on f5 can no longer be driven away. Black now has evident weaknesses on both wings and Lasker exploits them without any particular trouble.

46.Bc2 Bc5 47.Ra1 Reb8 48.Bc1 Qc7 49.Ba4 Qb6 50.Rg2 Rf7 51.Qe2 Qa6 52.Bc6

Threatening 53.b4.

52...Ne7

At last he manages to oust the intruder at f5, but meanwhile White has grown too strong on the Queenside.

53.Nxe7 Rxe7 54.Ra4 exf4

Desperation. There followed:

55.gxf4 f5 56.e5 Nf6 57.Rxc4 Ng4

58.Rxc5 Qxe2 59.Rxe2 dxc5 60.d6 Ra7 61.e6 Ra6 62.e7 Nf6 63.d7 Nxd7 64.Bxd7 1-0.

This fine game is instructive as illustrating the struggle of united Bishops for open space in which to maneuver.

The following game won a brilliancy prize in the New York tournament of 1927.

Game 42

Nimzowitsch-Marshall
New York, 1927

1.c4 Nf6 2.d4 e6 3.Nf3 c5 4.d5 d6 5.Nc3 exd5 6.cxd5 g6 7.Nd2

To establish himself at c4.

7...Nbd7 8.Nc4 Nb6 9.e4 Bg7 10.Ne3

Planning a4-a5 and posting the Knight anew on c4. Black would have done better to exchange Knights on his 9th move. White now gets the advantage.

10...O-O 11.Bd3 Nh5 12.O-O Be5 13.a4 Nf4 14.a5 Nd7 15.Nc4 Nxd3 16.Qxd3 f5 17.exf5 Rxf5 18.f4

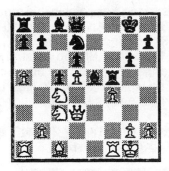

The prelude to a complicated attacking operation which was unexpected since 18.Ne4 gave White a good position without any effort. But for once, I wanted to go in for a combination.

18...Bd4+ 19.Be3 Bxc3 20.Qxc3 Nf6 21.Qb3

White gets compensation for the d-pawn, as it is difficult for Black to develop his Queenside.

21...Rxd5

The answer to 21...Nxd5 would have been 22.Rae1!!, by which 22...Be6 would have been prevented because of 23.Bxc5. Black would then have been quite helpless, and White could have won by playing his Bishop to d2 and doubling Rooks on the e-file.

22.f5! gxf5 23.Bg5

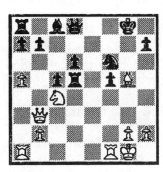

There is a peculiar point in this move. If now 23...Be6 24.Qxb7 (threatening 25.Bxf6 winning a piece), 24...Rc8 25.Rae1! and the Bishop must give up the defense of one or the other of the Rooks, on which Bxf6 would lead to the win of whichever is left undefended.

23...Rd4 24.Nb6+ c4 25.Qc3 axb6 26.Qxd4 Kg7 27.Rae1 bxa5

28.Re8

Violent but intelligible.

28...Qxe8 29.Qxf6+ Kg8 30.Bh6 1-0.

Game 43

Nimzowitsch-Alekhine
Semmering, 1926

1.e4 Nf6 2.Nc3 d5 3.e5 Nfd7 4.f4 e6 5.Nf3 c5 6.g3 Nc6 7.Bg2

Black's Kingside seems somewhat boxed in, but as compensation his center is more mobile.

7...Be7 8.O-O O-O 9.d3 Nb6

9...d4 would have been bad because of 10.Ne4 and the Knight is centrally

established. On the other hand, 9...f6 was well worth consideration. For instance, 10.exf6 Bxf6 and Black controls the center.

10.Ne2 d4!?

Black wants to score the Knight move as an error, for now the Knight cannot get to e4. This is a mistake, however, and therefore it would have been better to play 10...f6 instead of 10...d4. For example, 10...f6 11.exf6 Bxf6 12.c3 e5 13.fxe5 Nxe5, and Black would not stand badly.

11.g4 f6

This move, which Black has twice passed over, leads now, thanks to the weakness of e4, to a result which promises little fruit. The "prophylactic" defense, 11...Re8 12.Ng3 Bf8 13.Ne4 Nd5 would have been better.

12.exf6 gxf6

There was also no joy for Black in 12...Bxf6 13.Ng3 e5 14.f5.

13.Ng3 Nd5

Black seeks to defend his threatened Kingside from the center. This plan

---

should not have been sufficient to save the situation.

14.Qe2 Bd6 15.Nh4

Threatening 16.Bxd5 followed by Nhf5.

15...Nce7 16.Bd2

Sharper here would have been 16.Nh5 Ng6 17.Bxd5 exd5 17.Nf5 with a winning attack.

16...Qc7 17.Qf2

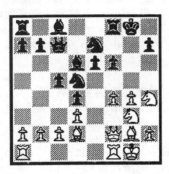

17.Nh5 was still to be preferred.

17...c4! 18.dxc4 Ne3!

With this ingenious diversion Dr. Alekhine succeeds in bringing his opponent's attack to a standstill for some time.

19.Bxe3 dxe3 20.Qf3 Qxc4

The position is to a degree cleared up. Black has a passed pawn which is sick, but very highly insured against death. We mean that the diagonals a8-h1 (after ...Bd7-c6) and a7-g1 are compensation for Black with his two Bishops. Instead of chasing after the dubious win of the pawn, it would have been more to the purpose had White gone on with his

Kingside attack with the immediate g5. Neglect of this move sets White back.

21.Ne4 Bc7 22.b3 Qd4 23.c3 Qb6 24.Kh1

White has localized the enemy thrust.

24...Nd5

24...Bd7 was certainly better.

25.f5

Here White misses his opportunity to play 25.g5 with a win. For instance, 25...fxg5 26.Nxg5 Rxf4 27.Qh5; or 25...f5 25.Qh5 fxe4 26.Bxe4.

25...Nf4 26.Rfd1 Kh8

Better, according to H. Wolf, would have been 26...e2 27.Rd2 Qb5 followed by ...Qe5.

27.Bf1 exf5 28.gxf5 Be5 29.Re1 Bd7

Now it happens as was indicated in the note to move 20. White wins the pawn, but Black keeps the pressure by means of his two Bishops.

30.Rxe3 Bc6 31.Rae1 Nd5

With 31...Rg8, Black could have increased the pressure.

32.Rd3 Nxc3

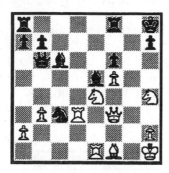

Pretty but insufficient. True, the acceptance of the sacrifice would have been ruinous (33.Rxc3 Bxc3 34.Qxc3 Qf2), but White has a truly startling counter at his disposal.

33.Ng6+! hxg6 34.Qg4!!

The point. To strike at once would have been bad. For example, 34.fxg6 Kg7 35.Qh3 Rh8 36.Rd7+ Bxd7 37.Qxd7+ Kxg6 and White is threatened by mate.

34...Rf7

34...Rg8 would have offered stiffer resistance.

35.Rh3+ Kg7 36.Bc4 Bd5 37.fxg6 Nxe4 38.gxf7+ Kf8 39.Rxe4

Simpler would have been 39.Qg8+ Ke7 40.f8=Q+ Rxf8 41.Rh7+ Ke8 42.Qxd5.

39...Bxe4+ 40.Qxe4 Ke7 41.f8=Q+

The passed pawn's lust to expand!

41...Rxf8 42.Qd5 Qd6

42...Qc6 would have led to the loss of Black's Queen. 43.Rh7+ Ke8 44.Bb5.

43.Qxb7+ Kd8 44.Rd3 Bd4 45.Qe4 Re8 46.Rxd4 1-0.

Game 44

Illustrates in an instructive manner the connection between play in the center on the one hand, and diversions undertaken on the wings on the other. The dependence of a flank attack for success on the "state of health" of the center is very clearly brought out. This was one of four simultaneous consultation games.

E. Andersson, R. Enstrom, and O. Oeberg-Nimzowitsch
Upsala, 1921

1.e4 e6 2.d4 d5 3.Nc3 Bb4 4.Bd3 Nc6 5.Nge2 Nge7 6.O-O O-O 7.e5 Nf5 8.Be3 f6

Black has overcome the difficulties of the opening.

9.Bxf5 exf5 10.f4 Be6

Obedient to the law that a passed pawn must be blockaded.

11.Ng3 Bxc3! 12.bxc3 Na5!

It was only reluctantly and after much deliberation that I determined on this diversion on the Queenside. It appears risky, since the situation in the center is by no means secure. For one of my leading principles lays down that a flank attack is only justified if the center is secure. Yet in the present case White cannot force his opponent to play ...fxe5, and if White plays exf6, he gets, it is true, the square e5 (after ...Rxf6), but Black brings up his reserves and mitigates this danger.

13.Qd3 Qd7 14.Rf3 g6 15.Ne2 Rf7! 16.h4 h5 17.Kh2! Raf8!

The reserves. See last note.

18.Rg3 Kh7 19.Ng1!

Aiming for g5 or e5. It will be seen that the consulting players are thoroughly exercised in the art of maneuvering, and are opponents to be taken seriously.

19...Rg7 20.Nf3 Qa4

Black at last proceeds with the attack to which his 11th move was the prelude. This slowness is all to his credit.

21.exf6 Rxf6 22.Ng5+ Kg8 23.Bg1 Nc4 24.Re1 Bd7!!

This simple strategic retreat reveals my plan of defense. As my system lays down, the ideal aimed at by every operation in a file is the entry to the 7th and 8th ranks. However, here the points of invasion, e7 and e8 are safeguarded, and the Rook on g3 cannot co-operate since he is deprived of the square e3.

25.Nf3 Bb5 26.Qd1 Qxa2 27.Qe2

27...Nd6!!

With this retreat a maneuver is started which is designed to neutralize the enemy's strong hold on the e-file. Less effective would have been 27...Qa3 (with the idea of getting home safely with the booty) 28.Ne5 Qd6 29.Nxc4 Bxc4 30.Qf2 Re6 31.Re5! and White still has drawing chances, whereas the text move wins.

28.Qe5 Ne8!

With this, the regrouping ...Rd6 followed by ...Nf6 is threatened. The Rook and

Knight will have exchanged stations. If White prevents this by 29.Ng5, (29...Rd6?? 30.Qxe8+ mating) he will undoubtedly be strong on the e-file, yet the distinctive characteristic of the position, namely the spearhead station of White's Queen will prevent him from taking full advantage of the file. For instance, 29.Ng5 Bc6 30.Rge3 Qxc2; or 30.Re2 Qc4 (Blockade!) 31.Rge3 a5 and wins, for 32.Ne6? is impossible because of 32...Re7 and White has no other effective move on the e-file at his disposal. The game continuation was:

29.Nd2 Rd6 30.c4 Bd7 31.Rc3 Nf6

Now the difficult regrouping maneuver (under enemy fire) has been carried out.

32.cxd5??

A gross mistake, but even after 32.Qe2 Re6 33.Qd1 Rge7, White's game would have been hopeless.

32...Ng4+ 0-1.

In the following game two armies out of contact with one another operate in the center and on a flank. It is interesting to see how contact between them is finally established.

Game 45

Yates-Nimzowitsch
London, 1927

1.e4 c5 2.Nf3 Nf6

The innovation introduced by me in 1911 at San Sebastian.

3.e5 Nd5

The relationship between Alekhine's Defense and this treatment of the Sicilian will be noted.

4.Bc4 Nb6 5.Be2 Nc6

White has lost a tempo with his Bishop. The Black Knight on b6 is not well placed, however, so the Bishop maneuver is not to be blamed.

6.c3 d5 7.d4

Better would have been 7.exd6 e.p.

7...cxd4 8.cxd4 Bf5 9.O-O e6 10.Nc3 Be7 11.Ne1

If the attack planned by this move, namely f4 to be followed by g4 and f5 should really prove possible to carry out, this would be a proof of the incorrectness of 8...Bf5, and that would be an absurdity. In point of fact the matter stands as follows: No particular result is achieved by the move 11.Ne1, and this diversion would better have been abandoned in favor of a systematic utilization of the c-file. For example, 11.Be3 0-0 12.Rc1 followed by a3, b4, and Nd2-b3-c5, and the establishment of an outpost advocated by my system would have been attained.

11...Nd7! 12.Bg4!

Well played! The answer to 12.f4 would have been, of course, 12...Nxd4 13.Qxd4?? Bc5. 12.Be3 would also have been bad because of 12...Ndxe5 13.dxe5 d4 14.Bd2 dxc3 15.Bxc3 Qc7 with advantage to Black. By the move 12.Bg4! Yates is able in a quite startling manner to play f4, the move at which he has been aiming.

12...Bg6 13.f4 Nxd4 14.Nxd5! Nc6

If 14...Bc5, then 15.b4 would have been strong. 14...exd5 would also have been bad because of 15.Bxd7+ followed by Qxd4.

15.Nxe7 Qb6+ 16.Kh1 Nxe7

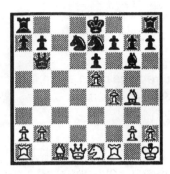

17.Qa4?

A typical sin of omission!

In the face of Black's obvious plan to occupy the central points, White should, by also centralizing, have disputed this with his opponent. Therefore, 17.Qe2 (intending 18.Be3) 17...Nd5 18.Bf3 Qc5 19.Bd2 N7b6 20.Rc1 Qe7, and White has more of the center than Black. Even if "more" of the center were not attainable, White should have fought for whatever share he could get. As it is a just punishment now overtakes him.

17...h5 18.Bh3

Forced, for if 18.Bf3, then 18...Nf5 with a further gain of terrain in the center. There would then also be a mating threat in the air, namely ...h4 followed by ...Ng3+.

18...Bf5 19.Qa3 Qb5

Making room for the Nd7 to maneuver to d5 via b6.

20.Kg1 Nb6 21.Qf3 Nbd5 22.b3 Qb6+ 23.Rf2

23...Rc8

This move in conjunction with the next leads to a decentralization of one of his Rooks and so to a defect in his position which has been so harmoniously constructed. On the other hand the continuation 23...0-0-0! held out the promise of untroubled harmony, for after 24...Kb8 and 25...g6 nothing stood in the way of employing the two Rooks centrally. Perhaps even better might have been 23...Bg4! For instance, 24.Bxg4 hxg4 25.Qxg4 Rxh2 26.Qxg7 0-0-0 27.Kxh2 Qxf2 28.Nd3 Qe2 and Black must win. Lastly, it was also possible to combine the two plans. 23...0-0-0 24.Ba3 and now 24...Bg4. If then 25.Rc1+ Kb8 26.Bc5 Qxc5 27.Rxc5 Bxf3 28.Rxf3 Rc8 with a victorious incursion on the c-file.

24.Bd2 Rh6

Interesting, for when all is said and done, Black's position, centralized even to the extent that it is, can support an adventurous raid; yet 24...0-0 with ...g6 and ...Rfd8 was certainly more correct.

25.Rd1 Bxh3 26.Qxh3 Nf5 27.Qd3 Rg6 28.Nf3 Rg4 29.h3 Rg3 30.a4 Nh4

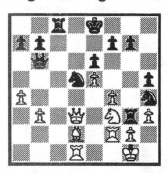

Black's structure suffers under an inner discord. The position of the cut off Rook makes a mating attack seem desirable; but the disposition of the rest of the army is rather directed towards the endgame, in which the Nd5 would have enormous effect, while the light squares would be in Black's undisputed possession.

31.Kf1 Rc6

To neutralize White's threat of Qh7-g8+, the Rook flees the back rank. Black must maneuver cautiously.

32.a5 Qd8 33.Kg1 Nf5

If 33...Nxf3+ 34.Rxf3 Rxf3 35.Qxf3 g6 would be bad for Black because of 36.f5!

34.Kh2 a6 35.Qb1

To threaten 36.Nd4 (attacks the defender of the Rg3).

35...Qe7

Black does not mind the threat, and actually has his eye on the move ...Qc5.

36.Nd4

Loses; 36.Rc1 was better.

36...Qh4!

All of the detachments which have been cut off cannot get back to the army, so the army comes to them.

37.Be1

If 37.Nxc6?? Rxh3+! followed by mate.

37...Nxf4

Black threatens mate again, this time by 38...Rxg2+!

38.Rxf4

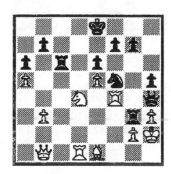

38...Rxh3+!

The simplest.

39.gxh3 Qxf4+ 40.Kg2 Ne3+

And mate follows. **0-1**. This game was awarded a special prize "for the best played game" of the tournament.

There follow five games of historic interest.

Game 46

A most instructive game from A to Z, one which I regard as the first in which my new philosophy of the center was exhibited.

Nimzowitsch-Salwe
Carlsbad, 1911

1.e4 e6 2.d4 d5 3.e5 c5 4.c3 Nc6 5.Nf3 Qb6 6.Bd3 Bd7 7.dxc5 Bxc5 8.O-O f6

Black hungrily attacks the last remaining member of the once-proud White pawn chain. His war cry is "Room for the e-pawn!" But it happens quite otherwise.

9.b4

In order to be able to provide e5 with an enduring defense. 9.Qe2 would also have been a defense, but not an enduring one, for there would follow 9...fxe5 10.Nxe5 Nxe5 11.Qxe5 Nf6 and the blockading Queen at e5 will be easily driven away.

9...Be7 10.Bf4 fxe5

Once again we have the exchange operation which we have so often discussed. This time it is not really justified, for the new blockader, the Bishop, proves to be very stout .

11.Nxe5 Nxe5 12.Bxe5 Nf6

12...Bf6 would be met by 13.Qh5+ g6 14.Bxg6+ hxg6 15.Qxg6+ Ke7 16.Bxf6+ Nxf6 17.Qg7+.

13.Nd2 O-O 14.Nf3!

The blockading forces are to be reinforced by the Knight.

14...Bd6

14...Bb5 would yield little profit for 15.Bd4 Qa6 16.Bxb5 Qxb5 17.Ng5 wins a pawn.

15.Qe2 Rac8 16.Bd4 Qc7 17.Ne5

The immobility of the Black e-pawn is now greater than ever. White has utilized his resources very economically. The possibility of a successful occupation of the points d4 and e5 hung on a hair, on taking small advantage of the terrain.

17...Be8 18.Rae1 Bxe5 19.Bxe5 Qc6 20.Bd4

Forcing the Be8 (who was looking at h5) to come to a decision.

20...Bd7 21.Qc2

The decisive regrouping.

21...Rf7 22.Re3 b6 23.Rg3 Kh8

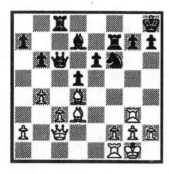

24.Bxh7 e5

24...Nxh7 lost because of 25.Qg6.

25.Bg6 Re7 26.Re1 Qd6 27.Be3 d4 28.Bg5 Rxc3 29.Rxc3 dxc3 30.Qxc3 Kg8 31.a3 Kf8 32.Bh4 Be8 33.Bf5 Qd4 34.Qxd4 exd4 35.Rxe7 Kxe7 36.Bd3 Kd6 37.Bxf6 gxf6 38.h4   1-0.

Game 47

Of special interest historically as being the first game in which what has been called the "Ideal Queen's Gambit" was played, where Black forgoes altogether the occupation of the center by his pawns. It was played in the all-Russian Tournament in Petrograd, 1913.

Gregory-Nimzowitsch
Petrograd, 1913

1.d4 Nf6 2.Nf3 e6 3.Bg5

In answer to 3.c4 I had planned 3...b6. The point d5 is to remain permanently unoccupied.

3...h6 4.Bxf6 Qxf6 5.e4 g6

Black owns the two Bishops, and in what follows concerns keeping them.

6.Nc3 Qe7

In order after ...d6, not to be exposed to e5, opening up the game.

7.Bc4 Bg7 8.O-O d6 9.Qd3 O-O 10.Rae1 a6 11.a4 b6 12.Ne2

The mobility of White's center must be rated as very slight, for any thrust would be intercepted without any trouble. For example 12.e5 d5!, or 12.d5 e5!

12...c5

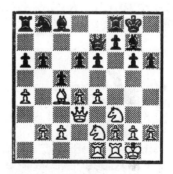

A strategic device which the Hypermodernist may care to note, makes its appearance here. I mean the continuity of an attack directed against

---

a pawn mass. This is to be understood as follows - The threatened advance must first have its sting drawn in this game this was done by 6...Qe7. It is only when this has happened that we may regard the mass as semi-mobile and attack it, for only those objects which have been made immobile should be chosen as a target.

13.c3 Bd7 14.b3

14.Nd2 was to be considered. For instance, 14...Bxa4 15.f4 with definite chances.

14...Qe8 15.Qc2 b5 16.axb5 axb5 17.Bd3 Qc8 18.dxc5 dxc5 19.e5 Nc6 20.Bxb5

If 20.Ng3, then 20...b4 and if 21.c4 Be8 with the superior game.

20...Nxe5 21.Nxe5 Bxb5 22.Nf3 Qb7 23.Nd2 Bc6 24.f3 Rfb8

Now the Bishops assert their rights.

25.Ng3 Qa7 26.Rf2 Bd5 27.Kf1 Qa2 28.Qxa2 Rxa2 29.c4 Bd4 30.Rfe2 Bc6 31.Rd1 Rb2 32.Rc1 h5 33.Ke1 Ra8

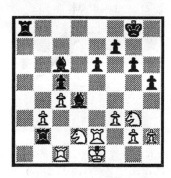

Threatens complete paralysis by

34...Raa2, since 35.Rb1 is impossible because of 35...Rxb1+ followed by ...Ra1.

34.Nh1 Raa2 35.Nf2 Rxd2 36.Rxd2 Rxd2 37.Kxd2 Bxf2

The win is still a considerable way off. In what follows Black maneuvers against the c-pawn, but also keeps before him the possibility of an incursion of his King at g3. This however, by itself would not be sufficient. Black has also still to play out the duel on the Kingside with his pawn majority, and in doing so his position will become broken up, and with all of this the c-pawn is a constant worry.

38.Rb1 Kf8 39.b4 cxb4 40.Rxb4 Ke7 41.Rb8 Bd4 42.Rc8 Bd7 43.Ra8 e5 44.Kc2 Bc6 45.Rc8 Ba4+ 46.Kd3 Bd7 47.Rc7 Kd6 48.Rb7 Bg1 49.h3 h4

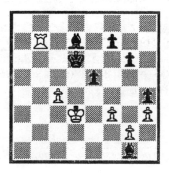

The square g3 now looks ripe for invasion by Black.

50.Rb3 Be6 51.Ra8 Bb6 52.Rh8 Bf2 53.Ra8 Bf5+ 54.Ke2 Bb6 55.Rh8 g5 56.Rg8 f6 57.Rf8 Ke7 58.Rb8 Bd4 59.Rb5 Bg6 60.Ra5 Bf5 61.Ra6 Bc8 62.Rc6 Bd7 63.Ra6 Bc5 64.Kd3 Bf5+ 65.Ke2

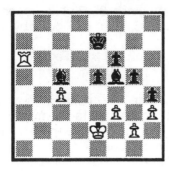

65...e4!

At last the right moment has arrived.

66.Rc6 Bd4 67.Ra6 Be6 68.Ra4 e3 69.Kd3 Bc5

Now the King threatens to journey to g3.

70.Ra6 Bxc4+ 0-1.

After 71.Kxc4 e2, the pawn decides matters.

Game 48

This was the first game in which the thesis of the relative harmlessness of the pawn roller was stated.

Spielmann-Nimzowitsch
San Sebastian, 1911

1.e4 c5 2.Nf3 Nf6

This set Spielmann thinking. After some minutes I raised my eyes from the board and saw that my dear old companion in arms was quite disconcerted. He looked at the Knight now confidently, now suspiciously, and after much hesitation gave up the possible chase started by 3.e5 and played the more circumspect 3.Nc3. The next year I tried 2...Nf6 on Schlechter, and in the Book of the Congress we find the following note to this move by Tarrasch: "Not good, since the Knight is at once driven away, but Herr Nimzowitsch goes his own road in the openings, one, however, which cannot be recommended to the public."

Ridicule can do much, for instance embitter the existence of young talents, but one thing is not given to it, to put a stop permanently to the incursion of new and powerful ideas. The old dogmas, such as the ossified teaching on the center, the worship of the open game, and in general the whole formalistic conception of the game, who bothers himself today about these? The new ideas, however, those supposed by-ways, not to be recommended to the public, these are becoming today highways, on which great and small move freely in the consciousness of absolute security.

3.Nc3 d5 4.exd5 Nxd5 5.Bc4 e6 6.O-O Be7 7.d4 Nxc3 8.bxc3 O-O 9.Ne5 Qc7

What now follows is play against the hanging pawns, which will soon come into existence.

10.Bd3 Nc6 11.Bf4 Bd6 12.Re1 cxd4!

This exchange in conjunction with ...Nb4 is the point of the proceedings started by 9...Qc7.

13.cxd4 Nb4 14.Bg3 Nxd3 15.Qxd3 b6 16.c4 Ba6

The hanging pawns, which come under heavy fire, prove in the end to have much vigor. The game is about equal.

17.Rac1 Rac8 18.Qb3! f6 19.Qa4?

19.c5 Bxe5 20.dxe5 would have led to a draw.

19...fxe5 20.dxe5 Ba3! 21.Qxa3 Bxc4 22.Re4 Qd7 23.h3 Bd5

With his Bishop posted here, Black's advantage is clear.

24.Re2 Qb7 25.f4 Qf7 26.Rec2 Rxc2 27.Rxc2 Qg6 28.Qc3

White cannot well give up the c-file. If 28.Rc3 h5 29.h4 Rxf4.

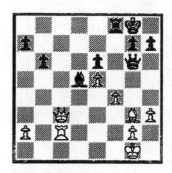

28...Bxa2! 29.Bh4

On 29.Rxa2 comes 29...Qb1+.

29...Bd5 30.Be7 Re8 31.Bd6 Qe4 32.Qc7 h6 33.Rf2 Qe1+ 34.Rf1 Qe3+ 35.Rf2 a5 36.Be7 Qe1+ 37.Rf1 Qe3+ 38.Rf2 Kh8

Directed against the possibility of Bf6.

39.Bd8 Qe1+ 40.Rf1 Qe3+ 41.Rf2 Qe1+ 42.Rf1 Qg3 43.Rf2 Rf8 44.Qxb6 Rxf4 45.Be7 a4

A passed pawn and a mating attack - these make a wicked affair.

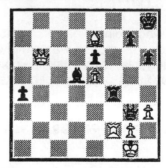

46.Kf1?

Black was lost in any case.

46...Qxg2+ 0-1.

Game 49

This was the first game in which my idea of a sacrifice for the sole purpose of establishing a blockade was illustrated.

Nimzowitsch-Spielmann
San Sebastian, 1912

1.e4 e6 2.d4 d5 3.e5 c5 4.Nf3 Nc6 5.dxc5 Bxc5 6.Bd3 Nge7 7.Bf4!

Overprotection of the strategically important square e5.

7...Qb6 8.O-O Qxb2

This was no ordinary pawn sacrifice for the attack. Its motive was simply and exclusively this: to maintain the point e5 in order to use it as a base for blockading action.

9.Nbd2 Qb6 10.Nb3 Ng6 11.Bg3 Be7 12.h4

This is no attacking move in the ordinary sense. Its meaning is: "Get away from the Key Square e5."

12...Qb4 13.a4 a6 14.h5 Nh4 15.Nxh4 Bxh4 16.c3 Qe7 17.Bh2 f5

This move, which throws open all lines of approach to his opponent, must be made by Black in order to give himself air. With it White's attack first appears in evidence.

18.exf6 e.p. gxf6 19.Nd4 e5 20.Bf5!

and 1-0 in 44. For the continuation, see Diagram 76, page 66.

Game 50

From a match; the first game in which the idea of a pawn sacrifice in the opening is used not to obtain an attack, but to overprotect a strategic point with a view to cramping the enemy forces.

Nimzowitsch-A. Hakansson
Kristianstad, 1922

1.e4 e6 2.d4 d5 3.e5 c5 4.Qg4

My innovation.

4...cxd4 5.Nf3 Nc6 6.Bd3 f5 7.Qg3 Nge7 8.O-O Ng6 9.h4 Qc7 10.Re1

White's plan is now clear. He has given up a pawn, not caring when, if ever, he recovers it, provided e5 is maintained as

---

an instrument to cramp Black's game. There was no idea of attack in 9.h4. Its idea was only to pave the way to the removal of some of the pressure on the e5 square. The pawn sacrifice clearly comes within the category of sacrifice for the sake of blockade.

10...Bd7

10...Bc5 was essential here in order to leave f8 for the Knight in the case of the pawn push h5.

11.a3 O-O-O 12.b4

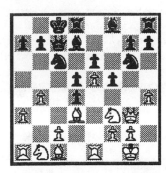

White if he had wanted, could have won the exchange here by 12.h5 Ne7 13.Ng5 Re8 14.Nf7 Rg8 15.Nd6+, but with his undeveloped Queenside and his unprotected pawn on h5 he would have had some difficulties to contend

with. The text move is the logical continuation.

12...a6

Better would have been 12...Kb8 13.c3! dxc3 14.Nxc3 Nxb4 15.axb4 Qxc3 16.Be3 Qxd3 17.Bxa7+ Kc8 18.Rec1+ Bc6 19.b5! Qxb5 20.Nd4 with complications. White, had he wanted, could have avoided all of this by playing 13.Bb2.

13.h5 Nge7 14.Bd2 h6 15.a4 g5 16.b5 f4 17.Qg4

The Queen is actually well placed here.

17...Nb8 18.c3 Re8

Black's only move. It will be noted that the overprotector, the Re1, now has the c-file opened for him without any trouble. In order to avoid loss of material Black has to submit to a curious regrouping of his forces.

19.cxd4 Kd8 20.Rc1 Qb6 21.a5 Qa7 22.b6 Qa8

The Queen finds herself in a position which would normally only be seen in a problem!

23.Rc7 Nf5 24.Nc3 Be7 25.Nxd5 Nxd4
26.Nxd4 exd5

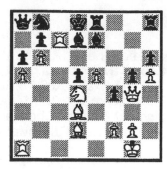

27.Qxd7+.

Mate by the Knight follows. A beautiful
finish. **1-0.**